Pirate Modernity

Cities in Asia, Africa and Latin America are now increasingly shaped by technological networks. Low cost media have blurred the boundaries between technology, culture and everyday life for large urban populations. This media urbanism has come in the context of a long drawn crisis, rising inequality and accelerating social conflict. Unable to grapple with this scenario, modernist planning designs of the 1950s and postcolonial control models of the city now lie in disarray. Nowhere is this more apparent than contemporary Delhi, India's capital and one of the world's largest cities.

Using Delhi's contemporary history as a site for reflection, *Pirate Modernity* moves from a detailed discussion of the technocratic design of the city by US planners in the 1950s, to the massive expansions after 1977, culminating in the urban crisis of the 1990s. As a practice, pirate modernity is an illicit form of urban globalization. Poorer urban populations increasingly inhabit non-legal spheres (unauthorized neighborhoods, squatter camps) and bypass legal technological infrastructures (media, electricity). This pirate culture produces a significant enabling resource for subaltern populations unable to enter the legal city. Equally, this is an unstable world, bringing subaltern populations into the harsh glare of permanent technological visibility, and attacks by urban elites, courts and visceral media industries. The book examines contemporary Delhi from some of these sites: the unmaking of the city's modernist planning design, new technological urban networks that bypass states and corporations, and the tragic experience of the road accident terrifyingly enhanced by technological culture. *Pirate Modernity* moves between past and present, along with debates in Asia, Africa and Latin America on urbanism, media culture, and everyday life.

This pioneering book suggests cities have to be revisited afresh after proliferating media culture. *Pirate Modernity* boldly draws from urban and cultural theory to open a new agenda for a world after media urbanism.

Ravi Sundaram is a Fellow at the Centre for the Study of Developing Societies (CSDS), Delhi. In 2000 he founded CSDS' Sarai programme along with Ravi Vasudevan, Monica Narula, Jeebesh Bagchi, and Shuddhabrata Sengupta. Sundaram has co-edited the critically acclaimed Sarai Reader series that includes *The Cities of Everyday Life* (2002) and *Frontiers* (2007).

Asia's Transformations
Edited by Mark Selden,
Cornell University, USA

The books in this series explore the political, social, economic and cultural consequences of Asia's transformations in the twentieth and twenty-first centuries. The
series emphasizes the tumultuous interplay of local, national, regional and global
forces as Asia bids to become the hub of the world economy. While focusing on the
contemporary, it also looks back to analyse the antecedents of Asia's contested rise.

This series comprises several strands:

Asia's Transformations

Asia's Transformations aims to address the needs of students and teachers. Titles
include:

Debating Human Rights
Critical essays from the United States
and Asia
Edited by Peter Van Ness

Hong Kong's History
State and society under colonial rule
Edited by Tak-Wing Ngo

Japan's Comfort Women
Sexual slavery and prostitution during
World War II and the US occupation
Yuki Tanaka

**Opium, Empire and the Global
Political Economy**
Carl A. Trocki

Chinese Society
Change, conflict and resistance
*Edited by Elizabeth J. Perry and
Mark Selden*

Mao's Children in the New China
Voices from the Red Guard generation
Yarong Jiang and David Ashley

Remaking the Chinese State
Strategies, society and security
*Edited by Chien-min Chao and
Bruce J. Dickson*

Korean Society
Civil society, democracy and
the State
Edited by Charles K. Armstrong

The Making of Modern Korea
Adrian Buzo

The Resurgence of East Asia
500, 150 and 50 year perspectives
*Edited by Giovanni Arrighi,
Takeshi Hamashita and Mark
Selden*

Asia's Great Cities

Each volume aims to capture the heartbeat of the contemporary city from multiple perspectives emblematic of the authors' own deep familiarity with the distinctive faces of the city, its history, society, culture, politics and economics, and its evolving position in national, regional and global frameworks. While most volumes emphasize urban developments since the Second World War, some pay close attention to the legacy of the longue durée in shaping the contemporary. Thematic and comparative volumes address such themes as urbanization, economic and financial linkages, architecture and space, wealth and power, gendered relationships, planning and anarchy, and ethnographies in national and regional perspective. Titles include:

Singapore
Wealth, power and the culture of control
Carl A. Trocki

The City in South Asia
James Heitzman

Global Shanghai, 1850–2010
A history in fragments
Jeffrey N. Wasserstrom

Hong Kong
Becoming a global city
Stephen Chiu and Tai-Lok Lui

Asia.com is a series which focuses on the ways in which new information and communication technologies are influencing politics, society and culture in Asia. Titles include:

Japanese Cybercultures
Edited by Mark McLelland and Nanette Gottlieb

Asia.com
Asia encounters the Internet
Edited by K. C. Ho, Randolph Kluver and Kenneth C. C. Yang

The Internet in Indonesia's New Democracy
David T. Hill and Krishna Sen

Chinese Cyberspaces
Technological changes and political effects
Edited by Jens Damm and Simona Thomas

Mobile Media in the Asia-Pacific
Gender and the art of being mobile
Larissa Hjorth

Literature and Society

Literature and Society is a series that seeks to demonstrate the ways in which Asian literature is influenced by the politics, society and culture in which it is produced. Titles include:

The Body in Postwar Japanese Fiction
Douglas N. Slaymaker

Chinese Women Writers and the Feminist Imagination, 1905–1948
Haiping Yan

Routledge Studies in Asia's Transformations

Routledge Studies in Asia's Transformations is a forum for innovative new research intended for a high-level specialist readership, and the titles will be available in hardback only. Titles include:

The American Occupation of Japan and Okinawa*
Literature and memory
Michael Molasky

Koreans in Japan*
Critical voices from the margin
Edited by Sonia Ryang

Post-conflict Heritage, Post-colonial Tourism
Culture, politics and development at Angkor
Tim Winter

Education and Reform in China
Emily Hannum and Albert Park

Writing Okinawa
Narrative acts of identity and resistance
Davinder L. Bhowmik

Maid In China
Media, Mobility, and a New Semiotic of power
Wanning Sun

Northern Territories, Asia-Pacific Regional Conflicts and the Åland Experience
Untying the Kurillian knot
Edited by Kimie Hara and Geoffrey Jukes

Reconciling Indonesia
Grassroots agency for peace
Birgit Bräuchler

Singapore in the Malay World
Building and breaching regional bridges
Lily Zubaidah Rahim

Pirate Modernity
Delhi's media urbanism
Ravi Sundaram

* Now available in paperback

Critical Asian Scholarship

Critical Asian Scholarship is a series intended to showcase the most important individual contributions to scholarship in Asian studies. Each of the volumes presents a leading Asian scholar addressing themes that are central to his or her most significant and lasting contribution to Asian studies. The series is committed to the rich variety of research and writing on Asia, and is not restricted to any particular discipline, theoretical approach or geographical expertise. Titles include:

Southeast Asia
A testament
George McT. Kahin

Women and the Family in Chinese History
Patricia Buckley Ebrey

China Unbound
Evolving perspectives on the Chinese past
Paul A. Cohen

China's Past, China's Future
Energy, food, environment
Vaclav Smil

The Chinese State in Ming Society
Timothy Brook

China, East Asia and the Global Economy
Regional and historical perspectives
Takeshi Hamashita
Edited by Mark Selden and Linda Grove

The Global and Regional in China's Nation-formation
Prasenjit Duara

Pirate Modernity

Delhi's media urbanism

Ravi Sundaram

Routledge
Taylor & Francis Group

LONDON AND NEW YORK

First published 2010
by Routledge
2 Park Square, Milton Park, Abingdon, Oxon OX14 4RN

Simultaneously published in the USA and Canada
by Routledge
270 Madison Ave, New York, NY 10016

*Routledge is an imprint of the Taylor & Francis Group,
an informa business*

© 2010 Ravi Sundaram

Typeset in Times by
RefineCatch Limited, Bungay, Suffolk
Printed and bound by
MPG Books Group, UK

British Library Cataloguing in Publication Data
A catalogue record for this book is available from the British Library

Library of Congress Cataloging-in-Publication Data
Sundaram, Ravi
Pirate modernity : Delhi's media urbanism / Ravi Sundaram.
   p. cm.
   1. Mass media and culture—India. 2. Piracy (Copyright)—India.
3. Globalization—Social aspects—India. I. Title.
   P94.65.I4S86 2009
   302.230954—dc22   2008054731

ISBN10: 0–415–40966–7 (hbk)
ISBN10: 0–203–87542–7 (ebk)

ISBN13: 978–0–415–40966–7 (hbk)
ISBN13: 978–0–203–87542–1 (ebk)

Contents

Figures

Preface

During a conversation in 1997 with a colleague, who is India's best-known critic of technology and Western modernity, came a frank admission. Even he, my colleague said, could not keep away from the mundane, addictive pleasures of post-industrial techno-culture. This conversation threw light on a larger, more noticeable transformation. At some point in the late 1990s, the experience of living in India's cities became intertwined with technology in ways that could never be imagined earlier. Media technology has played an important part in this. The consequences of this shift have been far-reaching, if not visceral and limitless. "Technology", once the preserve of planning and scientific debates, now seeped into the everyday lives of urban residents, their debates, their conflicts, their dreams and desires. With this, city life in India has never been quite the same, an experience that has reverberated all over Asia, if not the world. In Delhi, once seen as the dull city of political elites and former empires, this change has been particularly dramatic. "Media" now permeates not just the lives of Delhi's residents, but inflects political and cultural processes: court judgments, road deaths, video piracy, encounter deaths and terrorism, and the displacement of the urban poor from river-front settlements. Public discourse is now technologically coded with reference to air quality, electricity theft and transportation, privacy, polluting industries, and gated high-rise suburbs. The list is endless.

In *Pirate Modernity*, I attempt to make sense of this significant shift in the experience of the urban. Rather than media analysis, it is the sensate properties of the material world that I have been largely drawn to in this book. Instead of providing a new definition of technology or the technological, I have searched for archival fragments, media surfaces, maps, experimental cultural practices and residues from planner's files – all in the effort to find clues to this process.

Like many who now live in Delhi I was not born in the city, but arrived as a migrant in my high school days. Like Delhi, Bangalore, the city of my birth, has also changed dramatically over the past decade. Unlike most cities however, Delhi demands a tough love from its residents, perhaps even more from its migrants. Over the years the relationship has turned into that blend of intense affection and periodic frustration with which many of Delhi's residents are familiar. The migrant is now at home in the city, in a way that only Delhi allows.

It was in 1980s Delhi that I became part of the radical student movement, and entered what Giovanni Arrighi calls the "Marxist century". Since 1989 and the collapse of Stalinism this relationship has loosened considerably. However, in light of the recent economic catastrophes in the capitalist world economy and the public bankruptcy of the neoliberal agenda, perhaps Marx, if not the Kingdom in his name, becomes accessible once again, albeit filtered through the disturbing lessons of the twentieth century.

If Marxism did not live up to its promise, and the neoliberal era ended in global collapse, then neither did the techno-social dreams of the US liberal planners of Delhi in the 1950s. This world began coming apart in the late 1970s, and offered a productive site for the out-of-joint media urbanism described in this book.

Acknowledgments

This book would have been impossible without the unique environment provided by the Centre for the Study of Developing Societies (CSDS) in Delhi, a rare institution in this part of the world. At CSDS I enjoyed the intellectual freedom and debate that the Centre is justly known for along with constant conversation across disciplines, regions and continents. In particular, I would like to thank D.L. Sheth and Suresh Sharma for hearing me out with patience over the years, and giving feedback whenever demanded. Aditya Nigam, as always, was prompt and regular with comments, which I have used with profit. With Ashis Nandy, I have had the privilege of constant intellectual dialogue and debate over a range of topics; and he was always the perfect conceptual provocateur, pushing me to think in ways I had never imagined.

A major part of the writing of this book was shaped by the remarkable context provided by Sarai, a programme of CSDS that I have been intimately involved in since 1998. Sarai was conceived of as an experimental research/ practice space on urban life, and the interactions with colleagues and fellow researchers played a key role in developing many of the ideas in my book. Like many such experimental endeavors, the intensity of collaboration often matures into friendship, sharing moments of intellectual exhilaration, loss, joy, sadness, and anger. Ravi Vasudevan has been part of the original design of Sarai, and with him I have shared long conversations and debates on cinema, media, urban life, and the merits of Old Monk Rum. With Jeebesh Bagchi, Monica Narula, and Shuddhabrata Sengupta, members of the Raqs Media Collective and co-initiators of Sarai, there have been many shared journeys, collaborations, fierce debates and laughter. Their feedback on my work has been invaluable. From Awadhendra Sharan, my colleague at CSDS and Sarai, I have learnt a great deal – many of the ideas on planning, risk, and law in this book have emerged through conversations with him. Ravikant Sharma took me back to the world of contemporary Hindi writing on cities, much of which is in evidence in this book. Ashish Mahajan, as always, was a huge backup for my long absences during writing, patiently helping out with long-distance requests and text messages.

In Sarai, I helped coordinate (with Ravi Vasudevan) a research program on the media city called PPHP, short form for Publics and Practices in the History of the Present. PPHP was lucky to see a remarkably talented group of young researchers, who produced a large corpus of written and archival material, available online and in the Sarai archive. Bhrigupati Singh began the first PPHP fieldwork forays, followed by many others: Rakesh Kumar Singh, Bhagwati Prasad, Lokesh Sharma, Anand Vivek Taneja, Ritika Shrimali, Yamini Jaishankar, Tripta Chandola, Faizan Ahmed, Ankur Khanna, Debashree Mukerjee, Puloma Pal, Mayur Suresh and Jawahar Raja. I have benefited from all the PPHP researchers. The texts produced by Rakesh Kumar Singh, Ankur Khanna, Lokesh Sharma, Bhagwati Prasad, Khadeeja Arif, Mayur Suresh and Jawahar Raja are cited in various chapters of the book; each one of them has produced original insights on media culture in the fast-changing years after 2000.

From the Cyberhohalla (CM) media labs in working-class areas of Delhi I accessed a treasure of subaltern stories on the city; texts produced by practitioners and residents. From the labs in LNJP colony, Dakshinpuri, and the now tragically demolished Nangla site came an unending body of unique writings, collected in online archives, artworks and books. Shveta Sarda, who works in Cybermohalla, offered help and insight on my work, and forwarded texts whenever requested. The record of the demolition of the Nangla settlement on the river banks of the Yamuna by the local lab remains with us as a tragic record of those dark days in the city.

In the Sarai Media Lab I have benefited greatly from conversations with Mrityunjoy Chatterjee (Joy), Iram Gufram and Amitabh Kumar. Joy readily shared the images in the Media Lab Archive and helped in preparing the montage for Chapter 4. Amitabh Kumar's work on Raj comics was an eye-opener for me, and indeed some of those images may be found in this book. Amitabh worked closely with me in preparing the images for the book; for this I remain forever thankful.

At the Department of Urban Design. School of Planning and Architecture, where I also teach as visiting faculty, thanks to K.T. Ravindran for inviting me to SPA and for his original insights into urbanism and the development of Delhi. He was gracious enough to read the chapter on planning and respond with comments. Thanks also to Ranjit Mitra for hosting me when he ran the department and for his constant good humor with fellow faculty and students. And finally to all the wonderful students whose class and studio work regularly provided me with new insights into Delhi and its development.

This book has benefited hugely from long collaborations and friendships with people outside Delhi. From Bangalore, Lawrence Liang's pioneering critique of the intellectual property regime, his encyclopedic knowledge of the law and his personal generosity with books, articles and films have benefited this project tremendously. Solomon Benjamin showed me a wild urbanist sensibility with his work on Vishwas Nagar in Delhi and his continuing critique of civic liberalism in Bangalore. I have learnt much from Rupali Gupte and Prasad Shetty, both Bombay residents and members of the urbanist collective CRIT.

Part of this book has emerged through conversations with friends in different parts of the world. Geert Lovink has been a regular interlocutor for many years, and from whom I have learnt a great deal. In addition I would like to thank the large community of readers on the nettime list where part of a chapter was first posted. I have been lucky to share a dialogue and friendship with Toby Miller, his good humor and critical insights have helped me a great deal all these years. With Radhika Subramaniam in New York I share a mutual interest for things urban; she was the first to introduce me to the writings of Elias Canetti. Nitin Govil has been a sharp observer of the media industry; his easy wit has been a source of constant pleasure in the past few years.

Although this book is fairly distant from my graduate student work, the shadow of my intellectual mentors may be visible, even indirectly. I want to thank Dale Tomich, Mark Selden, Giovanni Arrighi and Immanuel Wallerstein for all their input and support over the years. These are intellectual debts whose traces always survive – in surprising ways.

This book was finalized when I was a Davis Fellow at Princeton University in the spring of 2008. I want to thank Gyan Prakash, the then Director of the Davis Center, for his wonderful, easygoing presence, his generosity towards the Fellows, and for having run a great Fellows seminar. His comments on my work have been invaluable, and helped clarify some of the arguments. I also want to thank the other Fellows of that year for their comments and feedback: Lisbeth Haas, David Lederer, Alexander Etkind and Ronald Schechter. My thanks to all the great friendships in Princeton with faculty, students and staff: Bhavani Raman, Michael Gordin, Christina Lee, Helen Tilley, Michael Laffan, Anson Rabinbach and Piotr Kosicki. Jennifer Houle ensured my stay was perfectly organized and was ever available for help. With Bhrigu and Prerna, there were many evenings of great conversation with food and drinks. Aruna Prakash opened her house for regular dinners and film-viewing sessions, all of which provided the right atmosphere to deal with the stress of writing. In New York, I cannot forget Joan, Frank, Leela and Babu – whose hospitality and kindness I have regularly enjoyed for more than two decades.

At different stages of writing, various friends have given me comments and feedback on my work and to them I owe a great deal. These include Nivedita Menon, Usha Ramanathan, Rana Dasgupta, Aarti Sethi, Priya Sen, Curt Gambetta, Vivek Narayanan, Sadan Jha and Zainab Bawa. Parts of the book were presented in Bombay, Baroda, Bangalore, Lahore, Princeton, Taipei, Amsterdam and Berlin, and I have benefited from all the comments made by people at these events.

Old friends in Delhi and beyond have been a source of support over many years. Suzanne Goldenberg has been in constant touch despite her movement from Delhi, to Jerusalem, to Washington. Thanks also go to Siddharth Vardarajan, M.K. Venu and Chitra Padmanabhan. In particular I want to thank my old friends and fellow East Delhi neighbors: Shohini Ghosh, Sabina Gadihoke, Shikha Jhingan, Sumit Ray, Vibhu Mohapatra, Litha,

Prabhat Jha, Soumya Gupta and Sheyphali Sharan. Shahid Amin and Sanjay Sharma have been constant visitors to the Sarai basement café keeping a tab on the status of my manuscript. Prabhu Mohapatra has been an old inter-locutor for over a decade, and will continue to do so. In CSDS and Sarai I want to thank Ghanshyam, Ramesh, Vikas and Sachin for always being there to help out without any questions asked.

The material in this book has drawn from various archival collections. I would like to thank the staff of the Albert Mayer Papers in the University of Chicago Library, the Delhi State Archives, the Princeton University Map Library, and the Ford Foundation Archives in New York. Special thanks go to Tsering Wangyal Shawa at the Princeton library and Anthony Maloney of the Ford Foundation Archives in New York. From the Sarai archive I have been able to source an invaluable collection of primary and secondary material deposited by researchers. Without the able help of Moslem Quraishy, the custodian of the Sarai Archive until recently, this task would have been made even more difficult. At the CSDS library, Sujit Deb and later Avinash Jha were ever ready to help out with impossible-to-find sources.

I want to thank the Sarai Media Lab, Raj Comics, the Sarai Archive, the Raqs Media Collective, and the Geographische Institut der Universität Bonn for their kind permission for the use of images under copyright in the book. Sadly some other images could not be used, as one of the copyright holders demanded astronomical sums – a comment on the insanity of the current copyright regime, partly discussed in the book itself.

I am grateful to the series editor Mark Selden for his support, and crystal-clear comments on the manuscript; I am also grateful to my two reviewers for their suggestions, all of which have helped me clarify the arguments in the book. At Routledge, I want to thank Stephanie Rogers for her regular feedback, support and patience during the writing process.

My extended family in Delhi – Ma (Vina Mazumdar), Baba (Shankar Mazumdar), Shaswati, Indrani, Surajit, Rajalaxmi, Akhila, Ashish and Rustam – kept me going all these years with great warmth and support, and with a healthy dose of debate on every conceivable topic from Marxism, to genetics, to Indian cricket. Although Baba is sadly not here with us today, I can imagine him smiling, whisky in hand, from the heavens.

My parents Appa (R.K. Sundaram) and Amma (Vaasanthi) have followed the progress of this book from Bangalore. My brother Hari has supported it from the United States. They have watched the progress of the book, at times with anxiety, but always with love and support, all of which ensured that this book finally came to see the light of day.

Ranjani Mazumdar has shared my love for the city; she has been a friend, an intellectual fellow traveler, a companion, and my best reader, critic and supporter. Together we have seen the world, South Asia and our city change before us over the past two decades. Without her presence this book could not have been written.

Introduction
After media

My first visit to Delhi was in 1972, when I was a child. Two things stand out in my memory. The first was the large decaying Red Fort, once the crown jewel of Moghul Shahjehanabad. I still remember the chipped walls of the Moghul palace inside the Fort, where eighteenth-century looters had scraped the precious stones that once decorated the rooms. My second memory of Delhi in 1972 was a trip to Delhi's first large "international" exhibition and trade fair, Asia 72. Laid out in the newly constructed exhibition spaces at Pragati Maidan, Asia 72 saw long lines of crowds (us included), who queued for hours to look at the technological marvels of countries in the West, the Soviet Union, the science exhibits from India, highlighting industrialization and its visible icons, power plants and the steel mills.

Asia 72 may seem like a tropicalized, if not delayed version of the European World Exhibitions of the nineteenth century. Walter Benjamin had called them "places of pilgrimage to the commodity fetish" (2002, p.17); the crowds that thronged the European exhibitions were drawn to nineteenth-century display, monumentality and the dream-like wonder of industrial modernity. Asia 72 also had technological spectacle and wondrous crowds, but the display of commodities was carefully enclosed in the mold of national sovereignty. The exhibition was designed to foreground the technological power of the Congress regime for the urban crowds who thronged Pragati Maidan. The architect Raj Rewal's innovative design of the exhibition complex used structural engineering and geometric patterns to create a structure that was futuristic for its time, and well ahead of any state-sponsored building in the city in the early 1970s.

I returned to Pragati Maidan in the early 1990s, and was struck by the changes. The old neo-futurist exhibition spaces were hosting a consumer goods exhibition and sales counters. The bulk of the visitors were out-of-town tourists, and local consumers hoping for large discounts. The comparisons with Asia 72 could not have been starker. The exhibitions of the 1990s were wild and chaotic, the stalls loud and kitschy, and the display of commodities was completely unregulated, suggesting a bazaar. Gone were the old crowds of 1972, the now-lost wondrous gaze at the industrial dream world. It was a flash, but it suddenly brought into relief the transformations of the past two decades. In the first place, the attempt to manage the circulation of commodities through the national control regime had gone awry; the technological monopoly of the state was in tatters, an unintended consequence of governmental economic liberalization in the 1980s. As growing sections of the population embraced forms of life that were increasingly both technological and commodified, the regime was mostly a confused spectator, often running behind events. India's cities have experienced these changes in dramatic ways. Cities and towns have seen the expansion of technological forms that have imploded, becoming sites of conflict and public debate. The technological has long exceeded the monumental spheres of the steel mill and the dam, which were promoted by developmental ideology in postcolonial India. Increasingly, the sphere called "technological" includes older infrastructures like roads, transport, electricity, modern housing, sewage, and water supply. Now, media formations have emerged as a second life, adding to and transforming the older infrastructures of the city. Together, they have produced a new sense of urban life in the past three decades as an equally dynamic but disturbed world.

It is this technologized urban experience that is the subject of this book. I examine postcolonial[1] Delhi through this lens, but the story is one that invites comparison with emerging technological urban cultures in Asia, Africa and Latin America. Delhi has been studied more for its history, urbanism and antiquity. However, in the last three decades, Delhi has seen the "technological" materialize itself more and more in city discourse. These range from debates over water, pollution, roads, buses, the "power of the media", privacy, urban spectacle and consumption, media piracy and terrorism. In taking Delhi as a site for looking at technological urban culture, I want to set it within a broader debate on postcolonial cities, going beyond the known examples of New York, Hong Kong, Bombay or Tokyo with which we have become familiar. Postcolonial cities are today also *media cities*, a tag typically reserved for the "global city." From the late 1970s various combinations of media consumption, circulation and production have rapidly grown in Asian, Latin American and African cities. Cassette and television culture have now expanded to digital media, with a cultural morphology that does not simply replicate forms of corporate and state control as in the broadcast age (Canclini, 2001; Ginsburg, 2002; Larkin, 2004) An increasing body of research from Mexico, to Nigeria and now Asia has shown that postcolonial cities are vibrant hubs for new media productions, spurred on by a range of low-cost urban infrastructures, mobile telephony, video and digital technologies, and parallel, informal distribution circuits. This produces a media experience that assumes constant breakdown, and recycling or using ways of bypassing existing infrastructures. Most city dwellers in India have grown up with the rhythm of technological irregularity, the ingenious search for solutions, or *jugaad* as it is known in Northern India. Electricity breakdowns are normal, the availability of a regular water supply a dream for a few, and official connections are available to only legal residents of the city. Urban populations do not just internalize the fragmentary time of infrastructure (water supply times, electricity breakdowns), they have resorted to a combination of bypass solutions, illegal sourcing from the official infrastructure for some, and private and semi-private infrastructure for most. Machines and technological gadgets are never thrown away, but reused, sold, repaired and used again. In his pioneering *Social Life of Things*, Arjun Appadurai (1986) spoke about objects entering and leaving commodification, as in a life. Postcolonial technological objects seem to be in the permanent Republic of the Living, with no traceable beginning or end.

I once lived for a year in the early 1970s with my grandparents in Chennai in a house that did not have electricity for the first seven months, as the landlord did not have municipal assent. Remarkably, life was smooth. We slept on the terrace, petromax lamps and lanterns lit the evenings, and the radio set worked on a battery. A life without some electric infrastructure is difficult to imagine today, even for the poorer inhabitants of cities. Electricity does not just light up dark spaces, it charges mobile phones, and powers simple music players and televisions, not uncommon sights even in Delhi's squatter settlements. "Media determine our situation, which – in spite of, or because of it deserves an explanation," once wrote the media theorist Fredric Kittler.[2] Media changed the flesh of infrastructure in urban India after the 1980s, by significantly expanding its material universe. Life in cities and towns today is also to inhabit a media urbanism, with its exhilaration and dangers, not just in India, but in most parts of the postcolonial world.

Media and technological cultures are constitutive of Delhi's development in the long decades after 1977, with the expansion of informal technological markets, the infrastructures of mobile telephony, cable television, and new forms of print and music. This proliferating media culture mixed with a proliferating city, with its palimpsest of technological infrastructures – electricity and television cables, expanding machines on the road (cars, buses, trucks, two-wheelers), new construction everywhere. Jean-Louis Comolli said that life after industrial modernity in nineteenth-century Europe was in the grip of what he called the *frenzy of the visible* (in Friedberg, 1993, p.15). India's cities have recalled this "frenzy" except through more intensive, cross-media forms. This was not simply a "frenzy" of the visible, but a wild ensemble of image and sensation, an urban *hyperstimuli*. When "crisis" began breaking out in the 1990s, it was this hyperstimuli that caused confusion, conflict, and an image of an out-of-control city. This was echoed variously through court decisions and reports of infrastructure breakdown, scandal, pollution and road accident stories that spread through the city during the 1990s. The mixing of technology and urban life was also an enabling moment for subaltern populations to access media. Low-cost technologies of mechanical and digital reproduction often blurred the distinctions between producers and consumers of media, adding to the diffusion of both media infrastructures (video stores, photocopy and design shops, bazaars, cable networks, piracy) and media forms (images, video, phone sms/txt, sounds). In the past, such "informal" networks were more vulnerable for incorporation by the state or large capital. Since the 1980s these networks have often taken on a life of their own, refusing to follow the mandates of legal accumulation. These non-linear networks act as vehicles of media circulation, changing and mutating with the environment. Urban populations across social classes entered this world in increasing numbers, posing great challenges for the state, expanding media industries and capitalist corporations, used to older technologies of management and control. This book uses this constellation to begin a discussion on technologized urbanism in India, with Delhi as its site.

The urban move

The last decade of the twentieth century drew attention to Indian cities in ways that could not be foreseen earlier.[3] After 1947 the urban's place in the nationalist imagination remained ambivalent, if not absent. Under Nehru, the postcolonial regime invested in developmental modernism, comparable to similar projects worldwide. Developmental modernism initiated state-centered accumulation strategies, and posited massive infrastructural projects like steel mills and large dams as crucial to a secular national consciousness. What was distinctive about the Nehruvian model was the seriousness with which it invested in development planning as a postcolonial ideal. It has been argued that the abstract space of planning gave Nehru relative autonomy from the day-to-day *sturm und drang* of Indian politics (Chatterjee, 1993; Kaviraj, 2000). In the event, planning produced an elaborate cultural architecture which set in motion a time-code for development. In the first place, the space of the "global" underwent a certain bracketing. In this fiction, the conquest of the national space and its consolidation was a necessary precondition for a thoroughgoing incorporation into the capitalist world economy. Development's abstractions displaced the older Gandhian allegory of the village with that of the nation *as economy* (Deshpande, 1993). The village and the city now dissolved into the broader schema of national modernization. For the new rulers, cities were mainly functional sites of political power, rather than contributing to national identity. The city was cited for its infrastructural modernity, as the possible future for the village within the broader schema of development. Said Nehru, "the fundamental problem of India is not Delhi or Calcutta or Bombay but the villages of India. . . . We want to urbanize the village, not take away the people from the villages to towns."[4]

By the mid-1970s the old developmentalist regime had run aground, grafted to a highly centralized and repressive state whose self-representation was dynastic rule by the Nehru-Gandhi family. "Development" was paralleled by state-sponsored compulsory sterilization drives aimed at the poor during the Emergency period of 1975 to 1977. This project ended in political defeat for Indira Gandhi and the Congress Party. The Congress was soon put out of power – but the old nationalist architecture was in considerable disarray. What followed were the "long" 1980s, where the post-Emergency period saw the unraveling of the post-1947 model. There were cycles of economic, political and social turbulence, Hindu nationalism and pogroms against the Muslim minority. This came with liberalization and faster integration into the capitalist world economy, agrarian crisis, and rapid cultural and technological transformations. The period after 2000 has witnessed a financial boom culture, and efforts to set up secure, tax-free Special Economic Zones (SEZ) of capitalist production in the countryside. To this dizzying and fast-changing list was added the rise of cities and urbanization.[5] In the late 1990s Ashis Nandy called this indicative of a larger seismic cultural shift, and the parallel "decline of the imagination of the village." Mixing allegory and his characteristically brilliant cultural critique of modernity, Nandy suggested that "few seem to love the city on its own terms in India"; the imagined journey from the village was a "fateful" one, beset by contradictions and inner traumas of selfhood (2001, p.28).

By the 1990s this fateful journey was in full evidence. The decade saw a series of concentrated shock experiences for Indian city dwellers, relentless expansion and spatial transformation, along with assaults on industrial areas seen as out of place by courts and liberal environmental activists. The technological sublime of the planner imaginary, so central to post-independence India, began giving way to a splintered urbanist sprawl in the main metropolitan cities. Planning bodies pushed for the privatized decoupling of infrastructures; transportation design privileged the automobile flyovers and private toll highways to facilitate rapid travel to the suburbs, and private builders took over from older, albeit limited concerns with social housing. This splintered urbanism is by no means unique to Delhi or to South Asia; it reflects a larger global process of rapid urban transformation in the contemporary period (Graham and Marvin, 2001). Most importantly, and perhaps dramatically, a vast new mediascape envelops cities like an all-pervasive skin.

Media lives

Walter Benjamin's suggestion in the 1920s that "the collective is also corporeal" intimated the mix of image, technology and experience that has defined contemporary cities (in Buck-Morss, 1990, p.270). That modern urban living can no longer be defined apart from the media experience is a truism of contemporary research; most recent cultural histories of the twentieth-century city include the sensory and imagistic world as part of their interpretive domain.[6] Benjamin's idea of a corporeal urban experience suggests an increasing entanglement of body and technology, where city dwellers process a range of shock-like visual stimuli, and develop disciplining techniques to deal with distraction, as well as tactile, playful appropriations of the rush of images. This changed phenomenology of nearness and distance brought about by the media has a productive and equally dark, visceral quality, tearing apart stable modes of contemplation. The dramatic "live" experience brought about by flickering film, television, advertising and mobile screens also disperses space, giving birth to new clusters that often bypass linear

networks of cultural and technological exchange. In the context of postcolonial South Asia where the media and the urban boom have coincided in
recent years, technological culture has become implicated in a broader social
theatre of boom culture and urban conflict.

Ever since India's independence from colonial rule in 1947, the nationalist
regime saw the media, most notably radio and later television, as primarily
pedagogic institutions, to nurture and shape a fragile citizenship.[7] The regime's
relationship to cinema, the main media producer in the country, put this
model to considerable test. On the one hand, cinema which was seen as
"commercial entertainment" was controlled through censorship and taxation.
The film industry's independent status complicated state control; the cinema
theatre's existence as a source of corporeal attractions and mass crowds
meant that demands that cinema conform to a "national cultural value" were
not always successful (Rajadhyakshya, 2003; Srinivas, 2000). It was through
the lens of the crowd that cinema was often viewed by the state a site of
immorality and danger, victim to the distraction/attraction machine that film
generated. As a symbol of a mass that disturbed bourgeois citizenship, popular filmic desire had to be managed rather than completely annexed to state
policy. Media outside cinema were more firmly yoked to developmentalism,
a model clearly underlined by the Chanda Committee on radio and television
in 1966.[8] Run by a technocratic elite, state-controlled radio and television
were clearly designed to stand apart from the city.[9]

All this changed significantly when state controls where loosened from
the 1980s onward, and the economy began a process of liberalization and
deeper integration with the global economy. This process significantly blurred
the lines between the media and the urban experience for millions of city
dwellers in India. In contrast to the earlier decades, the 1990s generated fast-
moving, tactile media. Low-cost computers, advertising, mobile phones and
digital images have transformed urban life. The experience is now a more
global one, incorporating design, telecom networks, architecture, software
and media industries, service workers, personal media objects and multiple
sensory environments. Elite suburbia designed on gated communities have
developed in city suburbs, offering refuge to affluent urban dwellers from
urban crisis.[10] The development of new elite suburbia and powerful media
industries notwithstanding, media urbanism in India has until recently, lacked
the spectacular force of its Western and East Asian counterparts. Continuous
immersion into a world of low-cost media forms is still the norm for many.
What is significant is the emergence of new forms of publicity, images now
crowd streets, walls and buses; electronically boosted soundscapes (music,
political campaigns, religious chants, car horns) expand and occupy roads
and neighborhood space. This media sensorium is often experienced in mixed
spaces – low-cost video players in working-class areas running makeshift
movie theatres. Cinema, that great archive of Indian cities (Mazumdar, 2007),
has been subject to fundamental transformation, splintering into unanticipated new formations. For cinema, movement from a feared but regulated

"mass" to a "dispersed media public, illicit, ungovernable, will remain a key dimension of media futures" (Vasudevan, 2004, p.72).

The evaporation of the boundary between technology and urban life in India's urban formations has produced a kinetic city – a delirious disorientation of the senses. The older categories of the city (i.e. the social, the political, the cultural, the separation of humans and machines) have all been subject to strain and transformation during this process. This is the context and intellectual provocation for this book.

The ruins of the modernist city

In an essay penned more than twenty years ago, Jonathan Crary declared that by the late 1960s the legibility of the (Western) city appeared near the threshold of oblivion." Beset by crisis, the Western city became a product of networks and the excess of speed and circulation, bypassing all plans to give the urban a coherent shape. For Crary, urban theory sought to desperately "impose spatial intelligibility to a locale that was being transformed by the anti-territoriality of capital" (1986, p.159). One form of the anti-territoriality of capital has been its flight from the old urban formations. In the advanced metropolitan centers a significant allegory of urban crisis has been of infrastructural decline, imaging empty peripheral landscapes of former industrial areas, which act as backbends to the endless urban sprawl.

As Western historic urban centers decline, a long line of social theorists point to the end of the classical landscape as a consequence of media networks. As landscapes changed, the loss of the autonomy of both technical objects and human species has been captured in science fiction, popular cyberpunk and contemporary television shows. Post-industrial landscapes in Western cities are paralleled by new generic spaces networked by communication fiber and "junkspace" design, a term famously coined by Rem Koolhaas. Thus for Koolhaas "Junkspace is a domain of feigned, simulated order, a kingdom of morphing. Its specific configuration is as fortuitous as the geometry of a snowflake" (2002a, p.177). A clutter of non-places has emerged – airports, malls, transit points (Augé, 1995). The old modernist models of the productive industrial city have long disappeared; their debris now clutters the landscapes of rust as dystopian afterlives (Picon, 2000).

Paul Virilio proclaimed almost wistfully that in the new urbanism the "architectonic element begins to drift" (1997, p.383). We confront the city primarily through screens and television. The old urbanism which harbored the tactile and creative now seems from a "pseudolithic era . . . a phantom landscape" (ibid., p.390). For Virilio, telecommunications have abolished the difference between surface and the inside; there is now an "overexposed" city of permanent, crippling visibility. The link between optics, speed and vision ushered in by twentieth-century modernity has turned from a destructive/creative dialectic into complete catastrophe.

This image contrasts with the European 1920s, where the encounter of media and urban life was taken as a significant site of analysis and intervention for writers like George Simmel, Siegfried Kracauer, Walter Benjamin and avant-garde movements like constructivism and Dada. If technologized urban modernity destabilized the senses through shock and speed, the European avant-garde used those very tools to "defamiliarize" everyday life with techniques of montage and shock-like assaults drawn from cinema, radio and electricity. Walter Benjamin's seminal essay "Work of art in the age of technical reproducibility" stages the encounter between film technology and modernity as one of revolutionary awakening,

> Our taverns and our metropolitan streets, our offices and our furnished rooms, our railroad stations and our factories appeared to have us locked up hopelessly. Then came film and burst this prison-world asunder by the dynamite of the tenth of a second, so that now, in the midst of its far-flung ruins and debris, we calmly and adventurously go traveling.
>
> (Benjamin, 1969, p.236)

In Benjamin's well-known argument, mechanical reproduction destroyed the aura around artworks, and film technology emerges as an optical unconscious where techniques of film montage fragment and penetrate the world as a radical disorienting tool. The optical unconscious was not only a radical expression of the encounter with technology, but also held out the "capability of returning the gaze" (ibid., p.188). Earlier in the "Artwork" essay, Benjamin had spoken perceptively about the "extension" of modern media after the arrival of print, with the public writing of reports, letters to the editor, comments and so on. "Thus," said Benjamin, "the distinction between author and the public is about to lose character" (ibid., p.232). Technologies of shock and reproducibility carried forward the slogans of the avant-garde – the destruction of the original context and a reordering of the object in a new setting. Similarly, Siegfried Kracauer suggested that media technologies like film represented a democratizing of urban life. Technological media expanded artificial surfaces in the city, and generated a mechanized mass public, which saw its "self-representation" in the medium of cinema. For Kracauer it was precisely in these technologized urban surfaces ("the outer skin of things") that the secrets of the city lay, to be decoded through writing and criticism. In differing ways, media technologies offered for both Kracauer and Benjamin a possible hope to decenter viewer reception, and to disrupt the homogenization of everyday life and the crippling historicism of bourgeois modernity.[11] This is what Miriam Hansen calls Benjamin's "gamble" with technology, where utopian possibilities of play and "innervation"[12] can be released by new technologies, "mixing" and exceeding its original capitalist purpose.[13]

This "gamble" with technology that German modernism took in the 1920s was buried by the catastrophe of fascism and war. Worse, postwar capitalist accumulation under US hegemony successfully integrated and normalized the very technologies in whose possibilities the 1920s writers had placed so much hope. Today the verdict among Western modernist scholars seems near-unanimous – that the last decades of the twentieth century are witness to the depressing closure of those very utopian sites of 1920s modernism, the dispersal of the city and its critical possibilities. In the endless landscape of post-urban sprawl, media corporations and globalized networks rule, a vast hyper space has destroyed the capacity to reflect on capitalist modernity, or as Fredric Jameson (1991) put it in his early critique of postmodernism, the ability to map it cognitively. The roots of this model can be traced back to the 1960s with Guy Debord's hugely influential 1960s polemic, *Society of the Spectacle*. In Debord's thesis, the combination of capital, media sign and spectacle represents the colonization of everyday life and the end of face-to-face interaction among populations. Debord famously argued that the modern world presents itself as an accumulation of spectacles. "All that was once lived directly," says Debord, "has become mere representation" (1994, p.12). Detached from life, images become autonomous, producing a reality that is but psuedo-real. The spectacle is the most general form of the commodity conforming to that historical moment when the commodity form completes its colonization of life. "The spectacle," wrote Debord, "as the present social organization of the paralysis of history and memory, of the abandonment of history built on the foundation of historical time, is the false consciousness of time" (ibid., p.114). Time and space now become abstract and lifeless; the former unity of the world is lost. Arriving in 1968, Debord's essay attained a cult status during its time and was widely read both among academics and student radicals.

Debord had proclaimed that "the spectacle had invented a visual form for itself." Jean Baudrillard clearly referenced this when he proclaimed that hyperreality had decisively overtaken the era of spectacle. For Baudrillard, spectacle belonged to the epoch of alienation, a modernist moment that has now attained closure. Like Virilio but with a different explanatory device, Baudrillard argues that the new technologies erode all modern divisions of spectacle and surface, inner and outer space, what he calls a forced "extroversion of all interiority" (1983, p.132). The legacy of the current epoch, says Baudrillard, "is the obscenity of the visible, of the all-too-visible, of the more-visible-than-the-visible" (ibid., p.131). The media surface, a source of critical inquiry for Kracauer and Benjamin, was now seen as an example of a crippling depthlessness, as if anticipating Jameson's (1991) model of the technological sublime in his essay on postmodernism. While Baudrillard was criticized by many at the time, the conceptual echo of his ideas is remarkable. With the problem of the legibility of the Western city, the recent efflorescence of the digital media has fed the obituary of twentieth-century Western modernism.

In the 1960s Marshall McLuhan (1964) had suggested that media is but a sensory extension of the human body. In McLuhan's reading, modernity had entered a third dimension, an "electric universe" capable of reciprocity (i.e. a television image was a "tactile" medium, an extension of touch). McLuhan's important insights were compromised by his pop-rhetoric and technological formalism; he was quickly rivaled in popularity by Debord and a renaissance in critical theory. McLuhan had famously suggested In *Understanding Media* that the content of media is governed by the technical medium, a point that came to the fore dramatically with the emergence of digital technologies of reproduction. The digital is today seen as a modernization of McLuhan's earlier vision of an "electric universe". There is also a renewed focus on the technical medium itself, as the digital is read through the transformation of surface, storage, and the relationship between spectator and screen. As a well-known writer on the phenomenon puts it, digital technologies as "new media"

> change our concept of what an image is – because they turn a viewer into an active user. As a result, an illusionistic image is no longer something a subject simply looks at, comparing it with memories of represented reality to judge its reality effect. The new media image is something the user actively *goes into*, zooming in or clicking on individual parts with the assumption that they contain hyperlinks.
>
> (Manovich, 2001, p.183)

Analog cinema, based on celluloid, was the twentieth-century quintessential techno-cultural medium. The coming of video and digital technologies has clearly decentered the old media geography constructed by cinema (Vasudevan, 2004). In his recent book *The Virtual Life of Film*, the film theorist D.N. Rodowick asks the inevitable question – is cinema's time over? Part of the idea of cinema, says Rodowick, is "already dead," with a future difficult to predict (2007, p.94). A vast new media territory that has emerged after the digital is "a landscape without image." Speaking as if for a whole generation of media and film scholars Rodowick goes on to summarize the problem:

> Here we confront a new kind of ontological perplexity – how to situate ourselves, in space and time, in relation to an image that does not seem to be "one." On electronic screens, we are uncertain that what appears is *an* "image," and in its powers of mutability and velocity of transmission, we are equally uncertain that this perception has a singular or stable existence either in the present or in relation to the past.
>
> (Ibid., p.95)

It has been argued that the so-called new digital media are nothing else but the further radical development of twentieth-century media archaeology (Elsaesser, 2006). Lev Manovich (2002) argues that computation-based creativity can be broken up into five core elements: manipulation of numbers, modularity, automated programming, variability and interactivity. Conceptually, manipulation, reproduction and easy distribution increasingly define all media, marking significant transformations in space and time.

Computational capacity and creative distribution transform the world of spectators and objects. Screens now become interfaces, transforming the older human–machine relationship. Manovich places this within a broader history of formal cinematic modernism, and new media mobilize its techniques from nineteenth-century computing technologies and Dziga Vertov's film experiments. The cinematic archive lives on as the logical cultural interface of the "new media." Manovich's argument is innovative, if not excessively formal, and may bring partial cheer to those attempting to perform a disciplinary rescue operation for film and media studies.[14]

This move has clearly not convinced others. In the opening pages of his pioneering book *Techniques of the Observer*, Jonathan Crary observed that the coming of the digital medium was a "sweeping reconfiguration of relations between an observing subject and modes of representation that effectively nullifies most of the culturally established meanings of the term *observer* and *representation*" (1992, p.1). Unlike Manovich, and in a Debord-like narrative, Crary indicated "that we were seeing the emergence of a world where visual images, now millions of bits of information, will no longer have reference to an observer in a 'real' optically perceived world" (ibid., p.2). This perception by one of the leading Western art historians refracts through a large community of Western modernist scholars. As if to reclaim a fragment of Western cultural life "before" the digital, a host of outstanding books on inter-war European modernism fall into this part-nostalgic constellation of a world of surfaces, observers and images.[15]

Postcolonial media urbanism has generated a whole new series of situations that prevent a recall of the modernist questions of the twentieth century. Populations have moved on from being seen as "recipients" of media in cinema halls, radio sets and televisions. This scenario, a staple of much of twentieth-century European modernity, based itself on experiences of initial shock and distraction in increasingly technologized cities. Populations now participate as part producers, part consumers and proliferators of media. At one level, media and cultural industries are a crucial asset for capitalist accumulation in India, playing an increasing role in the integration of finance, global expansion and political management. When the digital medium arrived in the 1980s, the Rajiv Gandhi regime designed panoptical computer networks for communication, with an all-seeing centralized node.[16] It was a nineteenth-century model of control that soon became irrelevant, a story that appears periodically in this book.

Pirate Modernity subjects the digital less to a formal analysis of its impact on a particular medium, but as a player during different vantage points: the staging of event scenes in the city, media piracy panics, security and surveillance pathologies, the articulation of urban fear. "The digital" was part of a larger destabilization of the media form in India beginning with cassette culture in the 1980s. Since then, more often than not, contemporary media emerged as a bad object, materializing itself in unstable assembleges that do not fit conventional accounts of media and modernity.

Pirate modernity

Postcolonial media urbanism produced an illicit form, *pirate modernity*. Piracy works through digital and mechanical reproduction, but becomes a life of its own. A media form, piracy also became a larger mode of replication for low-cost urban technological infrastructure. The world of piracy ranges from not just immaterial media goods of all kinds (software, movies, music, hardware) but also most mass-market commodities ranging from the counterfeit, to the "unbranded," the "graymarket" or the local commodity.

Pirate culture has utilized the technological infrastructures of the postcolonial city-electricity, squatter settlements, roads, media networks and factories. These are siphoned off, or accessed through informal arrangements outside the existing legal structures of the city. By disrupting existing technologies of control and expansion, piracy provides a key interface between media technologies and larger urban infrastructures.

Dramatically increased access to urban technological infrastructure, weaker bourgeois institutions and political mobilization by the poor provides a key context of pirate modernity. With its location in urban economic proliferation and media technologies of reproduction, piracy attracts subaltern populations, out of place in the contemporary city. Piracy's indifference to property laws produced a significant resource for subaltern populations unable to enter the legal world. This resource ranged from economic to media goods of all kinds. If pirate modernity's non-legality is its strength, it also makes it a subject of attack by globalizing elites. New liberalism's distilling of globalization as legal accumulation immediately transformed elite discourse in India. The civic side of this discourse suggested that pirate modernity was the city's problem, not its conditions of possibility. This set the stage for a series of attacks enacted by courts and anti-media piracy campaigners. New liberalism produced pirate urbanism as an illegal postcolonial descent into hell, a reason for globalization's impurity in India.

The anthropologist Brian Larkin once usefully called piracy a creative "corruption" of the urban infrastructure and media technologies that went on to create its own spatiality (2004). Parasitic attachment to urban infrastructures surely marked piracy, but it was much more than that. In its early years, media and economic piracy actually expanded the urban infrastructure in Delhi, in unauthorized factory zones, cable television for homes, and a series of markets devoted to media. This easy replication and adaptation marks urban piracy. Replication is not more of the same, but a giant difference engine, experimenting with possible openings in the city and becoming another. Each reproduction – of non-legal economic practices, media objects, software – creates a different form, and so on.

Pirate culture presumes and further expands the experience of the technological, at a time when the older boundaries between technology and culture have blurred in the contemporary city.[17] This blurring of the cultural and the technological has produced a vitalistic urban sensorium, dream worlds of consumption and spectacle, confusions of the natural and the artificial, and also terrifying enhancements of death and tragedy in a mediatized world. As it proliferated, pirate modernity disrupted not just capitalist control, but also the lives of the subaltern urban populations who were now part of the mediatized world. This is piracy's great aporia; even as it created radical conditions of possibility for subaltern populations in the city, it brought them to the edge of permanent technological visibility, and visceral circuits of media industries.

Piracy's strength was its ability to innovate and proliferate, and to disperse when attacked by new enforcement regimes in the 1990s. The informationalization of the postcolonial urban economy provided a key reference point for this. Informational control technologies (computerized land records, GIS city maps, biometric IDs) were initiated to make pirate modernity legible to property. In turn informational protocols were periodically broken, counterfeited and bypassed by pirate modernity. Bypass strategies had a high success rate for media goods, where movement was easy. In short, informationalization was a hydra, a possibility for capitalist profit and new liberal control technologies, electronic surveillance in the city, but also rescripted, and redeployed by pirate culture as it proliferated in the city.

Pirate culture is part of a world where "experience" as we know it is increasingly commodified. For the globalizing middle class in India commodification is happening through the more familiar modes of incorporation, credit cards and credit rating agencies, frequent flyers, vacations, niche marketing, ATM cards and monthly billing cycles, corporate consumer campaigns and brand environments, all generating vast amounts of information. This is the more conventional generic world of the new globalization. The networks of pirate culture, on the other hand, usually target the urban populations outside this world, but who are nevertheless drawn increasingly to the commodified forms of urban experience.

Pirate electronic networks are part of a "bleeding" culture, constantly marking and spreading in urban life. This emphasizes its resilience and is a nightmare to classify. In a world where information bleeding is part of the contemporary (SMS, television text scrolling, newspaper inserts, lamp-post stickers, internet pop-ups, event branding), pirate culture uses the ruses of the city *immanently*, not transcendentally.

Piracy is not an alterity, or a form of resistance, though it clearly offers creative solutions outside the property regime to subaltern populations.[18] Piracy disrupts capitalist control, but does so in a property regime that has little space for it.

Some years ago Zygmunt Bauman summarized the mood of the 1990s:

> Globalization is on everyone's lips; a fad turning into a shibboleth, a magic incantation, a pass-key meant to unlock the gates to all and future mysteries. For some, 'globalization' is what we are bound to do if we wish to be happy; for others 'globalization' is the cause of our unhappiness.
>
> (Bauman, 1998, p.1)

Pirate modernity may be seen as globalization's illicit and unacknowledged expression. In globalization's official script in India, "the market" replaces the state in fulfilling the developmentalist dream (Das, 2002). For radical anti-globalization activists it was the official script that mattered. For the managers of media industries and neoliberal civic campaigners it was usually pirate modernity, a form refusing the law, not anti-globalization radicals, that posed a greater threat to the official model of capitalism. Pirate modernity's world moved between the local city, the regional and the international. This was not just in Asian cities, but also in Africa and Latin America (Simone, 2006). In a recent essay Saskia Sassen suggested that the world economy was now seeing the proliferation of many cross-border systems, which assembled networks from national and global areas of territory and power. These were "bits" of an emerging reality. The assemblages were constituted by legal, financial, corporate and activist movements (Sassen, 2007). Pirate modernity could also be added to Sassen's list. Pirate networks move everyday goods, media, clothing and medicine, "reassembling" bits of local regional and transnational space – pursued by enforcement agencies, anti-piracy activists and lawyers.

More than a decade ago, Arjun Appadurai summarized the contemporary entanglement of media and modernity as "the Global Now," where "the modern and the global often appear as flip sides of the same coin" (1996, p.3). Appadurai later expanded on this, arguing that while modernity seemed everywhere, it was also a series of "somewheres" (Appadurai and Breckinridge, 2005, p.2). At the heart of the "somewhere" for piracy were the resources of the bazaar. Bazaars in India historically drew from knowledge resources of merchant communities, internal networks of credit and reciprocity, and a reasonable confidence to engage in long-distance trade across regions and countries (Markovits *et al.*, 2003). While integral to the postcolonial capitalist reproduction process, bazaars acted as contexts for legal ambiguity for both production and circulation – piracy's favored site. An interface between legal capitalist markets as well as non-legal urban and media proliferation, the bazaar/market references piracy's porosity. The bazaar of the postcolonial period has been surpassed by a hybrid market formation closer to its Asian counterparts, transnational, technologically innovative and developing para-legal trade networks in Asia and Africa. Increasingly, for intellectual property campagners and civic liberal activists, the new hybrid bazaar-market became a source of a threat to the city and its law.

The old modernist urban archive of the twentieth century produced the dualisms of the plan and counter-plan, the public and the private, control and resistance. Pirate modernity has no clear representative language, but a series of mutating situations. It emerged as a pragmatic appropriation of the city, perhaps more *in media res* than "marginal." Pirate modernity does not easily fit classic representations of the political, the resistant, the tactical, the marginal, the multitude or the "movement." The twentieth-century European avant-garde dreamt of transforming everyday life into a festival. Pirate modernity ignores the redemptive cast of either the early avant-garde or many subsequent political movements. *Pirate Modernity* suggests that pirate modernity is a contagion of the ordinary, which disturbs the very "ordinariness" of the everyday.

Delhi, Empire to machine city in the tropics

The 1965 manifesto-essay "Planning for Bombay" by Charles Correa, Pravina Mehta and Shirish Patel was published in a special issue of the architectural magazine MARG. It opened with a powerful metaphor: "Bombay, originally, was that finest of things, a city on the sea. From this grew its character" (1965, p.29). With this simple but effective image, Correa and his collaborators mobilized an image of a city organized around space and water. Meanwhile, shortly before the essay by Correa and his colleagues, a writer in the journal *Panchashila* passed his summary judgement on postcolonial Delhi: "What was meant to be a city of gardens and beautiful roads has grown into a city of endless uniform blocks of dull, drab, yellowish box-like houses, a city of squares and round-abouts, every square being a cul-de-sac for a cosmopolitan community" (Chitrasen, 1961, p.25). Filled with rootless migrants and government, "It is a city without a soul, a city without character" (ibid.). For India's oldest metropolis, which stood on the ground of various ruined empires for almost a millennium, the circle had turned fully.

Narayani Gupta has vividly demonstrated the brutal transformation of the Mughal city following the defeat of the rebels in 1857 by the colonial rulers. Delhi saw the systematic destruction of many parts of the city by the victorious company armies, and the management of the defeated populations first through terror, and later through limited municipal government.[19] Modest urban infrastructure was put in place to attend to colonial fears of disease and native proliferation. Sanitation, a significant colonial obsession, was added to an urban design that demanded the slow segregation of European and native parts of the city. While the obsessive concern with disease, epidemics and sanitation since the nineteenth century dramatized the public effects of colonial power in the city, it built a significant urban knowledge complex that combined statistics, disease control, urban bylaws and regulations. There were those like the Edinburgh designer Patrick Geddes who challenged the colonial urban eye in his writings and work (1946). His "diagnostic survey" offered experimental alternatives to colonial pathologies of disease; Geddes also stressed the importance of understanding native urban design. Mostly marginalized by colonial urban power, Geddes' greater success was with the princely states.

For the most part, Delhi after 1857 remained a poor cousin as compared to the colonial cities of Bombay and Calcutta in the deployment of colonial technological power. Electricity, piped running water, the railway, the electric tramway – all technological symbols of European power – came to Delhi well after they arrived in Bombay and Calcutta. The post-mutiny technological backwardness emerged as an allegorical form of the colonial shaming of Delhi's subjugated populations. More importantly, the defeat of the insurgents in 1857 inaugurated a move to a different model of urban life, where the display of colonial sovereignty slowly subsumed the urban pasts of Delhi. The Coronation Durbar of 1911 was the crucial turning point in this direction, and the colonial design by Edward Lutyens and George Baker for the new capital institutionalized it to perfection.[20] Lutyens' design was a mobilization of ceremonial power of Empire over the colonized, with a subtle incorporation of "local" influences (Irving, 1983; Metcalf, 2002). The urban form was based on an elevational display of the Viceroy's house and Kingsway, and a clear separation from the Moghul city and its traditions. A hierarchy of class and status was mediated through a combination of dispersed garden city design and baroque monumentality; vast empty spaces were included to give maximum exposure to colonial power and ceremony. New Delhi emerged as *the* city of the Empire all over the world where the volatile tropical nativisms were absorbed by a paternal universalism.

The colonial design paradoxically performed two double functions for Delhi's postcolonial successors; Lutyens' Delhi reincarnated itself as an integral part of both urban and Indian history.[21] The monumental form of colonial Delhi was repeated endlessly through visual representation at all state events since Independence. The colonial capital has thus provided a naturalizing locus for nationalist memory, the founding midnight myth of August 14, 1947 in Parliament, and the subsequent annual military parade in Rajpath on Republic Day. All this had the effect of almost erasing the 1857 revolt in Delhi's past, and the terrible slaughter and urban terror that the colonial regime wrought on the city after the rebels' defeat. Kingsway now became postcolonial Rajpath, and official Delhi. "The less memory is experienced from the inside," Pierre Nora warns, "the more it exists through its exterior

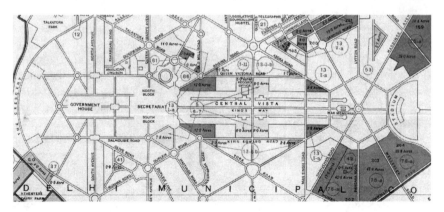

Figure 0.1 The colonial vision. Kingsway and the Central Vista later became Rajpath in the post-1947 city.

Source: Map III, *New Delhi Development Committee Report*, 1939.

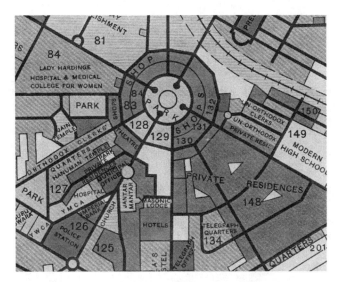

Figure 0.2 Connaught Place and surroundings in the colonial city. The elaborate hierarchy of the colonial design sought to overwhelm the perceived disorder of Shahjehanabad.

Source: Map II, *New Delhi Development Committee Report*, 1939.

scaffolding and outward signs" (1989, p.13). Until recently, Lutyens' Delhi seemed resistant to all the mutability and contingency that marks cultural artifacts; its success lay in the fact that the modernist elites of Delhi promoted the preservation of the colonial "bungalow zone" with missionary zeal.

The passing of Empire upset the smooth rhythm of colonial Delhi. The years of 1947 to 1948 saw periodic flashes of subaltern crowds in the city – in celebration at the Red Fort in August 1947; in fear and anger when Maulana Azad addressed the Friday gathering in Jama Masjid during Partition; and in sorrow when Kingsway was packed with mourners for Gandhi's funeral procession. This period was also marked by the terrible slaughter of Partition, the shameful expulsion of Delhi's Muslim residents, and the arrival of new refugees from former West Punjab. For the most part though, the memories of Partition's orgy of slaughter and displacement would return, but only decades later. The postcolonial elites who took power in 1947 had little identification with the pasts of Delhi, primarily seeing the city as a display window for nationalist sovereign power, in seamless continuation with the model of Lutyens' colonial design (Menon, 2000). Delhi was primarily viewed as a site from where national reconstruction and planning could be designed. The new rulers invested in a technocratic modernism for the city, to be produced and managed by experts and scientists.[22] For a capital city there was little time for experiments or utopias.

It was not without consequence that Nehru invested in Corbusier's Chandigarh as the dream city of nationalism free from the anxieties of

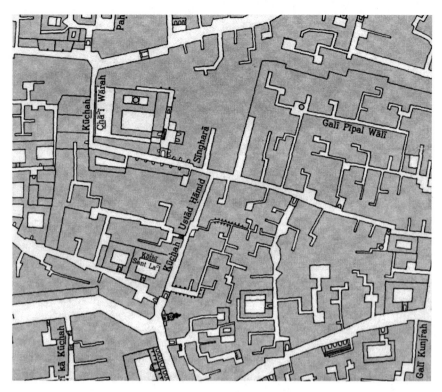

Figure 0.3 Shahjehanabad view, pre-1857. This is a fragment from a redrawn Moghul map. Technocratic modernism in the twentieth century reconstituted the old city as the prehistory of modern urbanism.

Source: Das Geographische Institut der Universität Bonn.

managing traditional detritus. Chandigarh's design suggested an abstract temporality, evoking one of the more noumenal visions of 1950s Nehruvianism – the urgent desire for modernity. This was a vision of an Ideal city where the chaos and uncertainties of the village would be banished. If nationalism's vision of the future was an eternally deferred not-yet, Chandigarh changed that into an architectural museum of the now. Chandigarh was conceived, or thought to be conceived on a *tabula rasa* that other Indian architects looked at with envy. The Chandigarh experiment could not be reproduced in Delhi, with its restless refugee squatter camps and politicized Parliament.[23] In Delhi modernism would be filtered for the public through a more familiar and reassuring optic – a healthy city, with attendant technologies of welfare and shelter. Urban modernism in post-Partition Delhi came primarily in the shape of urban planning – culminating in the 1962 Masterplan.

Le Corbusier had once asked the question "Architecture or Revolution?" in the early years of the modern movement, suggesting that it was a rationalist modernism, not the turmoil of social transformation that would answer the problems of the modern city. With a rational design and new "tools," revolution could be happily avoided. "Everything is possible by calculation and invention," wrote Le Corbusier, "provided there is in our disposal a suffi- ciently perfected body of tools, and this does exist" (1972, p.266). Elsewhere, Le Corbusier denounced the non-rational rhythm of the old city which he contemptuously called the "donkey track" view of urban life. Anthony Vidler has argued that modern urbanism has always been haunted by Enlightenment fears of "dark space," which is seen as a repository of superstition, non-reason and the breakdown of civility (Vidler, 1994). "Dark space" constantly invades "light space" through the fear of epidemics, urban panic, the homeless multi- tude and criminal activity. For the best part of the twentieth century, modern urban planning and architecture has sought to stake out the idea of transpar- ent space free from superstition, disease, myth and non-rational behavior. Modernism's use of glass and light, and the advocacy of the grid as a rational mapping of the city, went along with the establishment of governmental authority. The norms and forms of modern urban governance would separate the civic from the criminal, the public from the private, the human from the non-human, putting in place a model that would promise the visible and healthy interaction of human beings and things.

The Delhi Masterplan did not depart from this problematic significantly, but partly filtered it through the prism of Cold War liberal modernism, brought to the Plan by US experts. By this time, urbanism had purged the utopian elements from the modernist project, moving to the pragmatic and the technical. Technocratic urban design would answer problems of conges- tion, poverty and urban growth. Cast in a regionalist shell, the Masterplan involved a careful distinction between forms of labor and subjectivity that were seen as appropriate to modern urban life in India; those who did not fit this model could be open for displacement in the event of a failed assimila- tion into urbanism. As I argue here, the Masterplan did not simply put in place a "wrong" design that was widely believed to have "failed" by the 1980s. The plan's important innovation was to set in motion an implicit idea of the city as a machine, which was regulated by a technocratic apparatus. This idea of the machine city worked with a schema of decentralization with cellular neighborhoods, zoning, district centers, factory areas – all regulated by law. Technical instruments and expertise would generate urban knowledge, while counter-magnets to the core urban zone would contain inflows. This was not Le Corbusier's "machine for living" but a significant modernization. In the 1950s US urban planners were stressing that decentralization was not just appropriate for solving urban density, but was best suited for dealing with the threats of nuclear war. In the American variant, the decentralized city drew from cybernetic models where urban management would draw from information patterns and computer modeling to predict and calculate growth.[24] In the US debate, as within the American planners who worked on the Delhi Masterplan, the fears of density and an uncontrollable city were paramount.[25]

The Masterplan's public address was that of balanced growth and equity, which would be assured by a state development authority. In its technocratic language the plan sought to produce a double displacement. If on the one hand ceremonial order of the colonial city was replaced by a machine model of US urbanism, the forms of life that could not fit in the liberal city (economic proliferation, mixed-land use, "rural" industries) were set up for legal control and dispersal. "Discipline is a political anatomy of detail," Foucault once famously wrote (1977, p.139). The formal language of the plan hid a technological wish for diffused *legal* power. Foucault suggested that this was characteristic of modern regimes, a new political technology that was "more rapid, more effective, a design of subtle coercion for a society to come" (ibid., p.209). In Delhi at least this was not to be – for reasons discussed in this book.

The unraveling of the 1962 Masterplan has partially imaged the public discourse of the past three decades. The very forces that the technocratic machine sought to contain actively rebounded after 1977 – economic proliferation, urban sprawl, non-legal manufacture and commerce, migrant flows into the city. The very infrastructures that represented the plan's modernity (i.e. electricity, roads, water, health, pollution) became sites of public conflicts about the city. These conflicts were enmeshed in media infrastructures, strategies and techniques. This scenario is not unique to Delhi, but rebounds across the postcolonial world, where postwar planning regimes have collapsed in the face of failed economic models. The public debate has become cluttered with a cluster of responses, often at odds with each other. For the old planners the urban transformations suggest a crippled national sovereignty; for a range of Western and Indian orthodox radicals this marks the retreat of the state; for modernism in general the new urban is a catastrophic reversal of the critical possibilities of the twentieth century. For neo-liberalism in India, the current situation represents the long delayed modernization of Indian capitalism and the unleashing of market-based forces. The latter speak from a position of confidence – with easy access to media outlets, industry bodies and economic ministries of the government. In light of the economic catastrophes in Africa and Latin America following neo-liberal policies, this position is particularly fragile, and we may well see these strains in India in the near future.

This book offers a different path. I suggest that the recent transformations in postcolonial cities, Delhi included, involve a shift from the twentieth-century modernist heritage of urbanism. So fundamental is this move that it involves a significant rearrangement of the technologies of urban management that postcolonial cities have known after colonialism.

Power, politics, viral life

In his *Politics of the Governed*, Partha Chatterjee stages a conflict between modernity, committed to legal rights and civil society, as contrasted with the domain of populations and para-legal politics (2004). While modernity was the realm of legal subjects who could share in liberal citizenship, political democracy was the diffusion of governmental technologies of welfare and administration for subaltern populations who could not enter legal subjectivity. What resulted was a conceptual division between citizens and populations, where the latter were empirical categories of people who received administered welfare policies, while citizens were part of a homogeneous national body. The relationship between populations and the state was mediated through the domain of political society which was implicated in a series of complex social arrangements and political mobilizations, which could not be formulated within the classic state–civil society relationship. Political society, says Chatterjee, constituted a field which lacked the clarity of moral language and legal concepts that were supposed to define the relations between state and civil society. It meant bending the rules, recognizing that the legal fiction of equal citizenship did not always apply, that the laws of property and contract might sometimes need to be overlooked. To be sure, governmental policy treated population groups as discrete elements of "the heterogeneous social" (ibid., p.26). In turn political groups took it upon themselves to "mould the empirical discreteness of a population group into the moral solidarity of a community." Viewed through an urban lens, Chatterjee's argument offers a useful reconceptualization of the huge expansion of the non-legal in India's cities in the 1970s and early 1980s. It was representative politics mobilizing the "governed," rather than the liberal model of the Masterplan which produced a more diverse city. Through a political relationship to a governmentalized state and its institutions, urban dwellers would initiate back and forth struggles to expand claims on the city. Political society then is a post-liberal phenomenon, crossing boundaries of legal and non-legal. Independent of Chatterjee's essay, micro investigations by Solomon Benjamin in East Delhi's Viswas Nagar showed the development of a vast non-legal small industrial zone, built by complex para-legal strategies by local populations, tweaking classificatory categories, obtaining unauthorized electricity connections, cultivating political favors and tapping informal finance (Benjamin, 1991).

Chatterjee's "political society" is however surprisingly devoid of techno-cultural networks; it suggests a politics *before* media.[26] It emerges as the record of a postcolonial politics untainted by media technology, moving along familiar trajectories of citizenship and its outside, welfare and pastoral power, the domain of the legal and non-legal, mediated by the political. By the 1990s it was clear that techniques of the "political society" were significantly recast into a new uncertain domain, Strategies initiated by the "politics of the governed" (squatting, regularization of unauthorized colonies, informal infrastructure) suffered a major paralysis in Delhi in the 1990s, not least due to the emergence of new technologies of political control deploying radical media strategies. If the media zone allowed for the creative emergence of pirate modernity, it equally opened the gates for a new discourse of liberalism by globalizing elites. This was the birth of a new liberalism, which used the media as a significant site for new political discourse.

The implications of the shift in the cultural-technological landscape in Delhi and other Indian cities was quickly grasped by middle-class campaigners who posed the "problem of the city" in terms that had not been done by either political society or older Keynesian planning liberals. Ranging from neo-liberal activists to affluent resident welfare associations, environmental activists to transparency campaigners, they fell into a zone that may be called *civic liberalism*. Here the urban became an explicit site of discourse. Civic liberalism was the most ambitious intervention at an explicit urban discourse in India's cities, and the implications for Delhi were wide-ranging. Civic liberalism was nothing more than an innovative technology for a postcolonial "control society." It represented a bold, and for a while effective strategy by globalizing elites to reclaim urban discourse from political representation.

Technologies of civic liberalism refer to knowledges and techniques deployed to manage, map and understand the urban crisis of contemporary Delhi. These technologies emerge from both older and new sites of power in the city, urban resident welfare associations, hospitals, courts, civic groups on all issues, professional bodies, and media managers. The new technologies are innovative, intervening through media effects, publicized court judgments, TV campaigns, new physiognomies of identification and information gathering. Rather than care for a social body, the language of risk and uncertainty is increasingly the favored terrain for technologies of civic liberalism. Plunging into the new media (text campaigns, blogs, media management), these technologies suggest an out-of-control urban experience, needing radical new points of perpetual intervention.

In an era of globalization and uncertainty, "risk" has emerged as the main language of late (neo-liberal) modernity.[27] Risk is the management of danger, unintended consequences and urban fear. Risk technologies suggest that older institutions of governmentality (or political society) are ill-equipped to deal with the unknowability of the present. In this reading, contemporary crisis demanded a *new* kind of expertise. In the case of Delhi, the urban crisis of the 1990s led to a decisive shift in the language of urban governance. This was new liberalism's favored landscape of intervention. During the years of crisis Delhi witnessed a move away from the "classic" institutions of the city, which were now seen as contaminated by politics and therefore incapable of dealing with risk. The predictions of danger and risk assessment now emerged from a new domain of experts *not* accountable to the elected city government. This marked a big shift from the planner era when experts reported to the city and national government. The courts appointed the new experts during pollution case hearings on petitions filed by civic activists. The court case became a giant *event scene* in the city, with wide-ranging media effects involving experts, judges and affected populations. The new experts promoted techniques that embraced and accelerated the media experience, with new-style campaigns, bombardment of information on the airwaves, a frenzy of numbers, and graphs on pollution, safety and public health. The experts reported regularly to the Supreme Court and suggested rapid surgical interventions in the fabric of city life, almost all of which was implemented with court approval. Court-appointed committees supervised the removal of industry from the city, regulated buses and drivers, and forced the removal of working-class settlements from the river banks for allegedly "polluting" the river. The language of risk prevention now transcends the earlier allegiance to social justice in the planning documents of the 1950s. To date the court-supervised expert committees have removed more than 200,000 people from their old habitats, a scale inconceivable in the planning era. The evacuation of the civic from the "social" remains one of the most profound transformations in urban discourse in postcolonial India, the implications of which are in the process of being worked out.

Differing from the more prominent technologies of surveillance and control that have emerged in response to war, terrorism and social conflict, urban risk strategies in a postcolonial city like Delhi opened up a zone that is fraught with both media intervention and conflict. While the earlier language of urbanism had suggested that the urban body be mapped, enumerated and even disciplined to maintain its health, the new technologies of risk suggest that the problems of the city need to be resolved outside the language of the social. Abstract numbers on air quality, technical information on road sizes and so on have propelled legal discourse, a tactic that has successfully excluded the old formations of political society.[28] These new technologies suggest that modern urbanism's great wager in using architecture and planning to produce disciplined, healthy subjects may well be behind us. Civic liberalism's golden age was the 1990s, until it seemed to have peaked in 2006, after over-extending itself. In hindsight, it seems to have initiated the most significant transformation of urban discourse since planning, offering a new language to modernizing members of the political and corporate classes.[29] The strength of civic liberalism lay in its ability to produce *crisis scenes*, a dramatic intensification of media tactics and legal dramaturgies. Crisis scenes were hugely successful strategies for civic liberalism, but they disclosed a confusing blurring of boundaries between the human and the technological.

One of these instances emerged in the storm around road accident deaths in Delhi, examined in detail in this book. As a viral form – relayed instantly through text messages, repetitive live broadcasting and visceral media headlines – the road accident proliferated well beyond the control of media managers, city officials, the police and politicians. The "media" emerged as the signifying yet unstable archive of the event, where a body of images, news and text messages, all combined to produce a disorienting image of urban life, with machines and subjects spinning out of control. The divisions between human and machine blurred, and the roles seemed reversed at times. The machine, long seen as managed by humans, took on a subjective force in media accounts and court judgments. "Typically," says the philosopher Keith Ansell Pearson, "the machine is construed as a deficient form of life, lacking in autopoetic formative power and self-generative evolution" (1997, p.5). The road crash was a perfect but tragic site of the human/machine confusion, as causality shifted from event to event – errant bus drivers, failed brakes, exploding gas cylinders, bad roads and so on.

Courts faced similar problems when pushed by civic campaigners to intervene in the media city. The expansion of electronically amplified instruments from the 1980s in Indian cities posed the problem of managing public noise at a time when large sections of the urban population became actual or potential media consumers and producers. For the most part the existing technologies of sound management (Nuisance Law, the Factory Act) proved to be of little use. Proliferation of media, running parallel to the proliferation of the city, seemed unstoppable. Campaigns against "indiscriminate" use of loudspeakers and firecrackers were started by middle-class civic groups. Petitions reached the Supreme Court which ultimately banned the use of loudspeakers from 10 p.m. to 6 a.m. The Court judgment itself is fascinating, as it captures the problematic of media urbanism – the move from controlled and manageable spaces of reception (cinemas, factories) to a situation where media emerged from the public body, *as if without limits*. This is what the Court said:

> Noise is a type of atmospheric pollution. It is a shadowy public enemy whose growing menace has increased in the modern age of industrialization and technological advancement. . . . Noise pollution was previously confined to a few special areas like factory or mill, but today it engulfs every nook and corner of the globe, reaching its peak in urban areas. Industries, automobiles, rail engines, airplanes, radios, loudspeakers, tape recorders, lottery ticket sellers, hawkers, pop singers, etc., are the main ear contaminators of the city area and its market place.[30]

In suggesting that "noise" had emerged from the enclosed spaces of the factory to "every nook and corner" of the globe and the city the Court foregrounded the limits of the existing technologies of management. Mixing things and people as "ear contaminators" of the city, the Court judgment exposed the growing confusions about the effects produced by machines and humans. This was in a sense the dramaturgy of media urbanism. As urban populations embraced more media, producing unstable combinations of desire and conflict, civic liberal initiatives performed the role of a destructive reverse optics, dramatizing boundary confusions, rather than leading to "transparency."

A few years before his death, Gilles Deleuze suggested an update of Foucault's mediations on power and control, which at any rate had successively gone through the focus on discipline, governmentality and bio-politics. Deleuze mapped out an important change from disciplinary regimes, which in Foucault's original narrative had replaced the societies of absolutist sovereignty. New telecommunication networks and "flows" of information dislocated the technologies of confinement and designation distinctive of disciplinary regimes. What emerged were "control societies," a significant shift from the experience that Foucault had described. Now, "Enclosures are molds, distinct castings, but controls are a modulation, like a self-deforming cast that will continuously change from one moment to the other, or like a sieve whose mesh will transmute from point to point" (Deleuze, 1992, p.4).

Modulation, rather than old-style discipline, transforms the rhythm of movement, blurring entry and departure points. Says Deleuze, "one is never finished with anything – the corporation, the educational system, the armed services being metastable states coexisting in one and the same modulation, like a universal system of deformation" (ibid., p.5). Under societies of control the short term and the unbounded overtake the disciplinary models of the long term. The individual, the mass and the signature have been replaced by codes and passwords and databanks. Piracy and counterfeits replace sabotage, and capitalism is no longer confined to factories:

> [N]ineteenth-century capitalism is a capitalism of concentration, for production and for property. It therefore erects the factory as a space of enclosure, the capitalist being the owner of the means of production but also, progressively, the owner of other spaces conceived through analogy (the worker's familial house, the school). As for markets, they are conquered sometimes by specialization, sometimes by colonization, sometimes by lowering the costs of production.
>
> (Ibid., p.6)

Capitalism now works through dispersal, and debt rather than discipline is its primary tool. Deleuze's essay is but a rough outline, the economic analysis sometimes schematic and clearly Euro-centered.[31] In his characteristic style, Deleuze uses Foucault's work as a foil to bounce off his own ideas. Nevertheless, in his idea of a world that is "continuous and without limit," Deleuze illuminates the problem of collapsing boundaries of older control technologies. This was by no means a necessary "advance" over the previous epochs. In a conversation with Antonio Negri, Deleuze said that "Compared with the approaching forms of ceaseless control in open sites, we may come to see the harshest confinement as part of a wonderful happy past."[32] In this context, the problem of a politics appropriate to the new "technological" epoch was fundamental, a question that had also been raised by Benjamin in his Artwork essay. Except, unlike in Benjamin's time the choice today is not between "dreamworld and catastrophe," but responding to a capitalism that mixes technology and life in a destructive-chaotic expansion.

The book's structure

Michel Foucault wrote in his introduction to Georges Canguilhem's *The Normal and the Pathological* that a concept "must give access to a structure of intelligibility" (Foucault, 1991, p.19). To adhere to this injunction, this book is organized around a series of conceptual force fields. Rather than a historical sequence of postcolonial Delhi, I look at the way in which conceptual fields are enunciated. The elements of the fragmentary archive that I mobilize (planning documents, letters, everyday stories, media surfaces, interviews) all move through this method of exposure.

Chapter 1 looks at the liberal city imaginary of the 1950s through the making of the Delhi Masterplan. Planning emerged in the 1950s when a liberal urbanism posited a city of law and justice, based on an elaborate technology of urban management that would be inaugurated by planning. The plan did not just make the city legible for the postcolonial elites, it assured for them a model of sovereign control. Chapter 2 looks at the rapid unraveling of this model in the long decades after the Emergency, and the emergence of a media urbanism. The breaking of the Masterplan's careful separation of forms of work, residence and movement took place in the context of political transformation and media expansion after the Emergency and the Asiad of 1982. Media urbanism emerged during this period. I track this through the context of global urban debates on urban informality along with a critical take on recent catastrophic readings of the failed liberal developmentalist city. The chapter moves through the different sites specific to media urbanism, the event/spectacle, the market/bazaar, the "pirate city," the links of production and circulation in small informal factory zones.

Chapter 3 looks at the materialization of media piracy as the wild zone of media urbanism. Piracy spread rapidly all over India from the cassette era, reassembling local and post-national regional space in new technological infrastructures. Piracy was a corporeal zone that attracted urban populations transcending social class. By introducing a commodified zone outside "intellectual" property laws, piracy posed a vexing problem not just for the mainstream media industry, but also for older liberal/radical theories of the "creative" commons.

Chapter 4 looks at the experience of road travel for Delhi's bus passengers following the advent of private buses in the late 1980s. The planners had dreamed of the road as an integral part of the free circulation of goods and people in the modern city. By the end of the twentieth century Delhi's roads had moved into a dystopian world of speeding buses, and smashed bodies and vehicles. All events were magnified by a visceral media sensorium. This period saw everyday violent encounters between urban populations and speeding road machines, exposing public displays of technological death. This site of the city was the Accident. In every sense, the Accident captured the mixture of death, commodity worlds, technology and desire that marked the final decade of Delhi's twentieth century.

Walter Benjamin once spoke of the "actuality of the everyday," where the contemporary becomes *the* marker of the urban experience and foregrounds the time of the present. There are times when this "actuality of the everyday" suddenly takes meaning: London and Paris in the nineteenth century, Calcutta for the new urban elites at the turn of the nineteenth century, Berlin in the 1920s, Bombay from after World War II to the 1970s. For Delhi this surely was the time after the 1980s, when the city entered a new phase of uncertainty. It is to this actuality of the everyday and its prehistory that we now turn.

1 A city of order

The Masterplan

In July 1996 the Supreme Court of India began a series of far-reaching judgments affecting the city of Delhi in response to petitions by the environmental lawyer M.C. Mehta.[1] The issue was industrial pollution; a year earlier the Court had ordered the Central Pollution Board to issue notices to thousands of "hazardous" industries, demanding their relocation outside the city. In the 1996 order the Court decided that the industries be relocated outside the city by November.[2] The initial slot of units was around 168 in number, dealing with "heavy" industries, "hazardous and noxious" in nature, according to the Court. This judgment was only the beginning of a series of wide-ranging pronouncements; soon more industries were asked to move: hot-mix plants, "extensive industries" in residential areas, and brick kilns.[3] By the end of the decade the pronouncements expanded to "undisputedly polluting" industries in "non-conforming areas." This extended to "potentially polluting ones." By 2000 tens of thousands of workers were affected, and mass protests ensued. As one writer put it soon after the events,

> Suddenly all hell broke loose. Desperate workers were out on the streets alongside their employers, resisting the closures. There were roadblocks and violent protests as desperate workers, egged on by their employers – who themselves chose to remain in the background except in some cases – came on to the streets. For three or four days the city was in turmoil.
>
> (Nigam, 2001)

Anger in working-class areas of the city was widespread, given the scale of those affected. In 1996 the Court had asked the Delhi Pollution Control Board to conduct a survey of industries which put the total at 126,218 units with 97,411 "non-conforming" units (*Down to Earth*, 2000).

The Court judgment was hailed by the national media and the weary middle-class elites as a "landmark", and as the return of the rule of law in a city gone to seed under the assault of populist politics and "unplanned" growth. The Court now emerged as the authentic signature of a resurgent urban middle class for whom "legal activism" began to be seen as a way of producing a discourse on *their* city, long taken from them. The Court judgments were part of a series of spectacular pronouncements on the city which slowly moved to every aspect of everyday life, pollution, animals, and all forms of public behavior. Legal discourse now took on an uncontrolled master narrative on the city and its lives. In 2006 the court went even further, proclaiming that all commercial activity that was "non-conforming" would have to be "sealed" and forced to close. While in 1996 the affected were mostly workers in small establishments, now entire commercial areas, and shops and local establishments throughout Delhi were threatened with closure.

In both the 1996 and 2006 judgments the Court importantly referenced the 1962 Masterplan of Delhi as the Law of the City. The judgments followed the main document of 1962 with minor amendments by the Delhi Development Authority (DDA) in 1990 that largely preserved the original design. The 1962 Masterplan's land-use plan had delineated commerce, industry, work and home, and further distinguished between normal and hazardous and noxious industries, the latter to be displaced from the city (DDA, 1962, pp.83–85, 1990, pp.100–112).

The Court's judgments followed the pathogenesis of the plan's spatial argument. In the years following the Court judgment of 1996 the Masterplan emerged as the originary archive of the legal city, referred to in popular conversation and newspaper debates. The normative-disciplinary words deployed by the Plan – "non-conforming," "hazardous," "commercial" – now entered a larger universe of discourse on the city. As if displaced from the technocratic discourse of planners, the plan entered a realm of the imaginary.

In returning to the plan the Court hit upon a lost urban archive of planning in the 1950s. In the phantasmatic recall of the plan, the legal discourse shed light on postcolonial urbanism's urban design four decades earlier, based on a vision of order, the legal separation of work, commerce and industry, and proper civic citizenship.

Urban modernism in the 1950s, planning and dreaming

In March 1959 a significant gathering of India's architects took place in Delhi to discuss the future of Indian cities and the urban form. Present in the gathering were all the emerging architects, young and old: A.P. Kanvinde, Charles Correa, Aditya Prakash, Habib Rehman, Satish Gujral. Also in attendance was the British architect Gordon Cullen and representatives of the regional city movement from the USA, Catherine Bauer, and the planner Albert Mayer then leading a US team working on the Delhi Masterplan. The shadows of Corbusier and Chandigarh were in the air and there was palpable excitement among young architects. Modernism had arrived with a flourish, and had official sanction in Delhi. In a short, passionate speech, the young Charles Correa cut across the debate among older architects about the Indian "style." For Correa, architecture was about temperament, pure expression, a projection of the *auteur*, something that Corbusier's "savage" buildings successfully accomplished in Chandigarh. As an example, Correa reminded fellow architects about Corbusier's High Court Building in that city.

> The main entrance – it is one of the greatest *tour de force* ever pulled off in architecture. To enter that building, to stand under the columns is to know what justice is – superhuman justice, justice without mercy, the state above and beyond the prejudices of the individual. This is architecture, the feeling of command. . . . One would question it on one point alone. One would say, is this justice? Is this a picture of justice? Should justice be beyond the individual, superhuman, monumental, beyond mercy?
>
> (Correa, 1959, p.48)

While Correa distanced himself from Corbusier's vision, there was a clear admiration for modernism's *auteur* imagination, combining abstract freedom with the ability to imprint on built form. That mood reverberated through many speakers at the conference where architects spoke of the need for new materials and technologies, freedom from government regulation, and to develop new educational strategies of architectural expression and pedagogy.

The main event at the conference was the inaugural speech by Jawaharlal Nehru staking out his vision of the future urban form. Nehru's own sympathy for modern architecture's transformative potential was in little doubt; his enthusiastic patronage of Corbusier and the Chandigarh project was the clearest expression of that vision. In 1949 Nehru had visited the site for Chandigarh and exclaimed with considerable excitement, "The site chosen is free from the existing encumbrances of old towns and traditions. Let it be the first large expression of our creative genius flowering on our newly earned freedom" (Kalia, 1999, p.12). When he came to the Delhi conference, Nehru laid out his vision in clear, almost blunt terms. "The past was good when it was the present," Nehru declared, "but you cannot bring it forward when the entire world has changed into a technological period" (Nehru, 1959, p.7). At any rate, Nehru suggested that many of the beautiful old buildings in India date back a few hundred years before colonialism, as India and much of its architecture was "static" when the British arrived, as was the rest of society. Nehru exclaimed that despite their beauty, he found some of the older Southern temples "repelling":

> I just can't stand them. Why? I do not know I cannot explain that, but they are oppressive, they suppress my spirit. They do not allow me to rise, they keep me down. The dark corridors – I like the sun and air and not dark corridors.
>
> (Nehru, 1959, p.7)

In the new urban age, almost echoing Viennese architect Adolf Loos' older modernist slogan, Nehru asserted "function governs." Design without function may reproduce "ghost-like" buildings if it simply harks back to an earlier period. The built form was not eternal; Nehru even suggested that new buildings could have specifications that allowed them to be "knocked down" after a few years to allow new ones to be built (Nehru, 1959, p.8).

In this short speech delivered in his characteristically open style, Nehru articulated all the manifesto elements of twentieth-century architectural modernism, its critique of the past, the alignment of form with function, the creative-destructive potential of the new materials, and an impression of urban life that was suitably abstract to realize these goals. In his frank distaste of dark corridors and the ghost-like qualities of buildings modeled on the past, Nehru let slip one of Western modernity's classic secrets. As Foucault famously pointed out, the fear of urban darkness motivated a disciplinary order which sought to redistribute populations and environments to allow for the free circulation of light and reason. In turn, this redistribution led to new enclosures and hierarchies, nurtured by new surveys of populations and objects. This management of populations was of course pioneered by colonial technologies of government. In the postcolonial order this was supplemented by the larger question – what was the form of the new city? Nehru's address to the architects' conference offered no clear answer to this with its abstract modernist gesture.

One answer to the new form of the city was the idea of planning. For writers like Mulk Raj Anand and others grouped around the cultural journal *MARG*, planning offered a utopian dream site for the new nation, incorporating cosmopolitan virtues, internationalism, and an openness to new design. From its establishment after World War II, *MARG* emerged as a premier journal for discussions on architecture, design and art, with essays by prominent international and Indian writers. *MARG* was also a platform for progressive architects[4] in Bombay to generate what they saw as a genuine cosmopolitan discourse on the arts. *MARG* was founded in 1946, and its founding issue was significantly titled "Planning and Dreaming." In his seminal editorial which also functioned as a manifesto for the group, Mulk Raj Anand suggested that though power had not yet been formally transferred from the British, there was little time to wait. "We have to ask the meaning of our dreams," said Anand, "the dust of centuries which has settled on our souls must be swept and constructive ideas fostered" (*MARG*, 1946, p.5). In this new effort architecture was the "mother art," and the plan the utopian signature of sovereignty. *MARG* suggested that this was an urgent effort: "We have to be up and doing. As architects of the new India, this beautiful and glorious country of our dreams, we have to see for it that there are no loopholes in our plans for the future if we can possibly help it" (*MARG*, 1946, p.5). The old order was dying everywhere and a new world was emerging, and *MARG* suggested that the focus was going to be on the "man-centered cities, towns and villages" that would be built in sovereign India. Here Indians were at a great advantage.

> Whereas in European countries a great deal of the jerry-built, tawdry, tasteless architecture, whereas reconstruction and rehabilitation may only superimpose a layer of beauty in this uniform smoky ugliness, here in India, where there has been no widespread building for two hundred years, we are talking of construction, not reconstruction. And we have to start on a clean slate and have to build our industrial civilization. . . . And we can summon the courage to think in terms of a grandeur such as may surpass all our achievements in the past.
>
> (MARG, 1946, p.6)

This clean-slate model of construction would also derive from an enlightened ("non-slavish") appreciation of the Indian past along with the new tools of transformation, architecture and planning. *MARG* carried articles on Corbusier and essays on urban planning, articles on art and design in India, an appreciation of house interiors, and book reviews. *MARG* clearly saw itself as transmitting international modernism through a local lens for a new postcolonial modernity, and shaping the emerging sensibility of urban cosmopolitan bourgeois elites. The pages of the magazine were filled with discussions on the new architecture, the Bauhaus, Corbusier, Frank Lloyd Wright Neutra, and new construction and design materials used in homes and interiors, steel, cement, glass, chrome, deployments of light and shade. There were reports on art exhibitions, pre-colonial and ancient art in South Asia, as well as book reviews. Beatriz Colomina has written that media is "the true site within which modern architecture is produced and with which it directly engages" (1994, p.14), and MARG exemplified this perfectly.

Despite its own self-designated position, the first *MARG* manifesto ended with a distinct caveat about its own future status:

> Our love for the future and our faith in our ability to build it, our energism, however does not blind us to the many limitations which we suffer in the uncertainties and chaos of the present situation. And time alone will judge how far we are competent to act as self-appointed administrators of social and architectural hygiene in a world where our cities have become like running sores and our villages putrid cesspools.
>
> (MARG, 1946, p.6)

In the event, the *MARG* concerns turned out to be accurate; by the 1950s the utopianism of the early years had given way to the pragmatic. As nationalist sovereignty was proclaimed over colonial metropolitan areas, the regime was faced with vast inequalities in India's cities and had to address the demands for social justice that had emerged in the anti-colonial movement. In most major cities, the administration of "social and cultural hygiene" was displaced from the dreams of the *MARG* intellectuals to a more abstract structure of the urban Masterplan.

In Delhi the arguments for urban planning were emerging from a range of interests. The capital had been devastated by the Partition of the subcontinent, with considerable violence on the Muslim population, who had seen their houses destroyed, and many had been subject to displacement and ghettoization. The millions of Hindu and Sikh refugees who arrived from Pakistan overwhelmed the capital. For the years following Partition the Ministry of Rehabilitation, led by the astute Minister Meher Chand Khanna, quickly moved in to set up markets and housing colonies for the newly arrived residents of Delhi. In their later summary of this period, the Delhi Masterplan's researchers described this era as one of chaotic expansion of the city's built form, the originary moment of "unauthorized construction" a result of the emergency situation prevailing at this time. In short, "there was little time for careful planning or for proper coordination of services and even today, many of these colonies do not have the basic necessities such as water, sewage and electricity" (DDA, 1961a, p.187).[5] The infrastructural crisis of the city following Partition immediately began a debate on the legacy of colonial urbanism and its managing authority, the Delhi Improvement Trust.

Colonial urban policy in twentieth-century Delhi had been largely based on a need to manage the old city, decisively marginalized after the coming of Lutyens' New Delhi. The government-commissioned Hume report of 1930 identified acute "congestion" as a significant problem in the transformation of Delhi into a modern planned city. The metaphor of congested space with its catalog of disease and fallen colonial subjects suggested a regulatory regime of planning and urban redevelopment. The Delhi Improvement Trust (DIT) was a result of this report.[6] The DIT half-heartedly attempted to relieve congestion through various city expansion schemes, a process ultimately compromised by land speculation and little access to the new areas for the city's poor.[7] The Trust's role came under review from the years immediately following World War II, leading to the Delhi Municipal Organization Enquiry Committee, set up in 1946. The Committee members belonged to the old social elites of Delhi and their report suggested a gradualist acknowledgment of nationalist sovereignty while maintaining the social hierarchies of the colonial city.[8] The final days of the Committee were held in the chaotic circumstances of Partition, losing almost all of its Muslim members. Summarizing the final traumatic months, the report has this to say:

> [A]t this time disturbances on a large scale started in the city and further work became almost impossible for a few weeks on account of the complete absence of staff. In the middle of September, the Chairman also resigned as his services were urgently needed by the Government of Pakistan for the post of their Deputy High Commissioner in India. It was in these circumstances that the report was prepared.[9]

The Partition fractured the old elite coalition that managed the DIT; the latter was completely overwhelmed by the events of 1948 to 1950. In the annual administration report of 1950 to 1951, the Trust's chairman ended with a note of visible exhaustion, suggesting that lack of resources and public investment had reduced the Trust's meager activities to house the poor as a "mere drop in the ocean," and called for a national housing policy.[10] The funerary tone of the report suggests that the DIT commissioners were probably aware of the impending report of the G.D. Birla Enquiry Committee that had been appointed to investigate the DIT's working and social mandate in 1950, and whose report was released in 1951. The Birla Committee produced a comprehensive indictment of the Trust at every level, its failure to provide a healthy civic environment in the city, the disorganized management of Delhi, and the unplanned growth of the city without effective zoning or a comprehensive Masterplan. Hindered by financial limits, speculative land transactions ("selling lands to the highest bidder without regard for its anti-social repercussions"), the Trust failed completely in housing the poor. The Birla report provided key props to the emerging nationalist design of the capital. As a clear sign of changed sovereignty, the Enquiry Committee called for a powerful city-wide centralized body to plan and manage Delhi. This later gave birth to the Delhi Development Authority. The immediate requirement was a Masterplan and a civic survey which the Enquiry Committee placed at the beginning of its recommendations. The second sign of the new wind blowing was the Committee's acknowledgment of the postwar demands for social justice. The report suggested that the new authority must move to rapidly house the city's poor and ensure that no existing person be displaced without "alternatives."[11]

The Birla Committee was the first thorough examination of Delhi by the postcolonial elite. Headed by of one of India's best-known industrialists, the Committee also had three Members of Parliament, along with technocrats. This was a reasonable approximation of the post-independence coalition in the early 1950s. The report bore marks of industrialist G.D. Birla's stewardship, calling for active private participation in housing, and an amendment of the rent control acts.[12] More significantly, the Birla Committee report provided clear clues to the emerging elite consensus on the city's urban design: centralization, an acknowledgment of "social justice" and a "masterplan." There were also traces of classic colonial and bourgeois fears of urban collapse and decay caused by the "blight" of slums. These were now transposed to the postcolonial burden of governance, confronted by claustrophobic urban space.

> Bad environments affects us all alike; we are choked, each one of us, whether we realize it or not, by the meanness and squalor which stretches their tentacles upwards from the lives of our less fortunate citizens. The slums hold us back; while they exist, the roots of our civilization are rotten and our corporate existence as a people is diseased.[13]

The health of the postcolonial urban body was at risk; a speedy recovery needed an urgent transition to the new urban regime.

Figure 1.1 "A typical slum." Photograph from a Town Planning Organization leaflet in the 1950s. The slum was seen as a postcolonial burden, "holding us back," as the Birla Committee would put it. Notice the "village-like" framing of the slum image, which would be later theorized by US consultants.

Source: TPO, Delhi, 1957.

The epidemic

In the month of January 1956 Raj Kumari Amrit Kaur, the Minister for Health and Local Self-government wrote to Douglas Ensminger, head of the Ford Foundation office in Delhi, to ask for Ford's support for US city planners to "advise and guide" in the capital's planning efforts. Stating that she was greatly worried about the "haphazard growth" of Indian cities, Kaur said that "Delhi is ready and eager to undertake city planning and development" and requested the Ford Foundation to sponsor costs of the project.[14] It is no coincidence that Kaur's request came in January 1956, a month that saw the intensification of a major jaundice epidemic in Delhi which highlighted the city's crumbling infrastructure, and opened up a major public debate on hygiene, urban governance, and the lack of order.

The first reports on jaundice surfaced in December 1955, but began escalating in January. From the first week of January 1956 every passing day was filled with new stories of jaundice deaths. On January 4, a total of about nineteen deaths were reported, and scores more were admitted to hospital.[15] Other reports suggested the epidemic was more serious, the Delhi Medical Association reporting that on an average its members were receiving two new cases a day.[16] At a Medical Association meeting the consensus was that drinking-water contamination had caused the disease. The following day the "experts" appointed by the Government Director-General of Health services agreed, pointing to the contamination of the city's water caused by when the River Yamuna flooded in November 1955.[17] Meanwhile patients kept streaming into city hospitals and more deaths were reported. In two days the death-toll had mounted to twenty-eight and the Communist and Socialist Parties as well as the Delhi Congress demanded an investigation.[18] By January 11 the government gave in to immense public pressure and the Union Health Minister Rajkumari Amrit Kaur joined Delhi's Health Minister in announcing an official investigation into the epidemic which would examine both the issue of pollution as well as official negligence.[19] At the news conference the Health Minister went on to suggest that she was surprised more epidemics had not broken out earlier given the conditions in the city. For Kaur, the general unsanitary conditions were a permanent reminder of the "problem" of the city.[20] A few days later, R.N. Aggarwal, President of the Delhi Municipal Committee, went on to expand on the Health Minister's concern about the city's sanitation. He assembled a picture of urban detritus leading to pollution, sanitation dangers, and congestion. The list included "illegal and unlicensed dairies," customary rights of sweepers, problems of slums and *katras*, and the refuse loading platforms in Sabzi Mandi, leading to an impossible "fly menace."[21]

The jaundice enquiry committee report was placed in Parliament by the Health Minister on February 17, 1956.[22] The report calculated that the figure of those affected was larger than had been calculated, involving almost 400,000 people including those with severe and minor infections.[23] The report confirmed what had been widely suspected – the contamination of the drinking-water supply by the overflow of sewage from the city's Najafgarh drains. The report blamed city officials from both the water and health departments for severe negligence, leading to the spread of the epidemic. In a clear censure of the postcolonial ability to run cities efficiently, the report claimed that this was the first instance "in the world of a piped municipal water supply being responsible for a large-scale dissemination of the virus."[24]

The report led to a storm in Parliament with calls for the Health Minister's resignation. The more significant part of the jaundice report was its far-reaching narrative of overpopulation, lack of sanitation, congestion, and haphazard growth in Delhi. As the city's population was seen galloping from its post-independence size, the report spoke of sixteen colonies dumping their sewage into the Najafgarh drains which then spread to the main water supply. Most significantly the report argued that a "Masterplan" was the only way to manage the city.[25]

In his book *French Modern* (1989), Paul Rabinbow suggests that the cholera epidemic of 1932 in Paris catalyzed discussions on a move to a techno-social urbanism. For Rabinow, the incidence of cholera, which killed more than 18,000 Parisians, was a "watershed" event, suggesting that conventional moral explanations had to give way to a foregrounding of the "social question." Long seen as a tropical curse, the cholera epidemic moved urban debates "away from moralizing, philanthropic, liberal understandings of the world (and their associated technologies of order) and toward social ones" (p. 168). In Rabinow's story, the post-1832 discourse in France moved slowly from an initial techno-cosmopolitanism that combined scientific discourses, statistics and a governance model based on discipline and surveillance, to a middling modernism which called for "a normative administrative function guided by science and operating on an entire population" (p. 344). Middling modernism combined specific intellectuals and technocrats in a context of a disengagement from ideological explanations and a focus on specific problems and solutions.

Like cholera in Rabinow's story, Delhi's jaundice epidemic from 1955 to 1956 highlighted the problem of the city, already under strain from post-Partition migrations. All the technocratic and public discussions from the Birla Committee to the jaundice epidemic report suggested that the rational management of populations and urban environments had failed if not collapsed. While for the Birla Committee the city was compromised by colonial inheritance and the social "blight" of the slums, the epidemic report suggested that postcolonial knowledge was severely handicapped in managing a modern city. Mixing biology, technical knowledge, and the possibility of urban collapse, the plan emerged in the debates as the best solution for all concerned. Scientists, politicians, social movements, and municipal officials now all actively lobbied for a Masterplan. In a debate in Parliament in December, 1955 on a bill controlling unregulated building in the city, one member requested rapid government intervention so that Delhi could change from a city of slums and tombs to becoming a city of "beauty, pomp and pleasure."[26] The plan emerged as the postcolonial elite's answer to colonial inequalities, a rational model of management that would ideally combine both claims for social justice and a technological dream-world of the future.

US liberal modernism and making of the Masterplan

It was not out of place for the Indian government to request help with the planning of Delhi from the Americans, particularly the Ford Foundation. Ford's largest office outside New York was in Delhi, the center of an ambitious international grant-making network. In the 1950s the Ford Foundation was among the leaders of a Cold War liberal internationalism that underwrote an elite pluralism as an opposition to communism. From 1945 to 1949 the Foundation transformed itself from a small company-centered foundation into a large international body, with the single largest endowment at the time. The main vehicle for the transformation was a significant report commissioned by the Ford President Rowan Gaither, mapping out a world divided between democratic and "authoritarian" societies, a code word for communism. The report called for a broad range of interventions, including the "promotion of democracy," and made its key business welfare, knowledge, and education.[27] Domestically, Ford sponsored social science projects in US universities, and underwrote many large-scale social studies in the formerly colonial world.[28] Liberal modernism with a technocratic social science analysis of the once subject population by leading scholars from US universities was part of Ford's larger Cold War project that it saw as moderating the cruder elements of anti-Red hysteria in the USA in the 1950s. Within the USA the Foundation remained deeply concerned with issues of race relations and integration that it saw as detrimental to US foreign policy worldwide, Ford became increasingly involved in race relations projects from the 1950s.

US foreign policy in Asia was focused on directly countering the Chinese and Vietnamese revolutions through military-political efforts. Ford's own policy towards postcolonial Asia was mediated through the lens of modernization theory and development rhetoric. In its more basic versions modernization theory held out various arguments for the postcolonial world's slow transition to modernity, a list that included traditionalism, poverty and a weak middle class. This model soon became an article of faith for US foreign policy. Eisenhower had proclaimed that modernization of the former colonial world was the best "counter-measure to Soviet propaganda"; consequently the 1950s saw the rush of US social scientists, anthropologists, political scientists, sociologists, and urban planners all wanting to study non-Western societies, aided by private foundation-funded projects, and government consultancy. The impact on the social sciences of the 1950s was astounding. As one writer put it, "Carnegie, Rockefeller, Russell Sage, and a newcomer, the richly endowed Ford Foundation, virtually invented the label behavioral sciences and proclaimed it a new frontier in social research" (O'Connor, 2001, p.103). Behavioralism combined group and individual behavior analysis with a fetishized scientific method. Issues of inequality and difference were bypassed in the overall context of a Cold War liberal atmosphere of seeking solutions outside mobilization and direct agitation. The combination of professional "field" interests, modernization theory, and a war against "traditionalism" went hand in hand with intellectual arguments for the broader rubric of Cold War liberalism. Before the fires of 1968 swept away behavioralism along with much of Cold War liberalism, in the 1950s much of this was an article of faith, and a significant intellectual back end for US imperial planning worldwide.

While Ford's country reports as well as those of its US social science consultants would periodically draw from narratives of colonial difference, the focus of modernization theory lay in development, social integration, translation, and "citizen participation." As such this was a global model of the liberal social. For Ford, community action became a code word for poverty analysis globally, refracting from racially charged neighborhoods in the USA, to support for studies and rural community interventions in India (Connor, 2001; Topalov, 2003, pp.212–233). Although widely different versions of this proliferated, the perceptions of the "poor" were conventional, ranging from socially "disorganized," traditional, inadequately assimilated into "modern" notions of territory and solidarity. Structural inequality was carefully elided, and "action" was deliberately depoliticized. In such studies, liberal poverty analysts functioned as "change agents," armed with local statistical profiles and Foundation support, to "induce" community change. Although both Stalinist Marxism and Western liberalism promoted their own versions of developmentalism in the 1950s, the US model carried with it the attraction of a technically advanced society, with an evolving mass-consumption utopia. There was also little threat to local power structures as arguments about "poverty" and traditionalism were rigorously depoliticized and technical. The attraction of this model to postcolonial elites in the 1950s is evident; it offered a pathway to economic and cultural global citizenship, free from the clutches of "tradition" and the instability of revolutionary change.[29]

India emerged as an important focus of Ford's activities, becoming the largest single recipient of Ford grants in the post World War II era. Paul Hoffman the President of the Foundation in the 1950s was convinced that India was an important test case for Ford's philosophy of aid after the "loss of China." As one writer puts it, Hoffman saw this investment by Ford "for the good of the future of India and the good of the free world. Assistance to India would demonstrate what free men with wealth and wisdom could do to help other men to follow them down the same or a similar path of development" (Gordon, 1997, p.111). Hoffman visited India in 1951, and after meeting Nehru agreed to support projects in India with the approval of the Indian government. Ford contributed generously to projects in India in the 1950s, ranging from rural community development, population control, and support to universities. Rural projects played a prominent role, taking up almost half of the funding, in part as rural areas were seen as potential sites of peasant unrest.[30] Support to rural areas was also strong given the emphasis of Ford's India representative, Douglas Ensminger. Ensminger was an agricultural sociologist recruited by Hoffman and he remained India's head of Ford until 1970. Ensminger was an enthusiastic, larger-than-life figure, wielding considerable power not just in Delhi but also in New York. Leonard A. Gordon writes of Ensminger,

> He became, in time, the most powerful and longest-lasting representative of the foundation abroad. Not only did Ensminger develop a unique tie to the government of India through Nehru and other top officials, but he formed unusual ties to the trustees of the foundation in the United States that allowed him occasionally to go around administrators including the foundation's presidents in New York, who were supposedly supervising him.[31]

After receiving the Health Minister's letter urging Ford to support the planning exercise for Delhi, Ensminger moved rapidly, writing to New York and urging support given the strategic importance of the mission. Ford's support was crucial, as India expressed its inability to pay experts in dollars given the foreign exchange crisis in 1957. Ford would pay the team directly, and it was understood that the team members would work closely with the newly established Town Planning Organization (TPO). By May 6, 1956, the head office of Ford in New York had written to Rajkumari Amrit Kaur informing her of the approval of $215,500 towards the project.[32]

In her letter to Ensminger, Kaur had asked in particular that the urban planner Albert Mayer be invited to head the team, "since he is known to us in India."[33] Albert Mayer was a New York City planner who had been active in the regional planning movement in the USA along with Clarence Stein and others. Mayer founded the Housing Study Guild with Lewis Mumford and Henry Wright, intended to develop personnel for the public housing program in the USA. Mayer was an active public intellectual writing in newspapers and journals. In an early article in the *New York Times* that anticipated some of his later ideas, Mayer praised the green belt town of Radburn, which followed the model of the garden city designs of Ebenezer Howard. That model, argued Mayer, "seeks to establish urban-rural communities that will retain the suburb's theoretical advantages" (Mayer, 1936) The classic necessity of urban concentration had been relegated with the arrival of the motor car; instead Mayer held out an anti-urban utopia of decentralization.

> The citizen of the green-belt town rarely finds occasion to visit the city. . . . His children need not go to long distances to concentrated parks. They simply go through their own gardens to the green spaces within the block, or a little further if they want to play strenuous, noisy games . . . the entire satellite town is a pleasantly livable space place, its sections varied in character, but protected internally by planning and externally by the green belt.
>
> (Mayer, 1936)

The title of Mayer's piece ("Green Belt Towns for the Machine Age") was instructive, it was the motor car that freed the population from the city, and allowed a decentralized relationship to nature.

Mayer's ideas were part of the regionalist planning movement that had come to prominence in the USA by the late 1920s, and grew to wield considerable influence in housing debates during the New Deal. The regionalists notably took on the predominant "metropolitanist" tradition at that time. Metropolitanism argued for a continuation of the nineteenth-century urban form, i.e. a strong downtown with its urban bourgeoisie, a factory zone with working people – both forming the productive core of the city. This was a model of a productive city based on a labour–capital relationship, and a high centralization of infrastructure, with mass transit, and highways. The outer zone of parks and recreation would provide a healthy space of leisure for the city populations. Periodic and brutal "urban renewal" projects (tearing down working-class tenements), would create sites of monumentality and produce an urban form. Robert Moses' mega-projects in New York typified metro-politanism's combination of personality, centralization, and power (Caro, 1974). The weaknesses of the metropolitanist vision are apparent to a twenty-first-century observer. The model assumed a relationship between the urban bourgeoisie and space, and an endless commitment to a commercial downtown and a factory system in the city. The coming of the automobile and communication networks saw the decay of old downtowns in nineteenth-century cities, and deindustrialization transformed the older capital–labor relationship, displacing it on to a wider, global scale.

From the late 1920s regionalist writers like Lewis Mumford and Clarence Stein attacked what they saw as the inhumanity of the nineteenth-century city and called for active decentralization (Fishman, 1992, pp. 106–128). The regionalists were prominent in deploying the ideas of Ebenzer Howard and the English garden city movement to the USA. Centralization had promoted the domination of urban elites, and produced congestion, overcrowding and a sorry state of affairs. In the regionalist argument, new technologies of travel and infrastructure (automobility, electricity grids) made the case for a network of decentralized new towns, with green areas and open spaces, run by decentralized small communities. Human scale, in opposition to the giantism of the nineteenth-century city, was stressed by the regionalists. Clarence Perry, who along with Lewis Mumford and Henry Wright was among the original founders of the Regional Planning Association of America, argued that the urban neighborhood would play a significant role in the disassembly of the nineteenth century city. From his book *Neighborhood as a Social Unit* published in 1929 to his writings in the 1930s, Perry conceived of the neighborhood as a "cellular" space that brought together face-to-face intimacy, away from the automobile, and one which animated a "community spirit." The health of the city depended on producing a manageable unit like the neighborhood, which would incorporate living, work, schooling, and commerce. The neighborhood "superblock" was conceived of as a zone safe from traffic, and as a fortress, walled off from the intrusion of automobility. The neighborhood would nourish a healthy form of urban life for families and children, through technologies of social management and urban design. The community center, at the heart of the neighborhood, played a role of social integration and civic contact. Perry's ideas added to the regionalist horror of urban congestion by staking out the neighborhood as a fortress utopia, both animating and enclosing an intimate community with a careful delineation of space. While Perry was to go on to become a community planner, the neighborhood became the cell form of the regionalist escape from the city (Perry, 1939).

These were all themes that refracted in part through Mayer's early essay; his example of Radburn was one of the early new green belt towns. Regional-ism's cultural critique of the nineteenth century city reverberated powerfully in the 1930s; and the regionalists would play a significant force in housing programs of the New Deal. While regionalism's anti-urbanism held out the prospect of colonizing more space for the automobile, it clearly bypassed the more "classic" problems of the city. As the regionalists saw it, writes Christine Boyer, there

> was no other choice but to build a new urban order in the country. But the more the regionalists focused on norms of community life, and the new forms of group housing that encapsulated their ideals, the more they left intact the contradictory realities of the metropolis.
>
> (Boyer, 1983, p.196)

For many decades, the power of the regionalists was paramount in US planning, and in the 1950s regionalism promoted the British new town movement as an updated version of the 1930s models. Albert Mayer himself wrote sympathetic articles on the new town movement; the combination of regionalism and state control was an idea that fitted well with the atmosphere of the 1950s (Mayer, 1956).

In 1961, Jane Jacobs wrote *Death and Life of Great American Cities*, probably the most popular text on urban life ever written in the twentieth century. Writing as a "citizen" and not as a professional planner, Jacobs mounted a devastating critique of the regionalist advocates who she called "decentrists," whose ideas were "taken for granted in orthodox planning." According to the "decentrists," said Jacobs,

> The street is bad as an environment for humans, houses should be turned away from it and faced inward, towards sheltered greens. The basic unit of city design is not the street but the block, and more particularly the superblock. Commerce should be segregated from residences and greens. A neighborhood's demand for goods should be calculated "scientifically," and this much and no more commercial space allotted. . . . The Decentrists also pounded in Howard's premises that the planned economy must be islanded off as a self-contained unit, it must resist future change, and that every significant detail must be controlled by planners from the start and stuck to. In short, good planning was project planning.
>
> (Jacobs, 1961, p.410)

Many of Jacobs' criticisms of regionalism would re-emerge in popular questions about the future of Delhi in the 1990s.

The plans of Delhi

Albert Mayer first came to India during World War II as part of the US army, and he first encountered Nehru, at a meeting arranged by Humayun Kabir. Mayer returned to India in 1946 at Nehru's invitation, and quickly threw his energy into a number of projects, including a rural community project in UP that drew praise and attention from Indian leaders.[34] Mayer had prepared the first plan for Chandigarh, before he was ousted by Le Corbusier.[35]

After being approached by the Ford Foundation to lead the Delhi project, Mayer set out his vision for the plan in a letter to the Foundation's New York office. Clearly filled with a sense of the task at hand, Mayer argued that a successful plan "may be an important world example or pilot undertaking."[36] He went on to outline his design priorities, all of which would play out in the final Masterplan. Any plan, said Mayer, must be regional and "beyond the city". It should take in areas around Delhi, the economic form of the city – industrial or otherwise, the optimum size of such a city, with an effort to "minimize internal frictions of space, the tensions of functional and social mix-up."[37] It was the latter that would refract through the final document of the Masterplan and re-emerge in the public debate over Delhi's urban form in the late 1990s.

The final team for the Delhi project (apart from Mayer) included Gerald Breese, urban scholar from Princeton, Edward G. Echeverria, a physical planner, George Goetschius, London-based urban sociologist, Britton Harris, regional planner at the University of Pennsylvania, Bert F. Hoselitz, well-known economist from the University of Chicago, and founding editor of the journal *Economic Development and Cultural Change*.[38] Others were Walter C. Hedden, traffic expert, and Archie Dotson, government and administration specialist. Marshall Clinard, University of Wisconsin sociologist, was recruited to run the urban community project; and British architect Gordon Cullen joined the team in 1959.

There were many stories of international technical consultants in 1950s India who emerged in public memory – the aid to the steel plants in Bhilai and Bokharo are the most significant. In terms of scale and a model of managing urban space that would impact upon millions of lives, the Delhi Masterplan project was surely the "largest" of such projects although largely invisible from public memory.[39] Given its strategic importance to the Americans who hoped that Delhi's urban would emerge as a (non-communist) model to be emulated in other parts of India and Asia, the intellectual composition of the planning team stands out. With the notable exception of Mayer who had considerable experience in the subcontinent and intimately knew the intellectual and social-political milieu, the Masterplan consultant team was largely made up of people whose knowledge of India, let alone Delhi, was minimal if not non-existent. In his reminiscences, Ensminger agreed that the team could not have been more ill-prepared, as "there simply was not any one who had Asian planning experience that remotely resembled Delhi's problems."[40]

While Mayer worked largely out of New York, with extensive site visits and comments, it was the others who interacted on a daily basis with TPO research teams and officials. The atmosphere in the team was clearly inflected with the liberal paternalism of modernization theory. Marshall Clinard, the University of Wisconsin sociologist, summed up these feelings years later in a published address to US academics. Clinard detailed the role of the social science consultant:

> As a foreigner, he has a fresh approach to a local situation which may have been overlooked by local workers whose long association has conditioned them to a particular view and even inertia. . . . The consultant from a developed country is able to present an image of what things could be, particularly if similar conditions once existed in his own country. All too often persons in charge of social action in such countries feel that the situation has always existed and thus cannot be changed.
>
> (Clinard, 1963, p.210)

The main collaborator of the Ford Team in Delhi was the local Town Planning Organization (TPO). Composed of young US-trained Indian planners and architects, the TPO had drafted the Interim General Plan (IGP) of 1956 under tremendous strain, with lack of recognition by the government. The TPO planners were never properly consulted about the composition of the US team, and this produced tremendous friction when the team arrived. George Goetschius wrote a frank, confidential memo to his colleagues which made sharp, insightful comments on the situation. Not knowing the simmering anger within the TPO over the selection of the US team, Goetschius wrote, "We foolishly tried to sell them the 'O.K. boys this is the chance of a life time' type-line."[41] Goetschius went on,

> One of their [TPO] favorite stories [came] as a sort of half aggression, half joke. When the question came up in the Cabinet of whether or not to accept Ensminger's offer of a Ford Foundation Town Planning Consultant Team, Venkatasuban said to the Cabinet "No foreign team – let Indian planners make mistakes and learn. The foreigners will make the mistakes and leave the country; we will have the mistakes, we will not have learned. At least let our mistakes be Indian ones". After much discussion the Cabinet decided that since the advice of the foreigners was to be *free* . . . and since, as one member put it, we are not under a legal obligation to actually use the plan, the Ford offer would be accepted.[42]

The TPO staffers' early attitude reflected the way networks of power worked in Delhi for the US consultants. Mayer and Ensminger had direct access to Nehru – in all crises the Prime Minister's Office could be approached to directly intervene. While this did not always happen, and the US team was often mired in local battles with the TPO and the Health Ministry, Nehru remained a significant last option whom the Americans could call upon.[43]

The plan, assembling space

In *The Nation and its Fragments* (1993) Partha Chatterjee suggests that (national) planning represented itself as a process outside the domain of politics, to be managed by experts autonomous from the vicissitudes of party intrigue. Nevertheless, argues Chatterjee, while planning was part of the national state's strategy attaining legal-political sovereignty through economic development, it was equally tied to the "representativeness" of the state. In short, at the very moment when planning constituted itself "outside" politics it equally became an instrument through which sovereign power recognized *itself* as legitimate. Here Chatterjee refers to the "double deception" of planning. At one level planning rationally constituted and consolidated the diverse social as objects of power in a singular model through systems of information gathering. Nevertheless, the political process produced a process of reversal where traditional relations of subject and object were contested, even reversed. The most rational exercise at soliciting accurate units of "information" also left behind "an unestimated residue." The latter, "as the irreducible, negative, and ever-present 'beyond' of planning, is what we may call, in its more general sense, politics" (Chatterjee, 1993, p. 208). In setting up planning's rationality as part of the broader enactment of the political in postcolonial India, Chatterjee rehearses his broader thesis of "political sociality." There is an important insight to the overall formulation – the surplus of the political drew planning's discourse into the larger dramaturgy of sovereignty in India and the refraction of Western modernist techniques through a postcolonial lens. Chatterjee's argument works best as an explanatory technique for mapping the rationality of the national state, moving between politics and reason.

Urban planning shared the permeable boundary between politics and reason. In fact urban planning in India suffered from an excess of proximity, exaggerating its role as "media" offering a lens to reimagine and interpret the city. This was particularly evident in the Interim General Plan for Greater Delhi, released in 1956 by the newly formed Town Planning Organization, largely composed of local planners. Produced at great speed to provide an interim lens to view the "social question" of the city, the IGP represented the first major effort of a management model for the postcolonial city through the rational language of modern urbanism. Largely overshadowed by the main Masterplan that was conceived after the US planners entered the scene, the IGP nevertheless offers an interesting optic of early postcolonial urban planning. The plan's writers took great pains to stress the document's provisional and tentative suggestions. The narrative is marked by almost a representational anxiety, borne by the need to balance the claims of modern urbanism, the "social question" left by colonialism, and the legitimacy of the plan itself.

In her introduction to the IGP, Health Minister Rajkumari Amrit Kaur noted with alarm the "promiscuous" building that had cluttered the skyline of the capital and set up an alarming scenario of urban crisis:

> Matters have really come to a head. There are all-round discomfort and discontent. Traffic jams and accidents, sprawling colonies without the vital

conveniences of life in the matter of sanitation, over-crowding everywhere and particularly in miserable slum areas, miles of ribbon developed hut-shops, chronic water-shortage, all adds to the distress which is bad at any time but is well nigh intolerable during the rainy season.

(Ministry of Health, 1956, p.i)

Kaur was actually working with a draft supplied to her by Albert Mayer, and her own amendments incorporated the political importance of the Delhi plan, and muted some of Mayer's excessive descriptions of urban decline. Kaur nevertheless incorporated Mayer's main emphases – the need for a regional plan, the stress on a community pilot project that would develop a new urban sociality, and a green belt to contain the city's endless expansion.

What about the plan's legitimacy? The main text of the IGP was ambitious: "A democracy working for social ends has to base itself on the co-operation of the people and not on the 'power' of the state" (IGP, 1956, p.77). The Health Minister's introduction adopted a more Nehruvian form of address:

If we want the people's collaboration for a greater Delhi, the Master Plan must be thoroughly explained to them and therefore a technique must be worked out for securing genuine contact between the planners, their executive and the people. Time and learning by experience and infinite patience are required before this is attained.

(IGP, 1956, p.ii)

The main text of the IGP began with a pedagogical note explaining the functions of the Masterplan, undoubtedly aimed at a larger public. For the most part the IGP's formulations incorporated the main elements of international planning orthodoxy at the time. After indicting colonial urban design for dividing Old and New Delhi, the IGP called for a rational land use that would separate residential, commercial, and industrial spaces. It also called for the displacement of "noxious" trades and "non-conforming industries" outside the city, along with private dairies and gwalas, who were to be removed to designated areas. Slums were to be subject to clearance and renewal based on a survey and classification of slum areas (IGP, 1956, pp.viii–xiii). Again in line with planning doctrines, the IGP suggested that zoning was the principal tool for rationalizing land use and clearing urban overcrowding and clutter, and the intrusion of illegal commerce in neighborhoods. As a contrast to the migrant city marred by overcrowding and "blight," the IGP held up colonial neighborhoods as examples where zoning had at least "preserved" the urban form (IGP, 1956, p.20).

Zoning had been introduced in Germany in the nineteenth century, where it folded into the emerging idea of the city Masterplan. Reinhard Baumeister, urban planner for the town of Karlsruhe, initiated the idea of the Masterplan which would provide general directions to the urban form, and give predictions of developing urban space. Within the German tradition the Masterplan was supplemented by building regulations, followed by zoning. Zoning, which clarified space according to rational allocation of function, had the great merit of assembling the entire city under one larger conceptual unit, which drove modernist planners throughout the second half of the nineteenth century. The anticipatory logic of zoning was crucial; it drew both urban speculators as well as welfare advocates, as uncertainty was reduced and areas were mapped out with great clarity on the urban fabric. By its very nature zoning propelled a centralized model of urban planning; as local councils were seen as deficient in technical knowledge or subject to particularistic interests. This had a distinct advantage over the therapeutic models of the nineteenth century which exposed the moral geography of a city based on a social milieu. Here states of disease were located through surveys and typologies of health and crime, which in turn produced "unhealthy" environments. Emerging in France and England, this form of urbanism drew from medical theories of miasma and ill-health, leading to blight and "deviance." Miasma theory, perfected by Edwin Chadwick, held that disease was caused by invisible putrefied organic substances in the atmosphere as well as those emanating from human bodies. Concentration of populations (i.e. "congested" areas) generated more miasma, and to this was added the theory of "moral" miasma. The mixing of the social, the moral, and the physical drew equally from a range of disciplines – medical, scientific and statistical, in turn generating schemes of "improvement" at a frenzied pace in the nineteenth century. Planning's role was seen as interventionist, to manage and cure diseased parts of the city. Charles Booth's surveys at the end of the nineteenth century developed a comprehensive social map of London, based on a combination of statistical data and graphic representation. Moralism was explained statistically. Booth's social profile of the city was a moral map, where milieu, social type, and space were linked, albeit in a social scientific gaze. The graphic results were dramatic; the map was divided into seven classes of population, with class A ("lowest Class, Viscous, semi-criminal") attaining the darkest color: black.

The Masterplan's distinct advantage was its ability to transcend this moral geography of the nineteenth century. To be sure, the "social" milieu persisted along with moral and cultural typologies, but it was annexed to notions of law and technocratic design in the emerging centralized Masterplan model. Mass publics, the rise of a class of experts (planners, urbanists, sociologists), also led to the production of objectivized norms in planning. In the USA, working-class areas were now increasingly seen by social science and policy-makers as "neighborhoods," a term which would rise in value in American urban planning (Topalov, 1990). Not surprisingly, zoning grew rapidly in popularity, spreading to the United States, where a positive 1926 decision by the Supreme Court enshrined its place in urban planning, followed by the official recognition of the "Masterplan" in 1927. By 1933 the Athens Charter recognized zoning as a main thrust of urban planning, and the integration of plan and zone were complete. Ola Soderstorm argues that the visual representation of zoning made it a perfect candidate for its naturalization: "Synthesizing urban policy into a single, easily interpreted document, the zoning plan rapidly became a dominant form as a pure technical tool, which explains its extraordinary external efficacy" (Soderstrom, 1996, p.266). For the twentieth century city, increasingly seen as a machine for human living, zoning came to be seen as the adequate representation of a rationalized urban body, designed and implemented by technical experts. For American urbanism, the main influence on the Delhi Masterplan, "zoning represented the promise of scientific progress; technical efficiency experts would manipulate and manage the order of this new city" (Boyer, 1983, p.169).

The nineteenth century's moral geography continued to operate in twentieth-century colonial urbanism in India, with a replication of Improvement Trust sanitation schemes and congestion pathologies. In Delhi, the new colonial capital institutionalized a racial and class hierarchy. Not surprisingly, the mandate of the Improvement Trust was in areas of the old city where the bulk of the colonized population resided. As the first postcolonial plan for Delhi the IGP had to clearly break from the colonial model. In setting up the Masterplan–zoning–law triad, the writers of the IGP not only provided a visual and geographical device to interpret a new postcolonial Delhi in the 1950s, but also staked their claim as the legitimate technical guardians of that vision. It was a statement of sovereignty, not just from a colonial past but for urban planning as the naturalized science of the postcolonial city. Zoning was an emblem of urban health and banished clutter. As the IGP's praise of colonial New Delhi's managed urban form indicated, efficient zoning would represent the coming of age of postcolonial urbanism in the world. In allying with international planning modernism, most notably the US variant,[44] the writers of the IGP could legitimately claim to associate with a modernizing urban culture of the postwar period.

It was nevertheless an anxious modernism, where an unusually apologetic preface by H. Mukherji of the Delhi Improvement Trust went on to admit that "It is somewhat of a paradox that, though the Plan for a town depends on precise data, many of its long term proposals tend to be somewhat vague and indefinite." Nevertheless, Mukherji argued that in keeping with the times,

> a certain degree of idealism is perhaps a virtue in this matter. Whatever the ultimate shape of the proposals, they are bound to aim high and provide for living and working conditions which one would wish to have. And there is no harm in transporting a little poetry from its bucolic realms to urban planning.[45]

In an essay published only after his death, Foucault declared that in contrast to the nineteenth century's historical obsession, the current epoch "will perhaps be above all the epoch of space. We are in the epoch of simultaneity, we are in the epoch of juxtaposition, the epoch of the near and far, of the side-by-side, of the dispersed" (Foucault, 1986, p.22). Spatial anxiety of the twentieth century replaced the temporal anxiety of the nineteenth century. Following from this reading, urban planning may be seen as the quintessential science of the twentieth century, foregrounding the management of space. Foucault argues that "siting" has replaced the "emplacement" of Galilean space; his definition could well be seen as a summary of the planning imaginary.

> This problem of the human site or living space is not simply that of knowing whether there will be enough space for men in the world – a problem that is certainly quite important – but also that of knowing what relations of propinquity, what type of storage, circulation, marking, and classification of human elements should be adopted in a given situation in order to achieve a given end. Our epoch is one in which space takes for us the form of relations among sites.
>
> (Foucault, 1986, p.22)

Urban planning in India folded into the broader technocratic landscape of the 1950s where planning in general appeared as the mix of technology, information, and secular magic to propel modernization. India is "planning-minded," Albert Mayer noted with sarcasm in 1957, since the urban was subordinated to the broader project of modernization; the US planning imaginary in its post-urban phase found eager listeners. "Success" lay in the ability of the plan to address the problem of urban poverty, and equally order social space into rationally legible units. The burdens of postcolonial urban politics – the slum, the relationship between urban and rural, the problem of the form of the city – were all addressed in the Masterplan by drawing from and refining nineteenth- and twentieth-century planning doctrines.

Plan basics

The Ford Foundation Team's completed plan document was rendered into law on September 1, 1962. A draft Masterplan was put out in July, 1960 for discussion and to invite public objections. The draft was accompanied by a two-volume "Work Studies" publication containing the research produced in collaboration with TPO staffers in the run-up to the plan. The finalization of the plan was a significant source of pride for the Ford Foundation; it would soon begin support for a massive urban planning project for Calcutta. The Ford team had managed to navigate the various pressures that crept up on the project: the departure of Rajkumari Amrit Kaur as Health Minister, inter-ministry squabbles that threatened to harm the TPO's status, initial pressures for "quick results" over slum rehabilitation, and delays due to the 1962 conflict with China.

The document that emerged was remarkable for the near consensus it evoked at the time of its release,[46] in contrast to its less fortunate successor in

2007. The 1962 plan brought to an end the previous phases of the city's urban development, the 1947 to 1955 period, which was dominated by refugees and government-sponsored rehabilitation, and the 1955 to 1959 period, where private land development companies dominated urban construction.

The Plan was a regionalist model which worked to manage the "sprawl" of the city through a green belt and counter magnets – neighbouring towns that could deflect the population inflows into Delhi. The city was broken up into various planning divisions, as well as cellular neighborhoods, sub-centers, and district centers, to contain social life, commerce, and work. This was integrated with density and housing standards, balanced work–residence ratios and circulation patterns for different forms of traffic. The plan's language surveyed the city by reorganizing space, and ending the "clutter" of the past and the chaos of the post-Partition years. "One of the major principles is that in order to secure balanced development and minimize frictions, decentralization of places of employment and their right relationship with residential areas is necessary." [47] Strict zoning based on a rigorous land-use plan filtered through the regional vision as well as the various cellular units, combining modernist clarity with functional hierarchy.

> These are functional units reflecting their own pattern of development and land use, having certain individual physical characteristics, and social and cultural values. While the Old City is at present a chaotic mix up of incompatible land uses, New Delhi is lacking in compactness and social cohesion. The plan has allocated land for industry, commerce, living, play and other major types of urban land use in the most appropriate location for each use and interrelated to each other so as to produce orderliness and smooth functioning.[48]

This reflected the planners' clear desire to come up with a rational management of a new city, with representational clarity, along with a hierarchy of function. The ceremonial anxieties of the Lutyens design would be done away with, along with its structural inequalities. The chaos and clutter of the Old City with its congestion, slum-like conditions and unhealthy environments had to be transcended as bad examples of the prehistory of the postcolonial city. While links between the old and new city were to be forged through urban design,[49] the health of the new metropolis depended on a different model of land use and management.

In line with prevalent planning doctrines the plan orchestrated an ambitious

---

Opposite

Figure 1.2 The regionalist design. The first map was the then existing urban zone in 1962 and below it the design for the future city. The 1962 Masterplan expanded the urban area, while simultaneously managing it through strict zoning and demarcation of urban and rural forms of life.

Source: DDA, 1962.

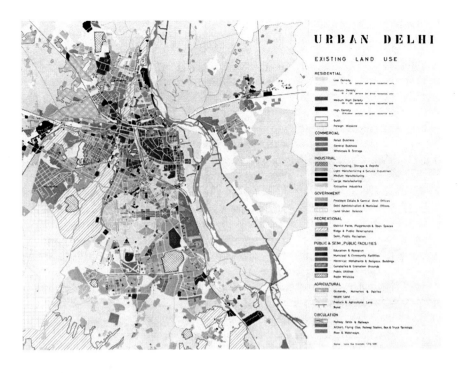

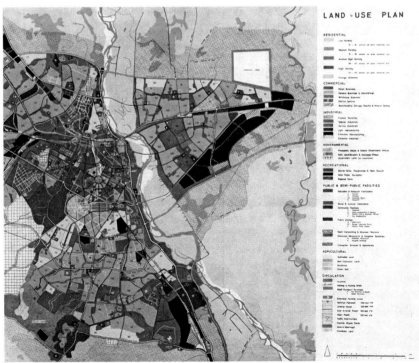

Figure 1.2 The regionalist design.

separation of industry, residence, and commerce. This separation was fundamental to most twentieth-century urbanism, underwritten by zoning. In the 1962 Masterplan industrial production was broken into a hierarchy where a shift was mandated to designated areas, with various time limits. The zones included areas for extensive, service, and light industry and "flatted factories" and work-cum-industrial centers for "non-nuisance" small and household enterprises, to be set up near places of residence, limiting travel time. Heavy industry was not permitted in Delhi as it would not fit the non-industrial "form" of the city – it would be based in the regional towns. "Noxious" and village-like trades and industries were prohibited by the Masterplan and had to be removed from the city.[50] Commerce was organized in wholesale markets, central business districts, sub-central business districts, and district centers, the latter to be built by the DDA. Some wholesale markets were to be shifted out of the old city. Most small commerce in planned neighborhoods was to be in designated areas, based on ratios specified in the plan.[51]

The plan set up an urbanizable limit of the city, based on the planners' statistical projections, to be enclosed by a green belt. Having done so, the planners also set in place what was arguably the largest land nationalization in Indian urban history, where the DDA was empowered to acquire a projected area of 34,070 acres for housing through the Land Acquisition Act, a major vehicle land appropriation in the colonial era.[52] This land would be auctioned by the DDA, and the surplus ploughed into public infrastructure. Public housing would also be built on acquired land. With one stroke, the plan produced a powerful image of sovereign control over land in the city for the new rulers, ventriloquized through the DDA and the language of "public purpose." It spoke to the atmosphere in Delhi and the clamor for a just city, by promising living space and control of speculation by a powerful, technocratic state body. Hostility to speculation was voiced periodically in Parliament and in the newspapers, and the DIT's dubious record on land speculation made sure that the Masterplan's anti-speculative gloss spoke to a receptive audience.[53]

The Delhi Masterplan of 1962 was followed by urban planning debates in Bombay and Calcutta. At the time of its promulgation the Delhi plan was among the most ambitious, and the DDA became the most important symbolic player in the city. Not surprisingly it has been subject to significant analysis, most of it critical, from planners, activists, scholars, ranging from the first major review in 1973 to reflections in the past decade, when the plan became a major reference point in public debate in the city.[54] There are two parts of the 1950s planning debates that would be recalled in the 1990s – the designation of practices that constitute the urban, and following this, their enclosure in the legal city.

The puzzle of the urban subject

In a lengthy text inaugurating the launch of the Masterplan 1962, a publicity article in the Sunday *Hindustan Times* suggested that "if Delhi is to be planned into a well integrated city, and is to be maintained as such, it *needs inhabitants with a primarily urban psychology*."[55] Seen here through a distilled modernization theory and sociology, the urban psyche produced specific practices of living, work, and community. Such social types were to be nurtured through planning practices and technologies of control and management. The search for an "urban psyche" contributed to the planners' orchestration of a complex system of zoning, social typologies, and regional dispersion. It drove endless discussions in the planning team as to the size of the city that would make it appropriate to separate the city from its neighbors. One of the main sites for discussion on the urban personality was the slum. Debates on the slum ranged from planners, politicians, and reform activists in Delhi, mixing narratives of health, sanitation, and moral welfare.

The slum represented the imaginative embodiment of urban decay and postcolonial shame. Colonial attitudes had been shaped by narratives on health, pollution, and congestion leading to the DIT; the Birla Committee argued that the amelioration of slum conditions in Delhi would be among the first tasks of any future Masterplan. In 1958 the TPO published a series of publicity booklets educating the citizens of Delhi on the making of the capital's Masterplan. Among them was a booklet on slums and urban renewal, which reflected the feelings of the planning elites as much as it sought to speak to a public realm.[56] Mapping out the reasons for slums, the TPO booklet suggested that the "pre-urban" ways of the slum dweller were incompatible with city living: "the obnoxious trades carried out by the slum families in their dwellings and the keeping of cattle and other animals have aggravated the problem of insanitation and congestion in the city." The strong solidarity among slum dwellers ("brotherhood ties") produced further "congestion" as migrants were drawn to their own and increased pressure on areas.[57] After the booklet retailed the usual catalog of slum horrors – disease, decay, filth, squalor, blight in general – a visit to the slum for the unacquainted "becomes a nightmare." The TPO went on to extend the slum issue to a problem of citizenship. If the moral decline of the slum dweller was complete with social vices like "gambling, drinking prostitution,"

> The total demoralisation of the slum dweller robs him of enthusiasm and makes him a backward citizen. National progress and efficiency suffer as a result. If India is to progress, the living conditions of slum dwellers must be improved.[58]

The TPO was clearly not speaking to the population at large. The pamphlet was aimed at the cultural and political elite of the city, making a case for new slum intervention technologies that would replace colonial "improvement." Those held up by the TPO were urban renewal, community development, and

Figure 1.3 Masterplan Publicity Planning Pamphlet, Town and Planning Organization, 1957.

"healthy neighborhoods," all typologies that would be expanded in the final
Masterplan.[59]

Slum anxiety was widespread among Delhi's elite in the 1950s, reaching a
crescendo in political circles. "I feel feverish when I think of slums," Nehru is
reported to have said, reflecting his personal horror and impatience with the
state of Delhi.[60] In 1956 Nehru was taken on a highly publicized slum visit
sponsored by the Bharat Sevak Samaj, a social service organization that
later published a significant survey of Delhi's slums. While Nehru angrily
declared to a slum owner that the tenements should be "burnt down to their
very foundations," the Samaj argued for a major program of education,
rehabilitation, and slum clearance.[61] In its survey published in 1958, the
Samaj significantly revised upward official estimates of slums. As opposed to
eviction and ad hoc removal, slums were to be addressed in a humane manner
– that included immediate measures addressing sanitation, removal of animals,
and "regeneration of slum life." While the Samaj's survey indicated a picture
where congestion was less of an issue among slum dwellers, its own model
was national-therapeutic, where slum justice would prepare the resident for
proper citizenship. In a memorandum submitted to Nehru soon after his visit
in 1956, the Samaj attacked the legacies of the DIT, citing Geddes with

approval, and calling for a humane approach to the urban poor. However, the therapeutic model of the Samaj was a mixture of economic analysis and moral categories, in line with the TPO's own thinking on the issue. Overcrowding and congestion could be traced to the "social degeneration and economic poverty of the slum dwellers." [62] The "miserable environment" bred "despair" and a "fatalistic approach" to life. The Samaj's own suggested solution to the slum problem partly anticipated the planning documents of 1962:

> Slums are indeed a standing menace to city life and the problem so viewed is of improving sanitary conditions, of the extension of civic amenities and community services, of dispersal of population from overcrowded areas and so of extending the geographical limits of the city. [63]

Equally the Samaj called for the removal of "cattle and obnoxious trades" from the city. Cattle and horses caused "over crowding and insanitary and un-hygienic conditions"; they would have to be removed and subject to a strict license system. [64]

While the Bharat Sevak Samaj's listing of "unhealthy" trades and practices were not explicitly cast in a broader argument about urban modernity, the TPO saw the slum as poverty plus the irruption of rural practices in the urban. This was the emerging consensus in the planning elite at that time. In an unpublished draft of a chapter on the Masterplan Albert Mayer listed various characteristics of a Delhi slum. Mayer agreed that Delhi's slums were the most "desperately severe and widespread of any city in the world. They can be identified by occurrence of or lack of certain minimal elements for humane existence which are readily seen in profusion in Delhi." [65] After listing the usual descriptions of slum conditions such as congestion and overcrowding, Mayer added another: "village-like habits of in-migrants." In adding rural practices as a reason for slum conditions, Mayer was echoing the words of the TPO brochure and speaking to the broader climate of Nehruvian modernity. Nehru's statement that the "village must be urbanized" now rebounded back on to the city in the shape of what was seen as demonstrably un-urban practices – low-sanitation literacy, animal rearing and continuation of "noxious" industries and practices. Planning's solution was surgical: the removal of persons practicing village-like trades to "urban villages" *outside* the city. The language of the Masterplan was categorical: village industries had no place in the city as they "cast an unhealthy influence on the urban setting." The scape was wide ranging – apart from diaries, tanneries, wood seasoning, it expanded further to artisan trades like pottery, zari, and artistic metal ware in the Masterplan's work studies. [66] This was in effect a program for a modernized form of urban apartheid, a purging of the village from the city through legal banishment to designated enclosures. *The Hindustan Times* article announcing the Masterplan in 1960 cheerfully told its readers that planning would "relieve urban Delhi of those members of its population whose occupations – and consequently ways of living – are primarily rural, and resettle them in the villages."[67] Awadhendra Sharan argues convincingly that the deployment of the trope of the rural in the Masterplan represents a nationalist modernization of colonial languages nuisance and environmental blight. In nationalist planning, "rural persons and rural industrial processes/trades being made to stand in the place of the native, as that which was prior and inferior and in need of transformation" (Sharan, 2006, p.4910).

The exile of village-like work practices left the existing city, whose inhabitants were still seen as insufficiently incorporated into urban living. This became the context for an ambitious pilot project instigated by US planners to promote neighborhood and community consciousness.

In search of the urban community

> To help people of village orientation adjust to city life, neighborhood clusters would be developed with 50 to 150 families each.[68]

In 1959, Douglas Ensminger, head of Ford in India, suggested that Indian cities lacked a sensibility of the urban that had developed in the West.

> Indian cities in general appear to exhibit less feeling, than in Western society, for what might be termed "city pride" or the "city as a whole". This can, in part be attributed to a continuation of attitudes which arose out of conditions as far back in pre-British India. During this period the population of an Indian city was largely distributed by caste, occupation and religion. . . . To a certain extent, this pattern continues today and inhibits contacts among groups.[69]

Not only did Indian city dwellers lack a neighborhood consciousness, said Ensminger, but there was an emphasis on "personal interest which does not extend beyond the immediate family or caste."[70] From a political point of view, said Ensminger, the situation in Indian cities was "dynamite" with large-scale poverty and neglect. The head of the Ford office in Delhi was in fact laying the ground for discussing an ambitious urban community project, to be carried out in conjunction with the Masterplan. Urban citizens "may be dissatisfied without recognizing the specific reason for their dissatisfaction," self-help, participation, and group action in the form of an urban community program would go a long way to solving mutual problems.[71] Most important, said Ensminger, urban community organizers could "translate people's problems in a way that can be interpreted by government and private agencies."[72]

Although Ensminger's note drew liberally from the internal drafts on the issue circulated by the planning team of US experts, it highlighted and expanded on issues of strategic importance to the Ford Foundation.[73] Ensminger suggested that urban community development in India could draw from its successes in the United States. Despite apparent differences, both countries shared the issues of "social integration," India with caste, religion and language, and the United States with many "subcultures." Ensminger pointed out that

> citizen participation in self-help programs may be found among the Mexican population of Houston, the southern Negro migrants in Chicago and Detroit, among Protestants, Catholics and Jewish groups. . . . This is the case in one neighborhood slum project where Negroes, Japanese, Filipinos, and Mexicans are now working together in a neighborhood council.[74]

The impetus behind the urban community project was twofold. The new neighborhood was an important item in the regionalist urban design; locality consciousness needed to be adequate to adapt to the decentralized design of the future city. From the outset, Mayer had campaigned for an urban community project to ensure the success of a regionalist Masterplan. The neighborhood would be governed by normative standards and self-control, and self-consciously break from older forms of hierarchy imposed by colonial design or rural difference. Social mixing was to be encouraged, and a new "organic community" built. The Masterplan's work studies suggested that without "a basic medium of cohesion of common civic interest and loyalty, the prospects of improved social contacts, which made urban life desirable now make it hazardous." While the neighborhood concept was "Western," it would speak to village migrants who had a "spiritual orientation" to "traditional" *mohallas*.[75]

While Mayer suggested that the neighborhood model was akin to the traditional *mohalla*, planning was motivated more by the culture of liberal modernism and modernization theory where Indian cities clearly stood at an earlier developmental path of the West. Bert Hoselitz, a consultant for the Delhi plan, argued that India's twentieth-century urbanization rate was comparable to Europe in the nineteenth century, and followed a reasonably similar trajectory. Hoseltiz contrasted the urbanization rate with "sociocultural difference," where India was seen as seriously deficient in autonomous urban politics. Hoselitz mobilized Max Weber's dubious example of the superiority of the Western city in developing an autonomous urban politics, guaranteed by burgher elites who mobilized independent power centers against autocracy. In contrast, Indian cities said Hoseltiz "always were appendages to a court or other administrative centre to a court or other administrative center, to a temple or other place of worship or pilgrimage, or to a colony of merchants" (Hoselitz, 1962, p.175). If India lacked autonomous urban elites, it was further compromised by caste which, despite losing vigor in some urban roles, continued to "play a divisive role, fractionalizing the urban population – especially in housing and community living aspects" (ibid.). Hoseltiz's list of deficiencies in Indian "urban thinking" also included no traditions of zoning, parks, and open spaces. In this context, Hoseltiz concluded, many of these elements had to now come from a "foreign culture." This bland if not crude statement of modernization theory represented a broad consensus among liberal elites in the USA and India. In the context of the Delhi plan it gave impetus to two forms: the neighborhood design around common civic facilities in the formal structure of the Masterplan, and a pilot urban community program also supported by Ford to develop territorial forms of solidarity and self-help in neighborhoods.

Although Mayer hard sold the "neighborhood" by suggesting that it was similar to the *mohalla*, he was careful to allude to only the "spiritual" aspect. In formal terms the Masterplan neighborhood was closer to cellular models of early regionalist/New Town designs. The residential area clustered around focal points like a community center or a school. It would be surrounded by roads "but not pierced,"[76] close to Park's community models developed in the USA. The community center cluster could be expanded to include offices, shops, health centers, even a cinema. In the planners' view the design was a deliberate attempt to stage civic solidarity and a break from urban anonymity: "the more efficiently it is done the easier it is for the community to function."[77]

The neighborhood model was clearly seen by planners as a Western (though productive) implant for a democratic urban life in Delhi, but faced possible failure in the context of weak urban secular consciousness that was inadequately linked to territory. As Mayer and his team saw it, genuine civic consciousness had to be evoked in a pilot community project in Delhi.

The first pilot community projects began in 1959, following a year of planning and training social workers with MA degrees who would act as organizers.[78] A total of six vikas mandals (citizen development councils) were initiated in six socially distinct areas of the city ranging from refugee squatter settlements, slum settlements of respective Hindu and Muslim concentrations, settled working-class areas, a low population refugee colony, and mixed slum areas.[79] These were scattered all over the city. Three vikas mandals evolved into larger neighborhood vikas parishads in Paharganj, Shora Kothi (Subzi Mandi), and Sadar Idgah. The organizers worked in group interview situations, with detailed question-answer sessions using "change agent" technologies generated by consultants. Campaigns for sanitation, general cleanliness, self-help, problem-solving, and civic action were launched. In line with liberal egalitarian principles, women and lower castes were encouraged to join.

Marshall Clinard, the US academic consultant, helped to shape the project considerably, and his views were symptomatic of much of liberal modernization thinking filtering through the behavioral social science climate of the 1950s. "There are few places in the world where the dignity of man has been more degraded than in Indian cities," Clinard authoritatively told a seminar in Hyderabad at the time of the project in 1959.[80] After a long, depressing list of urban ills, Clinard reiterated a favorite theme among community scholars at the time: the decline of face-to face, "intimate" communications in Indian cities. While individualism was part of urban modernity in general, in India there was no assumption of individual or group responsibility outside caste or region. The secular city as a whole or general welfare had no meaning in India. Community projects played a generative role in producing a model of general welfare for the public through community action.

The project moved crucially in the direction of behavior modification, a favorite of sociological theory at that time, and economic improvement was mostly subsidiary, despite complaints from local participants.[81] Action was often induced in a "tactful manner." As a review of the project for Ford put it, "While no organizer ought to force his value judgment on the community, he sometimes has to force the pace of community understanding. After all, a certain degree of value inducement would seem to be inherent in the very concept of community development."[82] Given the difficult situation of many of the project areas, techniques were deployed to utilize and channel conflict. The latter was seen as unavoidable, even productive. Conflict management, suggested Clinard, "demands extensive and careful organization techniques." The clear advantage of conflict was that apart from possible benefits, the "excitement and activity it generated sustained support of slum dwellers" (Clinard, 1963, p.327).

There were of course hundreds of local organizations in Delhi that were active on a wide range of issues in a public and sometimes militant fashion. Organizations included *mohalla* committees, colony welfare associations, and refugee organizations, bazaar committees of merchants, hawkers groups, and caste *panchayats*. The Masterplan's own work studies, particularly in the sections researched by Delhi-based TPO workers, document a wide range of such organizations, with reasonably high levels of solidarity and integration, even by the social science classification models that were often suggested by US consultants.[83] Many of these organizations could be territorial, while also mobilizing for a range of issues outside formal spatial categories. This was not lost on the US consultants, but the local organizations were seen as prey to traditionalist difference, denying women or lower castes easy entry. In contrast, the representational form of the liberal community model was a "citizen's organization," a potential new center of power distinct from existing bodies. The organizational elite of the vikas mandals cultivated by the project were encouraged to avoid leaders of existing political groups or traditional organizations (Clinard, 1963, p.293).

In his detailed analysis of the urban community project in Delhi, Mathew Hull (2009) usefully situates it within the transformation of democracy in community in postwar social science. Here group feeling and community identity combined with individual initiative came to be associated with democratic culture. Hull writes, "Democracy, conceived in terms of group solidarity and individual initiative and participation in collective objectives, was incorporated into the very conception and procedures of expert-directed social change" (ibid.). The Delhi project was the deployment of this "democratic technology," where consultants used a variety of coordinated methods to generate group feeling and neighborhood affiliation. Narrow statistical survey models showed that group sentiments resulted from the project, since many alternative forms were rejected. The "social change technologies" pushed by US experts in the context of postwar democratic ideology gave them the potential to become "aggressive instruments to undermine forms of sociality valued by many people targeted by the programs."[84]

On reflection, the community project must be put in a broader context of liberal modernist experiments to simulate a model of secular affiliation. Secular territory ranged against local politics and traditionalism would modernize colonial difference. The flat technocratic narrative of the Delhi project reports shied away from traditional categories, preferring statistical charts and secular designations of class or the unnamed "upper" or "lower" caste. This contrasted with the more vivid Bharat Sevak Samaj survey of slums or even the neighborhood studies of the Masterplan that were written by TPO researchers where caste communities were clearly named, and local traditional conflicts were referenced in descriptions.

The Delhi project was comparable to other international US social science research that worked with urban renewal projects in Europe and the USA. Mostly supported by the Ford Foundation, the projects worked in the context of liberal efforts to understand and manage class and racial difference. In Europe, older working-class areas also became neighborhoods and communities in social science, and social scientists located "traditional working-class neighborhoods" that could not easily assimilate into an emerging mass society of Fordism (Topalov, 2003, pp. 212–233). In the US, community research in "socially disorganized" urban areas became submerged under

Slums around Jama Masjid

Tomorrow's Dujana House

SCHEMES TO CLEAR UNSIGHTLY CONGESTION
AROUND JAMA MASJID

Figure 1.4 From Slum to the Planned City. Town Planning Organization publicity series. The contrast of the "congested" old city/slum with the model of planned neighborhoods was a recurring theme in Masterplan publicity.

Source: TPO, Delhi, 1957.

assimilationist models of "migration" where no distinction was made between African American and white migrants.[85] In the anti-communist liberal academic culture of the 1950s, if class seemed an antiquated relic from the nineteenth century, race was dissolved within the broader urban sociology of migration.

Liberalism's city

At the end of a study of Delhi conducted in the 1950s Bombay-based sociologist Bopegamage noted with alarm the sharp segregation in New Delhi, where one part of the city was unaware of how another part lived. A society needed "social health," declared Bopegamage, and this distance was disturbing given the context of centuries of "caste segregation":

> If we are dreaming to attain a socialist pattern of society and foster the democratic spirit we must condemn this sort of physical segregation ... and take greater care to plan the physical organization in order to bring various groups together for co-operative endeavor.... [T]he new planning should be so designed as to embody the vital concept of neighborhoods by making it possible for face-to-face contacts.
>
> (Bopegamage, 1957, p.201)

Bopegamage reflected international social science literature in his stress on face-to-face contacts and desire for planned areas, while his own research on Delhi seemed to indicate that some of the older unplanned colonies as well as the Dalit area of Regharpura showed great internal solidarity. Segregation was equally anathema to the liberal model of the US consultants given the US experience of race. The Masterplan warned that "segregation foiled the very concept of neighborhood integration," and called for neighborhoods to be open to different income groups and households "irrespective of cultural and social background."[86]

In this view, the cellular design of the neighborhood was to be a model of non-segregated urban citizenship, protected from the customary *sturm und drang* of urban life. It would be populated by freshly socialized de-tradtionalized populations, eager for community life. This model of the neighborhood was part of a larger orchestration of the urban, where the plan would define proper "limits" to the city allowing for the rational management of the various forms of life. This border of the urban would decide the division between urban and non-urban, the space where proper urban citizens could be cultivated, and where inadequately urbanized subjects and populations could be displaced in specific "urban villages."

The fears of imminent and rapid urbanization were on the planners' minds, with cultural projections of high rates of rural urban migration, leading to a sense of claustrophobic space, beyond the rational management of things and people.[87] In the early meetings of the planning team in New York the optimum size of the city was a prominent item of discussion. While Edward Echeverria wrote that the "psycho-social" limits of Delhi seemed to have been reached, Julian Whittlesey argued that setting a limit to the central city was the basis of the very regional model.[88] The plan arrived at the urbanizable limits of the city after calculations on work–distance ratios, density, and a balance between the core and the counter-magnet regional towns which would deflect migrants away. Having established the optimum size through technocratic design, the main zone would be a model of normative urban form and social justice.

This took three forms, all of which were integral to the liberal model of the planners. The slum was to be tackled not by head-on assault but by a mixture of conservation of existing areas, relaxing building standards in some and increasing support, and removing some areas while providing adequate alternative accommodation in new areas where slum dwellers were displaced.[89] Displacement without alternatives was out of the question. The political consensus at the time was hostile to slum demolitions, and regular protests in Parliament and angry attacks on the government by MPs on demolitions by the DIT[90] made it clear that dealing with the slum question was a significant item on the agenda of postcolonial planning.[91] Total clearance of slums was considered not feasible by the planners, "at least for the next two decades."[92] Even the new migrant poor would have recourse to specially earmarked zones in the city. These areas should not be in the periphery to institutionalize segregation, but be an integral part of the city, "with a proper layout and the space standards for the facilities like schools, open spaces etc. . . . . Building by laws should be considerably relaxed" for these spaces to enable low-cost housing.[93]

The order of liberalism required that justice be housed in a rational city. Mayer's early complaint against "functional and social mix-up" of space was common to all planning doctrines; other colleagues in the planning team argued that "an area must have a predominant function of land use that can be easily described and delimited."[94] The culture of planning demanded this simple clarity of purpose, since the order of the city was premised on it.[95]

"Failure" of planning

Paul Virilio once famously said that the accident was the diagnostic of technology; to invent the plane was to equally invent the plane crash. We could say that "failure" is the diagnostic of the plan. Like disaster diagnostics on television, where experts analyze the event for a viewing public, modern projects have always produced a surfeit of "failure analyses." As an event, failure's diagnostic is internal to planning's discourse, if not to much of modernist urbanism. The event re-enacts the "public" in whose name the design was launched, and suggests periodic recombinations of the technocratic constellation.

A decade after the 1962 Delhi Masterplan, a major review was undertaken by the Town and Country Planning Organization, the successor to the TPO.[96] The review panel was headed by Syed Shafi, and TPO member of the planning team for the 1962 Masterplan. After praising the Masterplan for initiating the first comprehensive plan for Delhi, the review went on to issue a damning report. Not only had the proximity of work and residence not worked out as had been hoped in the plan,[97] but the spatial segregation of the city was moving rapidly, with affluent districts in the south and poorer districts in the east.[98] One by one, the plan's meticulous model of land use, the separation of industry, commerce, and home was shown to be in tatters. Not a single "flatted factory" to house small enterprises had been built, and the work on the first district center in Pusa Road had only just begun, giving commercial establishments little or no place to go.[99] Given the inability of the city to come up with alternative facilities for housing, commerce, and industry, squatting was widespread, along with "unauthorized colonies" and "non-conforming industries." The review even went on to question the land-use philosophy of the Masterplan, based on "Western" planning models disregarding the "unorganized" sector in Delhi; and

> it is absurd to characterize the entire walled city of Shahjehanabad as a slum by adopting environmental and spatial frame wholly irrelevant to the life cycles of the traditional city and unrelated to the life of the common man. The unique feature of the indigenous city is that economic, social and cultural activities have endowed a spatial form and organization to the community whereby seemingly conflicting functions and process can co-exist together. . . . Unfortunately the very important link between people and their activities is disrupted by a superficial, rather, a mechanical separation of land uses implied in zoning superimposed on a city form evolved through centuries.[100]

This comprehensive denunciation of Western modernist planning in the name of an indigenous urban life was part of a larger review which called for better, more intelligent planning for the city. This 1973 document had been proceeded a few years before by an equally alarming review by the same TCPO on land values in Delhi. The report found that land prices had risen fourfold between 1958 and 1969 since the DDA was granted monopoly on land control in Delhi. This speculative jump was far in excess of what existed under the regime of "normal" private property in land in the 1950s. The few land auctions that the DDA had conducted commanded such high prices that most ordinary citizens were turned away, and social housing was modest if not laughable. Following in the footsteps of the hated DIT, the DDA had emerged as the main speculator. The report pointed out that the DDA's "exploiting its near monopoly hold of the land market with an eye on making financial gains damages the more important social objectives of land policy."[101] Forced off legal land, urban populations flocked to "unauthorized" colonies, where land was cheap and facilities could be negotiated through

Figure 1.5 Flyer of a private builder promoting a new neighborhood in the mid-
1950s. "Speculation" by private companies and the DIT would emerge as a
major concern of planners and politicians in public debates at the time.

Source: FF Archives.

political mobilization and local networks. Small industry also developed in
unauthorized areas, moving into cheap land in the east and the west of the
city.[102] Proliferation, the very demon that planning hoped to exorcise, was
now widespread in the city. Planning's rationalization eventually caused what
Jai Sen (1975) famously called the "unintended city," where the separation of
the spheres of urban/rural and formal/informal collapsed under its own
contradictions.

Planning and Delhi's twentieth century

In public discourse the Masterplan was posited as a break with colonial
urbanism. This feat was achieved significantly through the transfer of all land

control to the government. Planning was significantly associated with state power over land acquisition. As in the pre-colonial period, the control of land assured social power; in the nationalist incarnation this sovereignty would deliver justice and "the overall welfare of the city."[103] As if to reinforce the symbolic transference of colonial to nationalist power, the Masterplan documents valorized colonial power over land in Lutyens' New Delhi as a sound basis for planning. For the planners this policy had been ignored since Partition, leading to speculation and slum growth. If the Lutyens design had highlighted monumental display and political control of the Empire, the Masterplan's 1950s modernism emphasized secular sovereign power through land.

The proximity of the 1962 document to colonial urbanism was even more sustained than is commonly assumed.[104] The Lutyens design self-consciously drew attention to imperial power by separating Shahjehanabad from New Delhi. Some local artisan influences were carefully, if not deliberately, incorporated into buildings within a broader schema of European classicism and garden-city dispersal. In contrast, the Masterplan's modernist effect was non-historical, to the point of expunging the cultural archive of Delhi's urbanism in its vision of the future.[105] Following the path set by Lutyens, the Masterplan emphasized the supremacy of the new city by deploying Shahjehanabad as a negative example of urban chaos and decline. In the Masterplan's neo-Hegelian narrative, Shahjehanabad's once proud status almost inevitably moved towards successive tragedy and decay. Its contemporary status functioned as the other of planning. The old city imaged chaotic land use, "slum-like" conditions, lack of civic services and open space – a crowded, medieval, urban hell.

Instead of Lutyens' deliberate ceremonial supremacy of the new over the old, the plan used the model of Map and the Law. The Masterplan's land-use and zoning maps did not simply organize space into rational, manageable units for the new rulers. That had been done since the colonial era. As a specialist instrument of knowledge, the planning map of the 1950s fabricated urban expertise in Delhi. Planners and consultants now claimed privileged access to technical knowledge of the city, and consequently to political power. Law however remained the cement of the liberal modernist city. The land-use plan of Delhi's version of liberal modernism displaced rural forms of work and life to the periphery; commerce and industry were separated through an elaborate hierarchy common to planning. The plan as law sought to ensure this hierarchy – as indeed all plans did. The phantasmatic recall of the 1962 Plan by Courts and civic groups by the 1990s was to relive this mythic moment of liberal urbanism. The plan's more complicated narrative on the urban poor was passed over for an abstract legal urbanism in the neo-liberal *fin-de-siècle*.

The debate over justice passed over one of the more far-reaching techno-social implications of the 1962 regionalist design for Delhi. The city was conceived of as a *machine* with networks of circulation that included semi-autonomous cells (neighborhoods), and vectors that mapped on to a coordinated grid of technological infrastructure. While the machine was managed through a central regulatory engine, its decentralized design sprouted an endless mutation into non-linear networks allowing for new technological connections and assemblies by the 1980s. This was not a state of alterity, but akin to what Delueze and Guattari call a "line of flight":

> Lines of flight, for their part, never consist in running away from the world but rather in causing runoffs, as when you drill a hole in a pipe; there is no social system that does not leak from all directions, even if it makes its segments increasingly rigid in order to seal the lines of flight.
>
> (Deleuze and Guattari, 1988, p.204)

It is on the lines of flight, argue Delueze and Guattari, that "new weapons" are invented. Paradoxically the weapons that emerged in Delhi were not just the proliferation of forms of life outside the law of the city, but media culture – the great silence of the liberal city.

2 Media urbanism

At some point in the long decade of the 1980s the city of Delhi entered its own "very special delirium."[1] The ingredients of this delirium included a powerful mix of urban crisis and an expanding media sensorium that produced a feeling which was exhilarating for some, but equally terrifying and violent for others. Delhi's experience is also comparable to other rapidly growing cities of that "long decade," Mexico City, Karachi, Lagos, and many others, all places that experience similar concoctions of growth crisis and street media dynamism. In the fast-moving landscape of global event theory however, yet another genre has emerged which seeks to explain the turbulent expansion of cities in the South. This is a genre which can be best called "urban crisis" writing.

The most recent incarnation is Mike Davis' *Planet of Slums* (2006) which reads the urban crisis in the postcolonial world as heralding a new apocalyptic "slumming" of the world's cities. In Davis' narrative, a fetid, violent urbanism in the periphery is the future of modern capitalism, with collapsing cities and open sewage, vast migratory populations, and retreat of secular and state forms. To Davis' discomfort, welfare and self-help are now provided not by the state or radicals but by religious movements of popular Islam and Christianity. Davis' book recalls Victorian reformers' deployment of shock exposé and horror to focus on congestion, disease, and poverty in mid-nineteenth-century cities. In the postcolonial world, a version of the *Planet of Slums* has also crowded urban discourse in the past decade. This is the classic landscape of planners, and older reform elites. This discourse fills op-ed columns, widely publicized releases of status reports on the city, and media campaigns. For social liberalism and the inheritors of twentieth-century progressive urbanism, postcolonial urban catastrophes are signatures of weakened sovereignties, the rise of neo-liberal global urban expertise and private developers, and the failing dreams of a more equal way of urban life imagined by planners.

Others have taken an entirely different path. When flying over Lagos in a helicopter a few years ago as part of his research project, Rem Koolhaas (2002b) suddenly realized that the city that seemed on the ground to resemble a "smoldering, burning rubbish dump" was in fact a stunning post-plan metropolis. Koolhaas saw vast complementary coherences amidst the apparent chaos of Lagos, a self-organized rhythm of urban life, markets, traffic interfaces, network innovations that rendered its very "dysfunctionality" productive. When the post-independence order fell away, suddenly in the vast interstices of the planned city a new rhythm emerged, without mega-designs, first parasitic then productive and dynamic, or perhaps all of them together. Koolhaas' text has the merit of cutting through the apocalyptic critiques of urbanism. In his explication the dramaturgy of Lagos is filled with possibilities that speak beyond narratives of survival and loss. As a dramaturgy that evokes a different possibility of urban life to Western readers (to whom it is aimed at), Koolhaas' mediations on Lagos fail on one count; here the productive city of the South seems to have transformed the dead into the ever-flowing, and ever-living. If Mike Davis' doomsday narrative is aimed at shocking Western policy-makers and readers with his catalog of Third World shanty town horrors, Koolhaas' text flows (unintentionally?) well with the current vitalist moment in social theory. Koolhaas' narrative is the chapter of a novella to be written, the middle reel of a movie that has no ending. The lecture on Lagos may work as an abstract lesson for Western architecture, but it fails to capture an emerging urban media technics in the postcolonial world.

Crisis ingredients, proliferation and the informal

Both Davis and Koolhaas are right on one count: postcolonial urban life has imploded, the new expansion of cities has made classic urban management models irrelevant or simply inoperative. Proliferation, endless proliferation, marks the new postcolonial urban. Home workshops, markets, hawkers, small factories, small and large settlements of the working poor now spread all over the planned metropolis, or in regions where it was impossible to do so some years ago. Productive, non-legal proliferation has emerged as a defining component of the new urban crisis in India and other parts of the postcolonial world. The informality debates begun by ILO economists had begun to anticipate this emerging shape of the postcolonial metropolis in the 1970s.[2] Informal work and settlement lacked governmental sanction, rapidly drawing the new migrant poor, street traders, small workshops, and neighborhood factories. What has emerged right from the outset is informality's ambivalence about the law, both in terms of housing settlements and production sites which worked through de-facto tenure rather than formal title. Both Solomon Benjamin's (1991) work on East Delhi's industrial clusters and Timothy Mitchell's (2004) insights on informal housing in Egypt suggest that it is precisely this ambivalence about entering legal domains that accounted for informality's strength. As Mitchell's work on Egypt shows, urban populations identified as informal tended to stay away from legal regimes of property as the latter potentially destroyed local knowledges, and brought the informal into the extractive monetary structures of urban regimes.

Development and post-development planning literature tended to see informality more in terms of its opposition to or incorporation into the formal city and law.[3] Rather, informality's political stance was pragmatic to mercenary, working variously with local politicians and state employees to get services, local land speculators, small crime syndicates that provided protection, and religious self-help groups. Illegal lotteries known as chit funds were often used to finance low-cost constructions.

Informality was probably less unstructured than the early debates made it out to be; it also developed complex internal inequalities of work and gender. What is important for this discussion is that informality emerged from smaller academic and policy debates in the 1970s to become a form of urban life that took center stage in the dramaturgy of urban crisis in India by the end of the century. For state planners, neo-liberal civic groups, orthodox Marxists, and the old secular elite, informality became a model of wild, lawless urbanism that made a mockery of zoning. Lacking civic services, these zones emerge in civic reports as hellish sites of polluting industries, theft of civic services, and political vote banks. Informality was urbanism out of joint, a frightening Outside of the Law of the City.[4] A selective phenomenology of this urban informality as proliferating life clearly marks both Mike Davis' and Koolhaas' texts. For Davis, informality marks a morbid negation of any urban vision of collectivist solidarity, while for Koolhaas informality is *life itself*, with an organic rhythm, emerging from the bowels of the postcolonial city.

Koolhaas gets one thing right – the idea that the urban crisis has exposed new and old/new assemblages that mutate, incorporate, and displace populations, spaces, and things. The present becomes dramatically visible – in often disturbing ways.

Delhi

In his "Short Guide to Towns without a Past," Albert Camus called them places "without tenderness and abandon." They are, said Camus, "suited neither to wisdom or the delicacies of taste" (cited in Vidler, 2000, p.178). By the 1970s it was the fate of Delhi, the quintessential empire city almost a millennium old, that it was viewed by the rest of the country through the prism of a drab and cruel urbanism of the plan, and the rule of corrupt political and cultural elites. Other metropolitan elites regarded the city's largely migrant population as lacking in cultural capital – in Delhi, that most cosmopolitan of enlightenment virtues was now turning against itself. The great melancholy lament of Delhi's poets which began with the sacking of the city by Nadir Shah in the eighteenth century, the wholesale destruction by the Company's armies in 1857 to 1858, the caesura of Partition, all came to an end with the Masterplan's urban vision. Haunted by the dead, imprisoned in the ruins of the old city/slum, the new city suffered a representational paralysis. What was Delhi if not for politics and the plan? The more Delhi's inhabitants protested by showing the vitality of the new migrant neighborhoods and markets, the strength of its universities and intellectual discussion, the more the city seemed condemned to that derisive urbanist label of a capital – comparable to a Washington D.C. or a Canberra. The dream of a transparent city freed from congestion and health risks which motivated the planners may not have succeeded on the ground, but it set up a discursive terrain that seemed difficult to break.

To be sure, visitors to Delhi in the 1950s and 1960s may have observed a city lacking a modern urban rhythm, at least in comparison to Bombay and Calcutta. Urban civic and cultural life was muted; a very small cultural elite clustered around state cultural institutions could not intervene effectively in the public life of the city. Much of this took place in the Lutyens zone, which continued to be the site for institutional growth, including cultural centers, embassies, conference sites, hotels, all forming a model of abstract space that the original design had in mind. This was at a time when migration was steady: the city had expanded to 2.6 million by the 1970s. Urban planning bodies managed the city through zoning laws, housing schemes, and refugee resettlement. Housing construction was steady and colonies expanded rapidly in the south and the west of the city. The migrants from west Punjab reinvigorated commercial life in the city, markets expanded, and new networks of credit and circulation were built through family and kinship ties, all laying the ground for the rapid commercial explosions of the 1980s. By the 1970s a significant working-class presence, concentrated around small industries and the new export/industrial zones of Okhla and NOIDA, was recorded. These movements of working people to Delhi, along with the increase in small industry and commerce, gradually changed the urban morphology over thirty years with the three decades after 1971 showing the most dramatic shifts. In these three decades, not only did the population of Delhi rise from four million in 1971 to thirteen million in 2001, by 1998 there were 1080 squatter settlements housing approximately 10 percent of the population, and a further 24 percent of the population lived in "unauthorized colonies." In addition, there were illegal markets, street vendors, and weekly street bazaars, and a very dynamic small business culture, revitalizing markets. The footprint of Delhi now covers the "National Capital Region" which had a population of thirty-seven million in 2001. In short, Delhi had changed from the stasis of a political capital, dominated by bureaucratic elites, to becoming close to a "mega-city."[5]

Snapshot, the caesura of the 1990s

By the 1990s a feeling of crisis and constant breakdown in the city exposed the inadequacies of the 1962 Masterplan's confident modernist vision for Delhi. As if to suggest the failure of the Masterplan imaginary of ordered development, the bulk of Delhi's residents now lived in non-legal neighborhoods, ranging from working-class settlements to elite usurpations of public space. Crisis points of the city were rapidly mapped on to different landscapes, the liberal environmentalist demand to remove "polluting industries" from the city, chaotic public transportation, and the alarmingly high rates of deaths on the road. Paranoiac security discourses after insurgencies in Kashmir and Punjab overflowed in Delhi in the shape of terrorist incidents. In the event, constant urban crises prised open the existing political arrangements of the city. These had involved the grafting of political claims by local populations within the routine practices of urbanism, a phenomenon approximating Partha Chatterjee's description of "political society." This arrangement had accommodated the great expansion of the non-legal city after 1977, often with the help of local politicians. Since the mid-1990s, this older political model of urban growth was thrown into complete confusion. A significant cause of this has been a middle-class environmental civic campaign that petitioned sympathetic courts, portraying the city as a space on the brink of ecological collapse and transport disaster. Crisis scenarios by the turn of the century were identified and dramatized on a daily basis.

In this emerging scenario, intervention of both the Supreme and High Courts in the city was fundamental, woven in with media landscapes and narratives of urban catastrophe.

The courts had been shifting steadily towards interventionism in the 1990s, using the public interest litigations (PIL) initiated by civic groups as sites to generate an urban drama that occupied public life for more than a decade. As mentioned in the previous chapter, with the Masterplan as a referent, the courts declared different forms of urban life as non-conforming and illegal. While the court orders began as an ostensible critique of polluting industries and commercialization, they eventually touched every neighborhood, hundreds of squatter camps, and thousands of small shops, as well as simple extensions and modifications to homes. The court order acted as the master reference in the crisis, with daily violence when demolition squads moved in. Public anxiety was reflected in screaming headlines and non-stop new coverage. This brought to a climax and political crisis a discourse that emerged from the mid-1990s, when court orders periodically declared various forms of life to be out of conformity with the law, polluting small industries, speeding public buses, all settlement on land as "public land," squatter settlements. The court orders mobilized images of urban chaos, executive-style command, and a cinematic urgency of movement suggesting immediate action. Practices that were ordinarily part of the pastoral power of government were suddenly rendered visible through dramatic civic judgments. In doing so very publicly, the courts accelerated images of crisis, already in circulation in the hyper-stimulus of the city. Egged on by a sympathetic media and advocacy groups, the courts appointed special committees spread over every aspect of civic life, causing terror and fear in the neighborhoods they visited.[6] A phantom civic subject emerged in this very public legal discourse, identifiably middle class, post-political, and projected as the injured legatee of the urban body.

Like Koolhaas' almost revelatory description of Lagos, the court orders from the mid-1990s continuously dramatized a vast surface of a previously hidden city. These included new "unauthorized" neighborhoods, informal and non-legal settlements, working-class migrations and a vast network of small markets, neighborhood factories, and small shops. Horizontal networks of production, circulation, new work patterns, a dizzyingly complex world of infrastructure support, tenure and occupation emerged, a dynamic, productively chaotic mix, all of which became ingredients of the crisis narrative mobilized in court cases in the 1990s. Beyond the legal language of the Court, vast traffic, new smells of plastic garbage, industrial waste, food shops, and burnt fumes from buses and auto-rickshaws all transformed and inflamed the sense of everydayness, and produced a hyperstimulus of urbanism.

This hyperstimulus was predicated on a vastly expanded media, video, sound, digital print, telephony, and *things* of media – cassettes, televisions, screens, CDs, posters, phones, and flyers. These spread all over the city and became inseparable from the urban experience. This corporeal mix gave the urban experience a visceral, overimaged feel – it also dispersed the classic morphology of the planned city. It was clear that a different kind of city had emerged in the discourses of the 1990s from that imagined by the Masterplan. Proliferation, endless proliferation, was the secret of this new metropolis. Proliferation slowly mixed with a media sensorium to create a dynamic urban loop that seemed to push the city to the brink in the 1990s.

Figure 2.1 A Municipal Corporation of Delhi announcement, asking the public to provide information on "unauthorized constructions." The announcement also asks that the complaints be directed to Court Commissioners, reflecting the fracture of municipal authority.

Source: MCD, 2007.

The implosion of abstract space, rewinding to the "long" 1980s

As discussed in the previous chapter, the Delhi Masterplan of 1962 saw the city as a productive organism; urban design was subordinated to this broader aim. This involved a careful distinction between forms of labor and subjectivity that were seen as appropriate to modern urban life in India; those who did not fit this model could be open to displacement in the event of a failed assimilation into urbanism. The separation of work and industry, a discourse against congestion, and the marking of legal and non-legal habitation in the city was the central thrust of the plan. The plan's political thrust was abstract and vertical to assure sovereign control of the political elite over the city. This proximity to centralized power allowed for the emergence of bureaucratic planner elites with authoritarian fantasies. Among a section of the urban bureaucracy was a developmental modernist wing around Jagmohan, who incorporated nostalgia of urban memories of old Lahore and Shahjehanabad in his efforts to attempt Haussmann-like transformations in Old Delhi. In his book *Rebuilding Shahjahanabad*, published in the fateful year of 1975, Jagmohan suggested that certain parts of the old city had become "dead," and were now centers for crime and disease. He went on,

> In areas like Hauz Qazi, Lal Kuan and Turkoman Gate, bums and bad characters are all that can be seen after the nightfall. Only indecent remarks of cheap film songs are heard. The very sight of eating places, with broken chairs, stinking tables, and with shabby and shirtless waiters, is repellent. It is necessary to brighten up these areas; otherwise these will remain breeding grounds for criminals and rioters.
>
> (Jagmohan, 1975, pp.71–72)

Jagmohan's fascination with the old city was a mixture of nostalgia and necrophilia; it was Shahjahanabad's alleged combination of death, disease, history, and a mythic pre-colonial urbanism that made it a prime candidate for the planner-bureaucrats' schemes of social engineering.[7] At the close of his book, Jagmohan ended with a poem:

> I stand erect
> Restless and keen
> Willing to Fight
> Willing to Dream.

By the early 1970s it was increasingly clear that the Masterplan's timid projections of urban expansion and its classic divisions of work, industry, and commerce were breaking down. In the *Production of Space*, Henri Lefebvre suggests that "social space" could not be easily represented in any definitive map or maps. The French writer went on to suggest that it was doubtful if any number could do so. In fact, says Lefebvre, "what we are most

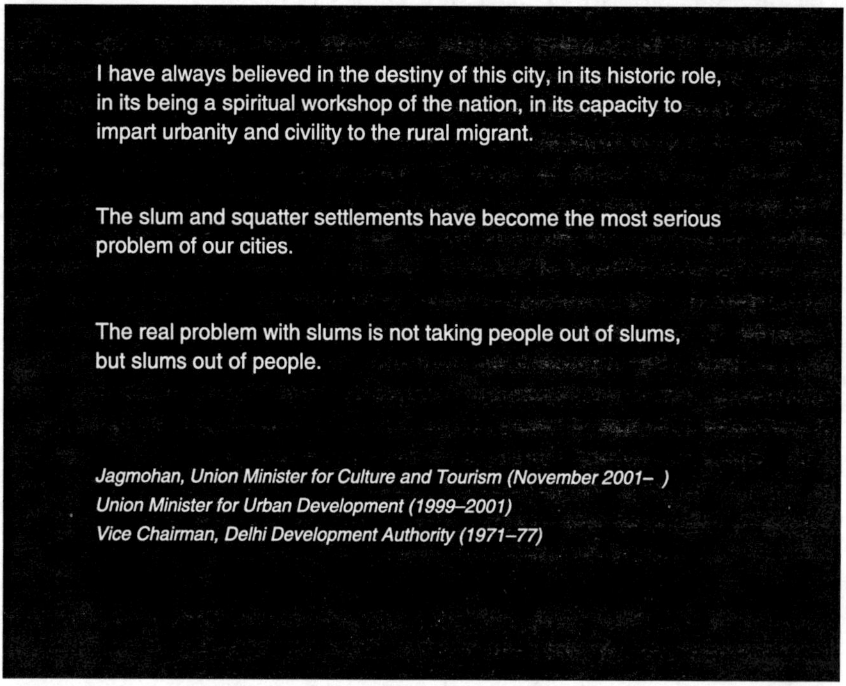

> I have always believed in the destiny of this city, in its historic role, in its being a spiritual workshop of the nation, in its capacity to impart urbanity and civility to the rural migrant.
>
> The slum and squatter settlements have become the most serious problem of our cities.
>
> The real problem with slums is not taking people out of slums, but slums out of people.
>
> *Jagmohan, Union Minister for Culture and Tourism (November 2001–)*
> *Union Minister for Urban Development (1999–2001)*
> *Vice Chairman, Delhi Development Authority (1971–77)*

Figure 2.2 The Jagmohan era became a significant allegory of slum dislocation. This is an exhibit from Coordinates of Everyday Life, Documenta 11, Kassel, Germany.

Source: Raqs Media Collective, 2002.

likely to be confronted with here is a sort of instant infinity, a situation reminiscent of a Mondrian painting" (1991, p.85). This "unlimited multiplicity" of space, as Lefebvre was to call it, was the kind of urban form emerging in Delhi barely a decade after the Masterplan. As the NCAER's survey of Delhi in 1973[8] showed, "unauthorized" colonies had expanded in the city, as had squatter settlements or *jhuggi jhopri* colonies. Unauthorized colonies spread as local private developers also encouraged people to settle on designated agricultural or lands planned to be acquired by the DDA (Bose, 1978, pp.1–42). Local promoters would attract people to settle on the land, a situation made more attractive given the DDA's sole monopoly on all land under the Masterplan. Part flight by workers from *basti* conditions and displacement, and part receptors of subaltern and lower-middle-class migration to the city, the unauthorized colonies were initially set up with a rudimentary infrastructure. This changed slowly through complex day-to-day struggles and mobilization of local political elites who used electoral politics to expand infrastructure and demand better services.

Molecular strategies of production, migration also punched holes in the plan's legal-rational containers. Productive activity in the city grew rapidly during the 1960s and 1970s; the NCAER survey also found that there were now 23,496 industries in Delhi, up from 5504 in 1950 (1973, p.180). By 1981 this had risen to 42,000 units.[9] At any rate the NCAER 1973 survey showed a remarkable morphology; most industries were small or cottage industries, and most were in "non-conformity" areas, i.e. outside the legal framework of the plan (ibid., pp.33–41). All over the city, particularly outside the NDMC zone, small industries appeared in neighborhoods, *bastis*, backyards, basements, ignoring zoning restrictions and Western-style planning separations. In *Production of Space*, Lefebvre also talks of the "collisions" of space, its wild interpenetrations and becoming more like flaky pastry than the "flatness" described in Euclidian/Cartesian models (1991, p.86). Any attempt to map this morphology would in fact be confronted with the kind of "instant infinity" that Lefebvre spoke about.

An expansion of space was implicit in the model of the plan. In the Masterplan's urban progressivist gloss, land assembly and development were concentrated in the hands of government. The vast expansion of the city outside the plan that became visible only in the 1990s was for the most part muted in public discourse in the early 1970s. Instead the image of the non-legal city was dominated by the classic demon, the slum. Slum demolitions, resettlement, and drives to clean up the old city dominated urban discourse by city technocrats in the 1970s. The first major displacements had begun in 1967, when poorer residents of various slum localities in Delhi had their homes demolished, and were unceremoniously dumped in the eastern part of the city (Tarlo, 2003, p.132).

The Emergency of 1975 to 1977 in Delhi violently dramatized this process of the dislocation of the working poor of the old city to the periphery. This model of dislocation was implicit in the urban designs of the colonial and planner city, but the Emergency accelerated this process through the use of police force and terror. Hundreds of thousands were forcibly relocated in settlements that were planned by the regime in the east, south, and west of the city. These resettlement colonies were based on a brutal transaction; those displaced got their plots regularized after agreeing to undergo sterilization of male members of the family. The resettled populace either agreed to get sterilized or "motivated" someone to do so. As Emma Tarlo convincingly demonstrates in her book on the Emergency, narratives of displacement were entangled in a complex web of everyday violence, market trading of sterilization certificates, and a deferral of judgment on the regime that sanctioned the move. Blame was often focused on lower level MCD officials, the DDA, and Sanjay Gandhi. Faced with relentless demolition before the displacements of the 1975–1977 period, the residents of new resettlement colonies could consent to the state control of their bodies in return for a permanence of settlement. Writes Tarlo,

While the sight of bulldozers razing whole areas to the ground was shocking to the elite, it was all too familiar to the inhabitants of slums and resettlement colonies. . . . Though sterilization was a new experience, and one that had incited considerable fear, suffering and resentment during the Emergency, people had survived it and had been able to secure a plot or two in the process. . . . These were narratives dominated not by the idiom of shock or guilt but by the idiom of survival.

(Tarlo, 2003, p.225)

The Emergency stories included all the elements set in motion by the discourse of planning in Delhi. These included elite fears of urban collapse due to congestion and poverty, and an authoritarian cultural politics of urban renewal led by Emergency personalities such as Jagmohan who suggested that radical and brutal solutions were needed to save the old city from collapse. Where the Emergency excelled over the older plan model was its fusion of high political and civic power, and a suspension of "normal" transactions of city government between planning bodies, city councils, and local units. These were subordinated to achieve totalitarian fantasies of control over productive male bodies, through sterilization targets. In retrospect it appears that the Emergency in Delhi represented more than just a drive against the urban poor as it seemed at the time. It represented a final authoritarian attempt by the government and technocratic elites to implement the legal rationalism of the Masterplan, and to reassert control over urban life at every level. Indeed, during that brief period of 1975 to 1977, the proliferation of habitation and production that were "non-conforming" came to a halt due to the fear and terror of the police regime. Migrants found almost no land to build shelter, and small-scale industries were now under the watchful eyes of the municipality. Thousands were displaced to the periphery from the city center, making way for beautification projects, clean-up operations, and parks.[10] People moved around the city desperately looking for habitation, and for ways to avoid the terrible scars of sterilization (Dayal and Bose, 1977; Tarlo, 2003; Benjamin, 2005c).

Thirty years later, hindsight tells us that the Emergency inaugurated the long process of the shift of postcolonial Delhi away from the classic image of the capital subordinated to political power and excess. By significantly expanding the physical form of the city through brutal resettlement, the Emergency developed new frontiers and settlements in Delhi. Large working-class peripheries emerged, becoming hubs for small-scale production, and interfaces opened up between the old city and the suburban towns in the NCR.

Within the new settlements (Mangolpuri, Sultanpuri, Dakshinpuri, Seelampur, Trilokpuri) smaller peripheries of non-legal tenements and rentals provided shelter to new migrants in the 1980s, when many original allottees also sold their plots to buyers. Connections between the markets of the old city and the resettlement colonies became important vectors for the movement of goods, labor power, and transport. In 1995, an appraisal of land policies in Delhi by the Town and Country Planning Organization (TCPO) confirmed the importance of the 1975 to 1977 period. In cold, statistical language, the TCPO review points out the implications of the brutal transformations of the Emergency years:

> The year 1977 can be considered a watershed ... for two reasons (1) DDA mounted the largest operation in the resettlement of squatters ever undertaken in any city bringing down considerably the extent of the squatter population and (2) though squatters were spread in all zones of the city to a greater or lesser extent the general trend after 1977 has been outward growth towards the periphery.[11]

In the post-Emergency period, the formerly policed empty spaces in the city filled up with poor migrants, and the squatter colonies exploded in their hundreds in a short space of time.[12] As migrants flooded into the city during the construction of the Asiad complex, the post-Emergency interregnum allowed a welcome political breathing space, which would only become clearer later in the grimmer atmosphere of the late 1990s. Nationally, an important Court judgment on pavement dwellers in Bombay even affirmed their "right to livelihood," which became a defense against their eviction by the Bombay Municipal authority.[13]

The defeat of the Congress in the 1977 elections and the overwhelming anti-Emergency feeling transformed the relationship between politics and urban power in Delhi. Technocratic power represented by Jagmohan and his cohorts suffered a serious setback. The legal rational days of enforcement and authoritarian planning were put on hold for the next twenty years, and consequently the ability of the government to implement bureaucratic decisions weakened over the long term. Post-Emergency local politicians entered into a practical contract with subaltern populations, enabling migrants to squat available space in the city and pushing moves to regularize "unauthorized neighborhoods." The Emergency defeat was a long-term enabler for Delhi's expansion; until the 1990s "anti-encroachment" drives were never as wide-ranging, and the hated bulldozer, a sign of Emergency excesses, only returned in force when demolitions resumed under Supreme Court directions in the 1990s. Even then, the orders were implemented more through slow, manual demolition squads given local animosity to the machines.

In short, during the Emergency the power of urban government expanded to its maximum possible, and fractured following the 1977 defeat. Planning's great technocratic model was subjected to authoritarian acceleration in 1975 to 1977, and burst at the seams.[14] By exorcising the ghost of congestion through brutal resettlement, the Emergency planners released new spirits of urban expansion and proliferation. In a sense this was the old regionalist nightmare scenario – the "urban sprawl," which Mayer and his colleagues had struggled to contain through the model of legal land-use enclosures, and urban–rural distinctions. But that urban regime was based on a powerful centralized authority, and older models of national power. After the defeat of the Emergency, it was difficult to argue for authoritarian models of urban governance.

To be sure, the city remained a difficult, even cruel habitation for the urban poor, but a temporary breathing space in the post-Emergency years allowed for the expansion of squatter *bastis* and unauthorized colonies. The increasing inability of the MCD to deal with non-legal proliferation or encroachment following the Emergency became clear within the organization itself. From the early 1980s both the Land and Estate and Vigilance Departments began issuing a series of urgent, almost repetitive circulars pointing to widespread encroachments on municipal land and "unauthorized" constructions. The language of the circular was almost generic: widespread encroachment, new constructions, expansion of molecular transformations in streets, markets, neighborhoods.[15] What is clear is that the local MCD officials simply ignored the circulars sent out from head office, preferring to make pecuniary adjustments on the ground. The language of the office memos offers a rare window into the changing nature of governmental power, where the centralized authority of the city slowly eroded, with neighborhood factors coming into play in the 1980s. In a circular dated 1983, the MCD admitted:

> It is seen the instructions contained in the various circulars issued by the Commissioner and the Directorate of Vigilance, Municipal Corporation of Delhi are not being complied with by the concerned officials in safeguarding Municipal Lands. . . . This is not only a matter of great and serious lapse but is a reflection on the working of Zonal authorities. . . . Most surprisingly the concerned Zonal authorities either express their complete ignorance or when required to take action, they only try and evade responsibility. The Zonal Authorities either pass on the case to the L & E Dept. or adopt dilly-dally methods thereby enabling the encroacher/builder in bringing a stay order.[16]

Zonal officials ignored circulars, fudged records, and mostly refused to keep count of "unauthorized constructions," a process that was more than just a generic feature of postcolonial urbanism.

Pirate cities?

A memory of the 1980s in Delhi is a clutter of events, the spectacle of the Asian Games in 1982, the assassination of Mrs. Gandhi and the pogrom against the Sikhs in 1984, the Rajiv Gandhi era, the arrival of terrorism and counter-terrorism, the anti-Mandal agitation by upper-caste students, and the rise of Hindu nationalism. Everything seemed to partly confirm Delhi's status as a shadow theater of national political acts, possessing no history outside that of the national state. Remarkably, by the end of the decade this entire image began spinning out of control following the destructive cycle of the anti-Mandal agitation in the city, quickly followed by the Hindu nationalist campaigns to demolish the Babri mosque in Ayodhya. Post Ayodhya, local politics in Delhi began slowly gaining in prominence.

Only today can we suggest retrospectively that the 1980s contained a secret unfolding history of Delhi. New productive sites and criss-crossing networks emerged, along with a vast economy of small and minor practices. The latter opened up a discursive space away from classic political acts of occupation of space, or older notions of resistance. I want to argue that these practices in Indian cities and perhaps in other parts of the postcolonial world went beyond classic post-Enlightenment discussions on everyday lives. To understand this point more clearly, we need to revisit the discussion of "minor practices" in social theory, notably the work of Michel De Certeau with whom the concept has been most closely associated. In his *Practice of Everyday Life*, De Certeau distinguished "minor" practices from dominant or "foregrounded procedures":

> A society is . . . composed of certain foregrounded practices organizing its normative institutions *and* of innumerable other practices that remain "minor," always there but not organizing discourses and preserving the beginnings or remains of different (institutional, scientific) hypotheses for that society or for others.
>
> (De Certeau, 2002, p.48)

For De Certeau minor practices are implicated in the *productive* power of the everyday. He approached the everyday less from the standpoint of popular culture, and more from a certain gesture to the Other. Thus for De Certeau the everyday is the "cultural activity of the non-producers of culture, an activity that is unsigned, unreadable and unsymbolized" (ibid., p.xviii). It is this productive banality that appealed to Meaghan Morris when she called for the adoption of De Certeau's work: "This is the banality which speaks in Everyman, and in the late work of Freud – where the ordinary is no longer the object of analysis but the *place* from which discourse is produced" (Morris, 1990, p.35). The logic for practice is tactical, it operates in the context of the marginalization of a large section of the population. Practice is not systematic, it is a multiple series of effects that non-producers of culture generate in the everyday, crucially through consumption. This alternative productivity is "characterised by its ruses, fragmentation (the result of the circumstances), its poaching its clandestine nature, its tireless but quiet activity, in short by its quasi-invisibility, since it shows itself not in its own products (where would it place them?) but in an art of using those imposed upon it" (De Certeau, 2002, p.31). There are no true and false needs, nor is De Certeau interested in motives of the tactical; he sees interest only in an *operational* logic of practice. De Certeau uses a Clausewitzian distinction between strategies and tactics. A strategy is the project of colonization of a particular place, the project of political, scientific, and economic rationality. A tactic is defined both by placelessness and a reliance on time. Although De Certeau warned against a "hagiographic everydayness," his *Practice of Everyday Life* is dedicated to the "ordinary man a common hero, an ubiquitous character, walking in countless thousands on the streets" (ibid.). It is the unrecognized producers, "trail blazers in the jungle of functionalist rationality," who make the everyday radical, even though it lacks the meaning of older politics. De Certeau's prose is comparable to the older language of Marxism, albeit without the old subject-object of history; in its place we have the "marginal" and the "ordinary." Although *Practice of Everyday Life* is devoid of an explicit discourse of resistance that has often been read into De Certeau's work, the utopian and psychoanalytic moments certainly offer space for such a reading.

De Certeau's important intervention needs a revision for our times while retaining the critical thrust of his work. "Minor" practices in Delhi and in many comparable urbanisms of Africa, Asia, and Latin America tended to be post-utopian, even post-political in the classic sense. When import-substitution regimes based on national geographies retreated under economic crises in the 1970s and 1980s new forms of urban strategy were deployed with great effect by migrants, squatters, and homeless populations. In urban Africa, as regimes failed to sustain the definitional aspects of rule (division of jurisdiction, policies), urban infrastructures were subject to heretical uses, with a multiplication of sites of non-legal production and innovative recombinations (Simone, 2006). This was the "pirate city," where the older infrastructure was either poached or incrementally built up by urban populations long abandoned by urban planning. Globalization increases the possibilities for this pirate urbanism by allowing the growth of low-cost (non-legal) networks to spread across regions, and generally weakening national sovereignty (ibid., p.357). Cities increasingly fail to apply normative boundaries as had been hoped for by planning; and multiple circulations of commodities and money through non-official channels further weakened civic authority, opening up new channels for migrants to flow into peripheral neighborhoods. This kind of pirate urbanism has been noticed in Latin America (*piratas*), in Africa, and the Middle East. Asef Bayat provides a vivid description of a similar world in Egypt:

> Cairo contains well over 100 "spontaneous" communities, or *manatiq al-ashwàyya*, housing over seven million people who have subdivided agricultural lands, putting up their shelters unlawfully. The rural migrants and slum dwellers, on the other hand, have quietly claimed cemeteries, roof tops and the state/public land on the outskirts of the city, creating largely autonomous communities. By their sheer perseverance, millions of slum dwellers force the authorities to extend living amenities to their neighborhoods by otherwise tapping them illegally.
>
> (Bayat, 1997, p.54)

This is a different "politics," often missed by older radical writers who tended to look for "resistance," public politics or worse, that catch-all phrase "civil society." Pirate urbanism could not fit any classic shoe, liberal or Enlightenment radical. Playing a complex game with the police, smaller local officials, and slum lords, and resisting periodic displacement by city authorities, the new urban encroachments actually vastly expanded postcolonial cities in the 1970s and 1980s. In this sense, though with significant local differences, India's capital city was no different.

In post-Emergency Delhi "minor practices" bypassed the normative framework of the plan, for the most part ignoring it. Neighborhoods, small factories, financing networks, new workplaces in homes, markets, and roofs spread all over the city, particularly in the Trans-Yamuna districts and parts of west and north Delhi. Almost all of these sites grew in non-planned or unauthorized parts of the city. This growth pre-dated the Emergency itself, but Delhi's pirate urbanism accelerated after 1977. As the unauthorized city grew, new municipal elections in 1982 opened the route for regularization of some areas, a mixture of neighborhood political mobilization, populism, and demands for infrastructure.

At any rate, the pirate city threw up a dizzying complexity of production sites, tenure, work practices, and agglomeration.[17] Every rule set up by the Masterplan was violated or "infringed," paradoxically contributing to the 1980 to 1996 years as the boom period, when production and markets grew at a hectic pace. Small, flexible sites of production and circulation contributed most to this new morphology, feeding into political patronage at the local level, raising demand for "regularization" and infrastructure. The productivity of these economies of the city was such that it was able to absorb the hundreds of thousands of workers who streamed into Delhi after the Asian Games construction and the Punjab crisis. By the time the counter-offensive came in court judgments of the 1990s, Delhi had unknowingly become a metropolis, with its own catalog of urban crisis and conflict.

New investigations reveal the remarkable fluidity of people, land tenures, things, and technologies across the city in the 1980s and 1990s, often hidden by the hyper-political montage of that time. After studying Viswas Nagar, an east Delhi neighborhood, for a decade, researcher Solomon Benjamin discovered that the classic worker/entrepreneur binary became fuzzy in small production clusters that dominated much of the non-legal city during that decade.

> Tracing life histories shows that these labels are interchangeable. Workers move on in three to five years to become foremen and after that, link to a variety of trajectories to start off their own firms in the main line of production, or into capital machinery. Some move to be trading agents. At times, these identities switch. Entrepreneurs and factory owners, even those from the financially astute group of the Marwari and Bania (trading castes), need to operate the machines on the shop floor to keep

in close contact with the technological options that open up, and to respond to complex and dynamic market demands. Much of small firm finance is driven by complex local mechanisms such as pooled funds linked to real estate markets. These financial systems draw in all – workers, factory owners, renters and land "owners" – even if in varied degrees. This intimate knowledge of financier circuits, even if power within these is unequally distributed, is critically important to make possible transitions between factory owners/workers/traders/innovators/artisans.

(Benjamin, 2005a, p.252)

The slow erosion of control models built along sovereignties of the city plan and the nation made possible not just fluidity of work but also considerable travel both within countries and across borders. Globalization radicalized this movement as states collapsed due to wars (Africa) or economic crisis (Latin America). Movements of illegal migrants from Africa into Europe and from Latin America into the USA have been accompanied by significant networks of small traders transporting goods across frontiers by skirting national import-export regimes. Simone (2006) speaks of illicit journeys not just to Europe but also to China and Taiwan as a source of cheap commodities that could be transported back home. Journeys were also made to Dubai, Istanbul, and Mumbai for similar purposes. These travel stories of small traders began surfacing in all my encounters with small businessmen in Delhi, an increasing number of whom began traveling to East and South East Asia from the 1980s. These people did not always come from traditional *bania* trading communities, similar to Simone's story of "new" African traders. Lacking proper infrastructure, these were the "suitcase entrepreneurs" of postcolonial cities from the 1980s, whose ambition was not just local and national but also international and regional. The traveling salesman was an old figure in modern capitalism; the 1990s' proliferation of small enterprise in India's cities saw a whole new generation of sales agents networking between pirate factories. Coined by Solomon Benjamin from his fieldwork in the east Delhi pirate-industrial neighborhood of Viswas Nagar in the 1990s, "suitcase entrepreneurs" are:

Marketing agents traveling with their suitcases filled with samples of shoes, plastic fittings, small electrical products. . . . They use a low cost but an extensive network of trains and buses to reach retail and wholesale markets in this wider territory. The Suitcase Entrepreneurs come from various backgrounds. They can be specialized marketing agents employed by the large traders in Delhi's wholesale market for electrical products Bhagirath Palace. They can also be marketing agents visiting Delhi from other smaller towns and cities.

(Benjamin, 2005c, p.25)

The rapid scramble for urban work practices and spaces may indicate a new threshold in the expansion of postcolonial cities. Some have mapped this phenomenon on to a broader context of a "splintering urbanism" in the wake of post-Fordist urban planning, where recent privatization of urban services transforms the very nature of urban life against which much of twentieth-century city writing had measured itself (Graham and Marvin, 2001). However the postcolonial expansion lacks the context of Fordism and a widespread public infrastructure. The expansion of infrastructure in post-1977 Delhi owed significantly to a pirate urbanism, which existed parasitically with official infrastructure.

The Asian Games and the constellation of media urbanism

In 1982 the Indira Gandhi regime organized the Asian Games (Asiad) in Delhi. From the outset, the Games were explicitly designed as a spectacular mix of technology and nationalism, to banish the bad memories of the 1970s, where protest, poverty, and social unrest marked daily life. Asiad was conceived as a carefully staged national television spectacle, where live broadcasts would collapse geography and unite the country through a common network. This was the first in a series of claims to technological modernity that were to reverberate in the 1980s. Television was the first, perhaps the most powerful vehicle of this transition. Martin Heidegger once famously described television "as the abolition of every possibility of remoteness" (1971, p.165), a phrase that captures well the moment of arrival when national network television broadcasts were introduced on August 15, 1982. "Liveness" now brought the space annihilating power of the network in ways that had never been felt before. Doordarshan, the national broadcaster, covered the country in shortwave transmitters, and used dedicated satellite slots to relay broadcasts. In a considerable pedagogic exercise, national maps of the linked shortwave transmitters were regularly shown to curious viewers. If the nineteenth-century railway network map of India was supposed to highlight the techno-spatial unity of colonial modernity, the television network map was to evoke the immaterial power of new technologies in safeguarding a weakened sovereignty.

Asiad 82 is often called India's first significant media event, heralding the growing gesture of politics to television. Asiad is also seen to contain the prehistory of globalization, where consumption and advertising were given a boost by media cultures emerging after mass television. The period certainly saw a shift from old-style nationalist policies which were seen by the elite as restricting initiative and growth. Under pressure from the IMF and the World Bank the old import substitution regime was gradually dismantled, and controls on domestic industry and transnational companies lifted. The process accelerated rapidly after the coming to power of Rajiv Gandhi. Behind all these moves was a decisive reconstruction of the old nationalist imaginary in ways that would dissolve it to the point of no recognition. Old-style "development" remained an issue, but was reconstituted as a problem of *communication*. The way forward was computerization, networking, and a new visual regime based on a national television network. With the coming to power of Rajiv Gandhi the network soon became the iconic space around which all representation, both state and commercial, cohered – the effect on nationalist discourse was incredible.[18] As opposed to the Nehruvian focus on nineteenth-century physical instruments of accumulation (steel, energy, coal), state discourse after 1984 posed a *virtual* space where issues of development would be resolved. Through public lectures, television programs, and press campaigns, state managers simulated this new space, which though unseen was viewed as transcending the lack inherent in Nehruvian controls.[19] In the event, the panoptics of Nehruvianism could not but undergo a subtle revision. The "national" was reaffirmed but through a new discourse, which complicated the notion of borders and sovereignty that were so central to the old visual regime. "Development" was redefined, *pace* Paul Virilio, as also a problem of speed and information. The more accurate and faster information you had, the better your chances in joining the West.

Along with television, the 1980s saw the setting up of a national data network which would connect all major district centers, state capitals of the country, and process vast amounts of information relating to development and administration. This was the development of NIC – the National Infomatics Center. The NIC had been set up in the mid-1970s to promote computerization in administration, but really took off in the 1980s with the inauguration of a satellite-linked network, NICNET. NICNET is easily the largest government network in the country today. Today it links up all district, state, and national centers, and runs large data bases on social science, medicine, and law; by 2000 NICNET had became the backbone of a massive egovernence program linking all the ministries and autonomous government bodies. At one level, the establishment of national television and NICNET in the 1980s suggested a modernized version of older nationalist surveillance models. While the 'national design' of the network was suffused with the cartographic anxiety of nationalism, it soon became apparent that the modernization initiatives unleashed forces that took on a life of their own.

The Asian Games of 1982 are a significant example of this shift. In popular memory the Games appear as a caesura, a sign of a significant transition, which saw construction projects, mass migration of construction workers to the city, new squatter camps, and the emergence of media urbanism, color television, VCRs, electronics in general, and the acceleration of consumption.[20] The Asiad emerges as the originary reference point for a morphed consciousness of urban expansion and media proliferation, and a general speeding up of the city.

In their book *Media Events, the Live Broadcasting of History*, Daniel Dayan and Elihu Katz suggest that the very publicness of an event renders the organizers vulnerable, even preceding the event. "Liveness" produces intense pressures to succeed, subjecting the organizers to tremendous stress (1994, pp.190–191). Asiad 82's particular constellation forced the regime into a peculiar situation; mounting a mass public event like the Games also meant suspending classic bureaucratic controls, and radically reworking the older import substitution regime. Internally, Doordarshan technocrats were given considerable operational freedom to design broadcasts, and all political interference was put on hold. The government opened the way for imports of color TVs and VCRs from abroad as gifts to ensure that the demand was met in time for the Games. Kits were imported from South Korea and West Germany for the assembly of TV sets in the country with licenses being given to twenty-two manufacturers, including various public sector concerns.[21] At a general level large-scale imports, both state administered and by individuals, were suddenly legitimized, opening the gates for dismantling the older regulation model. This was no longer limited to TVs and VCRs. Markets were soon flooded with smuggled electronic goods as the government looked the other way, and assembled electronics by local manufacturers through imported kits also made their presence.

Government officials suggested that the modernization of vision was also on the agenda. The old black and white TV screen, a symbol of import-substitution autarky, was to be junked. In the lead was the Information Minister Vasanth Sathe. "Black and white is dead technology. Dead like a dodo," said Mr Sathe in 1981. He went on: "If I had my way I will go in for the VCR right away. Cassettes can be produced in thousands and they are cheap. Every village and school can screen its own video cassettes" (*Deccan Herald*, November 13, 1981). As state officials began speaking a language of modernized optics where color played a significant part, what emerged was a new technique of transmission and consumption, enclosed within an increasingly fragile model of sovereignty. In the event, the older authoritarian model of cultural management was soon overwhelmed by events. Sponsorship of television programs was opened up, advertising revenues exploded; various critics proclaimed that "consumer culture" had arrived. The boom, initially middle class, saw the proliferation of TV ownership and credit networks. Journalist Amrita Shah sums up the situation at that time:

> Between 1984 and 1990 television sets rose from 3.6 million to 27.8 million. In 1988, five TV sets were said to be sold every minute and as many as 30 television brands were jostling for the buyer's attention. . . .
>
> The country's largest bank, The State bank of India disbursed Rs 400 million in less than two years (1988–9) for the purchase of TV sets, VCRs, washing machines, vehicles, sofa sets and so on.
>
> (Shah, 1997, p.41)

The increase of TV sets went hand in hand with a rapidly growing audio and video cassette market. Audio cassettes (led by the Gulshan Kumar's T-series group) tore apart multinational monopolies in the music business, establishing radically new distribution methods in neighborhoods, and introducing low-cost releases by a host of new talent. Video cassettes were entirely in the

Annexure A.

(TO be submitted in duplicate)

Form of application for Registration/Renewal of Registration as a Cable Operation

To

The Chief Postmaster
G.P.O. Delhi -110006

SUB: APPLICATION FOR REGISTRATION/RENEWAL OF REGISTRATION AS A CABLE OPERATION ...

1. a) Name of the applicant   :
      (Individual/Firm/Company/
      Association of Persons/
      Body/Individuals)

2. a) Address (Office)   :
   b) Telephone No. if any   :

3. a) Nationality   :
   b) By Birth/Domicile   :

4. a) Registration fee enclosed .... Yes/No.
   b) ACG-67 No. .... Date .... on ....
      .... Post office.

5. Area in which cable television :
   Network is working/proposed to be:

6. Number of Channells being provided/ :
   proposed to be provided(with Names)

7. a) Whether using TVRO   : .... Yes/No.
   b) If yes, Number and Size   :
   c) Location   :

8. Names of Doordarshan Setelite   :
   Channels included in cable service :

9. Copy of earlier Registration certificate enclosed ....Yes/
   (to be filled in only for renewal or registration)

10. Declaration, if Form No. 2 enclosed : .... Yes/No.

    I/We .... the applicant(s) (Individual/
   Firm/Company/Association of persons/Body of Individual (S) do
   hereby declare that the above facts are correct in all respect

Place :   (SIGNATURE OF APPLICANT)

Delhi :   Individual/Firm/Company/Associatic
                               of persons/Body of Individuals).

Figure 2.3 Mandatory registration form for local cable operators intended to manage unregulated cable media distribution.

Source: Sarai Archive.

pirate economy and spread like wildfire all over the country. Video libraries and video cinemas appeared in every part of the country, while restaurants, buses, and shops began installing video equipment. Within a few years, the production and consumption of sound and image was significantly decentralized. Video's geography of circulation was global as Hindi film releases soon arrived in India in their pirate form from couriers in the UK, Dubai, and Nepal. The situation was no different in the computer hardware market. By the 1990s when the market expanded, it was clear that the bulk of computers were in the assembled or gray segment, the parts sourced through smuggling from Nepal or visits by small businessmen to Singapore or Taiwan. This regional geography of the electronic trade was pioneered by audio cassette companies who first imported blank tape and cassette shells from Taiwan; it later became a regular feature of the traffic of electronic goods.

Wild zones

By the late 1980s the volatile mix of urban expansion, random violence, media explosions, and accelerating consumption set up the experience of living in Delhi as a series of kinetic shock experiences. Speed, an experience typically associated with the commercial capital of Bombay, had arrived in Delhi. The Hindi writer Uday Prakash captured this mood well in one of his stories: "All around the pace of change was incredibly fast. Delhi had become a kaleidoscope. It had hundreds of brands of soaps, thousands of different kinds of toothpastes, a million different watches, thousands of different kinds of cars, panties, creams, brassieres . . . compact discs, rifles remotes, cosmetics, designer condoms, tranquilizers" (2003, p.166). In the same story, the endless landscape of consumption exists in the background of vast suburban growth, terrorism, assassinations, and the loss of memory to a world of things. In Prakash's city commodities that were explicitly artificial were becoming preponderant in daily life. This experience of the contemporary for millions of people, of a life where "nature" referred to memories before migration or childhood dreams, is close to what Walter Benjamin had once called the actuality of the everyday. This is a life where most of the urban residents know no other products and objects other than those that are industrial, along with a perception of the present that seems never-ending, often mediated through the visual representations of events. Memories of the real "past" blur with memories of and identification with media narratives and experiences, television shows, cricket matches, film releases. This conceptual confusion, between real and virtual memory, between "newness" and an eternal present, between objects and human beings, shows a kind of untimely compression, where features commonly associated in the West with "modernism" and "postmodernism" seemed to blur in one decade of flux in India.

By the late 1980s some of those "authentic" experiences began to be transformed by media techniques. Religious events began to be staged publicly, using amplified music and video, something utilized with great effect by

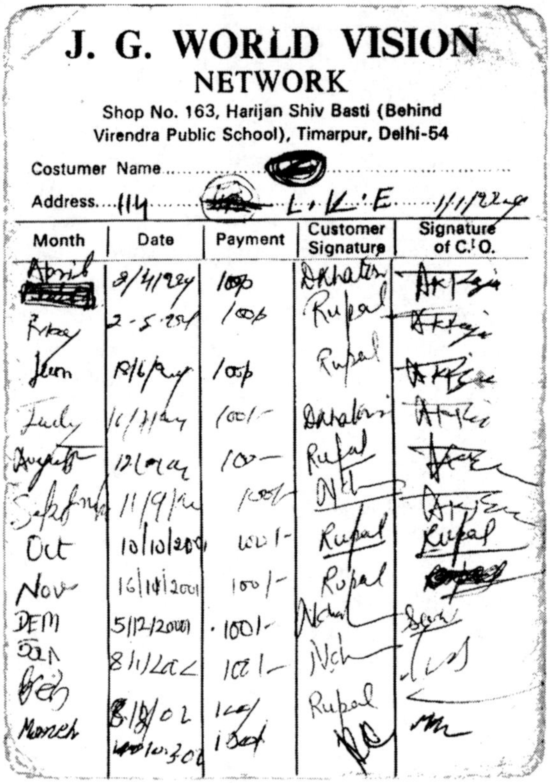

Figure 2.4 A neighborhood monthly membership card of a cable operator in a working-class neighborhood in North Delhi.

Source: Sarai Archive, 2004.

Hindu nationalist mobilization (Rajagopal, 2001). By the 1990s this had also spread to weddings and parties. Interviews with neighborhood DJs and music shops suggest that this transformation began in the mid-1980s when sound equipment costs dropped, but the deployment of sound and image for new forms of public expression in the city grew rapidly by only the mid-1990s. The levels of ambient sound that were always present in the South Asian city increased tremendously, causing conflict at every level. These ranged from the use of mosque and temple loudspeakers, car horns, loud *jagrans* in neighborhoods, and political rallies. What was once thought to be an assertion of middle-class modernity now expanded into a broader soundscape of the city to cover all social groups. In her book on the history of sound cultures of prewar America, Emily Thompson argues that a soundscape was not simply an aural landscape, but also included modes of listening and discipline (Thompson, 2002). Thompson also suggests that public sound generated a series of unforeseen urban conflicts that called for new technologies of civic management, which in turn emerged through regulation and a growing body of case law.

In retrospect, the great puzzle of the "long" decade is the relative stasis of government *vis-à-vis* the productive decentralization of media life. In part, the regime's paralysis with the new media may be explained by the pre-occupation with political instability, the implications of the 1984 anti-Sikh pogroms, political and military conflict in Punjab and Kashmir, terrorist incidents in Delhi and other cities, the fiasco of the military intervention in Sri Lanka, anti-Mandal agitation, the rise of Hindu nationalism, and the demolition of the Babri Masjid. This is by no means a short list, and while the Congress suffered long-term decline, governmental power never returned to the confidence of the 1950s and 1960s. Older models of control became increasingly inoperable as production and distribution of media commodities proliferated to multiple sites (small factories, pirate workshops, gray market networks), enmeshed with the broader proliferation of production under pirate urbanism. By the 1990s governmental intervention tried to distinguish between carriage and content, where the former (distribution of media) was part of regulatory control while "content" was under the purview of censorship and "social norms."[22] At any rate in the 1980s through the late 1990s public debates about the electronic media were almost entirely about media images and representation, ranging from gender, class, and later the rise of Hindu nationalism. For many, the media emerged as a larger-than-life reference for all cultural politics. Media was seen as the site of sexual transgressions and a battleground between secularism and a growing Hindu nationalist visual production. TV, and later video, became a central part of this debate. For popular critics, media was ubiquitous and expanding – while for the older literary elites it was a sign of cultural destruction wrought by globalization.

Writing in a North American context about media theory's assertions of TV's inherent "placelessness," Anna McCarthy suggests that

> The language of placelessness makes us forget that television is an *object* and, like all objects, it shapes its immediate space through its material form. The term is also quite vague; is placelessness really an adequate description of the range of ways in which we encounter television within spaces of everyday life, from the living room to the departure lounge to the department store?
>
> (McCarthy, 2001a, p.96)

In Delhi's context after the 1980s we could similarly ask: Was there more to the media than its centralizing mode or its encoding by subjects or power? Or, as I have suggested above, if the media exceeded its older representational structures in the long decade, what were the sites of its materiality?

In his *Speed and Politics* Paul Virilo suggested that cities are sites of "habitable circulation" (1986, p.6), despite the best efforts of official maps.

Distinguishing between territories and vectors, Virilio suggests that the former is space that is "defensible," even enclosed and managed. Vectors have *velocity* and refer to the movement of technology across space, disrupting its stability and enclosure. Virilio introduces the opposition between vector and territory to position his well-known model of technological speed overtaking older modes of travel.[23] Despite the customary excess in Virilio's formulation, I want to suggest that the dynamic between vector and territory offers us a useful tool with which to unpack the intersection between space and technological movement.

Vectors, bazaars, markets, neighborhoods, workshops

Delhi's pasts have been dominated by the strength and vitality of its bazaars. Merchant communities (Jains, Aggarwals, Khatris) dominated Delhi's markets which were easily the most powerful on the subcontinent in the Moghul era. Merchants ran informal communication systems, credit lines for trade, and were an important source of finance for trade. In the postcolonial era, merchant communities suffered a political setback, often marginalized by official planning regimes suspicious of unregulated commerce.

"Merchant society worked on secret, inward lines of communication and trust," wrote C.A. Bayly in his study of commerce in early modern colonial India (1983, p.372). While bazaar networks faced significant formal regulation and pressures from larger capitalist firms, it was this inner world of knowledge and continuing ambivalence about legal authority that made the bazaar a significant resource for commodified cultural resources not easily incorporated into formal capitalist models.

Bazaars have been called important sites for a vernacular modernism, irreducible to a larger, overarching logic of capital (Jain, 2003). I want to suggest that following globalization bazaars were indifferent to any specific form of aesthetic production. While particularly hospitable to vernacular forms (calendar art, local music, video), bazaars were contexts for all non-legal electronics and media. Bazaars today have transformed themselves into sophisticated networks connecting local, regional, and international markets. Urban bazaars are now proto-capitalist markets, with a significant number of non-Vasihya middle castes in their midst. Rahul Mehrotra calls the urban form of the bazaar city a kinetic form, both acting as cultural *doppelgängers*, switching roles. The kinetic/bazaar city is not representational in a two-dimensional built form. That the bazaar is a form of urban kinesis is itself a significant reformulation. The bazaar is not just the world of traditional merchants, but all forms of commerce, hawkers, iterant traders, street dwellers, "a city in constant motion" (Mehrotra, 2002, p.98). Prasad Shetty (2005) develops this by studying work practices in the commodified circuits of the city as "stories of entrepreneurship," where the ability to utilize everyday opportunities – in the street, in the neighborhood, in every part of the city – marks the movement of urban populations outside corporate or state employment.

In his multi-volume masterpiece, *Civilization and Capitalism*, Fernand Braudel advanced a three-level structure of social life. At the bottom was material life with unconscious patterns, the second level he called economic life or the market, with regular patterns, a division of labor, and remarkable transparency, and face-to-face interaction in which "everyone would be sure in advance, with the benefit of common experience, how the processes of exchange would operate" (1992, p.455). In contrast to the transparency of the market, the third level, capitalism, was shadowy, and based on monopoly power and violence. While capitalism was the world of unacceptable profits and speculation, the market was one of small surpluses and intimacy, overlapping with work. As Immanuel Wallerstein argues, in the Braudelian model, "economic life is the domain of ordinary people; capitalism is guaranteed by, incarnated in, the hegemonic power" (1991). For Wallerstein, despite its faults, Braudel's "upside-down" version of capitalism suggested flaws in the liberal and Marxist models of productive and unproductive labor where commerce, as part of the latter, was always a rung below industry, ethically compromised, and less capitalist. But Braudel made yet another claim – that capitalists were non-specialized and mobile, while the market was specialized and local. It was capitalism's lack of specialization and ability to move that accounted for its power and monopoly.

The empirical ground of Braudel's thesis is something we cannot engage with here. What is interesting is his model of small commerce and immobility, set against the structure of urban planning and models of social management. Delhi's commercial areas suggest a palimpsest – combining historic bazaars in the old city from the Mughal Empire, new refugee markets set up by the city after Partition, and designated new planned commercial districts including the district centers and sub-district centers. The Masterplan set up a model that attempted to strictly regulate commerce through zoning, decongestion of historic markets in the old city, and highly regulated models like the district centers.

Flowing from the plan, markets and small commerce in Delhi were subject to significant authoritarian controls, a design particularly bizarre in a city of historic markets and a large trading community. For many years iterant traders and hawkers were more strictly disciplined in Delhi than in Calcutta or Bombay, where they provided a vivid street culture of low-cost commerce for urban residents.[24] For Delhi's planning model, commerce worked best when enclosed in the designated zones and centers. On the other hand, traders formed associations to work with political parties at the local level to leverage moves towards regularization The Jan Sangh and its later avatar the BJP was the traditional party of post-Partition trading communities. The relationship between small commerce and urban government was a complex one, mediated by regular transfers of surplus and *hafta* payments to local officials and police.

Braudel's model of the face-to-face world of small commerce is an attractive if *simpliste* model, as is his contrast between a mobile capitalist economy and the more "local" specialized world of the shopkeeper. This is also the imaginative world of Jane Jacobs and non-modernist urban utopias, with a focus on the neighborhood street. In both Braudel and Jacobs, though in vastly different ways, the focus on the affective locality/market has great strengths, though the Braudelian historical model of market specialization versus capitalist mobility fades away in contemporary transitions, particularly in media networks.

I want to suggest that a new topography of urbanism emerged in the 1980s that linked media markets, parallel production centers, and neighborhoods. Almost entirely dominated by small commerce and industry, these sites were linked locally, regionally, and even internationally. Almost all were linked to each other through the transfer of goods, work, and technologies. Traveling salesmen moved between these sites using mobile technologies for up-to-date information, while skilled worker-entrepreneurs transferred technical skills between enterprises. This is a significant expansion of the older merchant caste bazaar; today, non-legal commerce draws merchants from across the caste spectrum.

In 2006 Lokesh Sharma met Akhtar Ali, a former worker who once worked in Cotina Radio, one of the many local companies that emerged in east Delhi in the boom years of the 1980s. Akhtar was a child in the old city when his dwelling was razed to the ground as part of the Municipal Corporation's clean-up drives in 1967, and the family was displaced to a squat in Seemapuri. Akhtar's recollection of that day still remains bitter:

> The government made us roofless with promises of a 22 sq ft plot but brought us to this open ground out of the city and dumped us here. We had not been able ever to gather our things, even take down the boards for keeping the household utensils when they brought everything down. They loaded us in a tempo and dumped us on this open ground in the evening.

Akhtar's full story, narrated in a remarkable text by Sharma (2004), captures the complex link between subaltern lives, bazaar economies, the drive to imitation, and its violent suppression in 2000.

From the 1980s media markets played a prominent role in this new 1990s morphology, attracting thousands of customers as well as distributors, head load workers, and booking agents for goods. Markets connected to small-scale electronic industries (Lajpat Rai market), grayware assemblers of computers (Nehru Place) and the demand for video cassettes and CDs (Palika Bazaar) from cable operators and the population at large. Significantly all the three media markets were postcolonial developments. While Delhi was a significant site for large markets and trading elites from the days of the Mughal Empire, the postcolonial expansion was significant since hundreds of thousands of Hindu and Sikh refugees flooded the city after Partition, many from former trading castes. The Department of Rehabilitation quickly set up sixty-three markets to accommodate refugees who had arrived in Delhi after 1947. These were initially temporary structures, but later became permanent for the most part,[25] with various tenancy and leasehold agreements with the shopkeepers. Lajpat Rai market opposite Red Fort was one of these markets. While other markets changed ownership, Lajpat Rai market continued with the Department of Rehabilitation until 2000, when it was passed on to the MCD. Located at a strategic point on the main Red Fort road at the entrance of Chandni Chowk, and adjacent to the important Bhagirath Place, Delhi's main electrical wholesale market, Lajpat Rai functioned as a perfect hub for different flows of visitors and commodities.

I visited Lapat Rai market as an undergraduate student in the 1980s and remember it as a mixed cluster of clothing, radio electronic shops, along with the stores for music instruments and marriage bands in the front row.[26] I visited Lajpat Rai market again in 1996 when my local cable TV supplier told me that this was the premier electronics market in Delhi. The change from the 1980s was nothing short of dramatic. The halls of the market were overflowing with new electronic goods, in the front were hand carts carrying goods for supply all over the city, and there were distributors for all the major audio companies, both legal and non-legal. The back of the market was now cluttered with large locally assembled satellite dishes for sale to neighborhood cable TV networks. The market jump-started the cable television boom in the 1990s with these inexpensive dish antennas, which were bought by dealers throughout the country. Today the market sells music systems to street DJs, television sets and VHS players, fake music, videos and DVDs, cameras, and thousands of electronic parts both new and recycled. All transactions are typically in cash, and most finished items are manufactured in small work-shops in the market, the nearby area of Angooribagh, and across the river Yamuna in east Delhi.

With its crowded passageways, brightly lit neon signs with advertisements of local brands, kitschy electronics of every imaginable shape, and black and white televisions with green, red, and blue screens, Lajpat Rai had a wild, energetic feel. So far was Lajpat Rai from the technological utopias being held out by India's cyber-elites in the 1990s that I was immediately reminded of Lefebvre's description of "representational space":

> It speaks. . . . It embraces the loci of passion, of action and of lived situations, and thus immediately implies time. Consequently it may be qualified in various ways, it may be directional, situational or relational, because it is essentially qualitative, fluid and dynamic.
>
> (Lefebvre, 1991, p.42)

There was a certain monadic quality to this space, where all features of the technological world of the 1990s seemed available: old and new media, tactility and distraction, density and dispersal, ruin and fantasy. For many years Lajpat Rai market had a mythic attraction for customers, small

Figure 2.5 Lajpat Rai market entrance.
Source: Sarai Archive.

manufacturers, and distributors. The technicians in the market repaired just about anything electronic, you got remotes for every television in the world, spare parts were no problem, and the locally assembled electronics could be reincarnated as a global brand with the appropriate stickers and cabinets produced in the market. Thieves and customers simultaneously went to Lajpat Rai and its sister market Bhagirath Place to dispose off and buy used goods. Lajpat Rai's reputation for fake brands was legendary among customers. The same reputation held among small electronic workshops that sold their finished goods in Lajpat Rai, and sourced spare parts from the market.

The characteristic Lajpat Rai style was to produce semantic twists on the original brand, a clutter of creative misspellings, in a tactic that ranged from international names to local products. The displaced Jamuna Bazar resident-turned-electronics assembly worker Akhtar Ali said about the market:

> they just replaced the 'i' in Philips with an 'e' and marketed the goods by just changing one single word. Neither is this very difficult. Lajpatrai is a market where number plate of any type can be had. They would change any company's monogram just marginally enough as not to impinge on

the customer's attention. Even if caught he would still insist that its produce is quite different. Our label is different. Our sound is different.

(Sharma, 2004)

Akhtar's own local firm, Cotina, was soon confronted by a Lajpat Rai look-alike called Motina.

Like all markets that bypassed the planned city's regulations, Lajpat Rai market developed an intricate model of incremental transformation, every shop expanded from the ground floor to basement and top floors which would house stores and small assembling factories.[27] A 1990s survey of the market by the MCD's Land and Estate Department claimed that 95 percent of the shops were marked by "large scale unauthorized construction and encroachments."[28] For many years, CREMA, the market's main shopkeepers association, fought a battle for legal ownership rights and better infra-structure with the Rehabilitation Department; the final solution that recognized ownership rights also gave the MCD the power to demolish "any unauthorized structure."[29] By 2000, the Public Interest Litigations by civic campaigners to the courts began targeting the market's wild urbanism, and by 2006 the Court ordered notices to the Municipal Corporation for its "laxity" in dealing with encroachments. The *Hindustan Times* reported that

Figure 2.6 Loaders in Lajpat Rai market.

Source: Rakesh Kumar Singh, Sarai Archive.

the Counsel for the petitioner, Arun Khosla, told the Court that the "illegal multi-storied structures posed a security threat to the Red Fort." He also said that the activities around the overcrowded market were causing traffic jams.[30] When MCD squads reached Lajpat Rai market on a Tuesday morning later that month, traders took to the streets and blocked traffic on Chandni Chowk, paralyzing access to the business centers of the old city.[31] Given its reputation, Lajpat Rai market came in for periodic attacks and demolition drives instigated by the court campaigns after 2000. For civic campaigners Lajpat Rai market symbolised the reckless urbanism that horrified the courts and its liberal supporters. The adding of "national security" to this list was in keeping with the times.

Unlike Lajpat Rai, Palika Bazaar in Delhi's central district, Connaught Place, was an enclosed underground market. Palika was planned during the Emergency to partly make up for the destruction of Coffee House[32] in the Central Circle. The market finally opened in 1978, and soon included seventy-nine shopkeepers displaced from Panchkuiyan Road, as well as those who came in later through a tendering process. Palika was India's first air-conditioned underground market, the pride of the New Delhi Municipal Corporation, which claimed that the market would give a big boost to tourism. Palika followed a zoning system, and in its initial years included clothing, handicrafts, furniture, travel agencies, leather, jewelry, tailoring shops, and fast food joints selling Indian, Western, and Chinese food.

When I came to Delhi from Lucknow as a student, I was told that this was the first place an out-of-town traveler visited. Palika in 1980 was thronged with excited crowds, with many new visitors from out of town; there was a buzz in the air, and the air-conditioning seemed shockingly efficient for Delhi. Apart from locals and new migrants like myself, there were visitors from every part of India, Russians and West Europeans, and even the stray American. This was the modern city of the 1980s, an underground market, air-conditioned and maintained by the public municipal authority, with a significant amount of displaced shopkeepers of other demolitions. The moment peaked with Asiad and then slowly Palika began to change. With the spread of militancy in the Punjab, bomb blasts and hoax calls began to plague Palika, and visitor numbers began to drop. By the end of the decade, the market had a decrepit air. When I visited the market in the early 1990s it was in infrastructural decline, as if imaging the plight of the postcolonial planned city. The air-conditioning plant was erratic, a nasty odor pervaded the market, and in response the shopkeepers began lighting incense sticks to deodorize the air. Palika's corridors were always labyrinthine, and with the incense smoke, the market had a claustrophobic feel to it. Rising rental demands by the NDMC led shopkeepers to pursue classic proliferation tactics. They carved out space in the front and sides of the shops which they then let out to small stalls. Rakesh Kumar, who researched the market in depth, summarizes the situation:

Times change. In a span of four to five years, the cracks emerged in the system. The NDMC did a shoddy job in maintaining cleanliness, air-conditioning. The rentals shot up five times from the original official values. The shops were being rented out with increased frequency rendering the zoning system futile. Responding to trade pressures, occupations changed. . . . Show windows became sale counters. Shopkeepers improvised and created two to three counters within a single shop. And each counter became a fresh source of enhanced rent. Very soon, encroachments became a pattern. What began as a demonstration in front of stalls quickly became mobile shops in common areas selling socks, purses, readymade garments, belts and electronic items.

(Kumar, 2002)[33]

Palika's great notoriety came with the video boom. Early on in the cassette and video years of the 1980s Palika emerged as one of northern India's major suppliers of video products, recorded tapes, smuggled VCRS, and cameras. Every major new audio and video company had shop outlets in Palika, ranging from T-series to regional productions from other states. As video and electronic shops increased in number and influence, Palika became Delhi's main hub for the circulation of pirate video, both Hindi and international, a feature that remains to this day. With the cable boom of the 1990s Palika became the nerve center of a complex web of operations linking local cable networks, neighborhood video rentals, and an elaborate courier system between shops and pirate factories in neighboring states, Pakistan, and South East Asia. Students, film buffs, and the public at large flocked to Palika as it gained the reputation of being India's major video bazaar. In contrast, and expectedly for anti-piracy enforcement detectives, Palika became a den of vice, a free zone of piracy. By the late 1990s Palika became a site of violent clashes between detectives and shopkeepers.[34] Here shopkeepers deployed the labyrinthine structure of Palika to their advantage, and the market gained a reputation among all detectives and policeman as a place where they often had to retreat after getting beaten. At any rate, shopkeepers used the fragmentation of many shops into smaller units to evade enforcement, since the sales counters were separated from display counters and storage units. When raids began, shopkeepers rapidly closed down shops and counters, and the fragmented structure made recovery of pirated material difficult.

A few kilometers south of Palika Bazaar in south Delhi is one of north India's most significant markets for computer hardware and software, Nehru Place. Nehru Place is both a media market and a commercial hub for software company offices. When I began visiting Nehru Place for initial research in the 1990s I entered a large complex of buildings, rundown as were most DDA built structures at that time. There was no electricity when I first visited Nehru Place and the entire market was thick with the smoke of scores of generators in the corridors, and a massive industrial-sized one that stood out

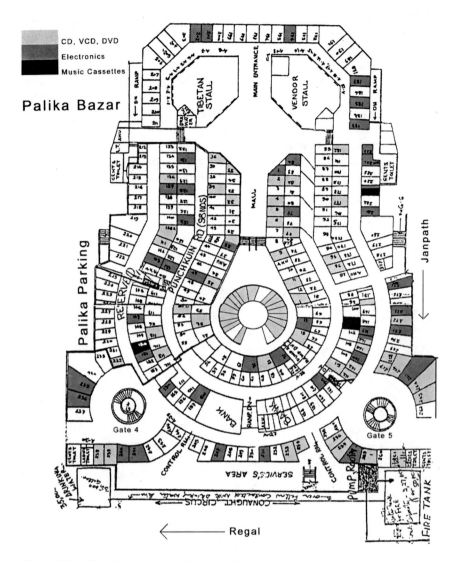

Figure 2.7 Palika Bazaar map, with marked electronic shops.

Source: Rakesh Kumar Singh and Sarai Archive.

in the middle courtyard. The inner corridors, peculiarly designed to keep out light, were pitch-dark, save for the stray shop lights lit by generators. Water dripped from the ceiling of one corridor, and the elevators were out of order. This was not unusual for most commercial markets run by the city at that time, but Nehru Place stood out for its combination of infrastructural problems for a main commercial center, irregular power, water supply and spatial claustrophobia; the worst excesses of international style design filtered through the DDA. In 1990s a revitalization proposal for the market summarized the situation:

> Public Amenities like toilets, drinking water, fountains, even basic seating, street plaza lighting, spittoons, garbage bins, are not provided for. Overhead electrical cables run haphazardly over the site. . . . Staircases in the plaza are too narrow and most are crumbling. The few planted areas are garbage dumps. Hawkers set up shops indiscriminately along the plaza disrupting movement of people. Shop signages are displayed on every conceivable surface, further adding to the virtual chaos one experiences.[35]

The 1962 Masterplan had spoken of commercial areas but they were the ones that were visible at the time, Chandni Chowk, Khari Boali, Sadar

Figure 2.8 Street computer vendor, Nehru Place.

Source: Sarai Archive.

Bazaar in the old City and Connaught Place among others. By 1972, sensing perhaps the southward expansion of the city, Jagmohan went ahead with proposing a new commercial center in Nehru Place around the district center model. Jagmohan's note was his typical evocation of European piazzas as a model for public life:

> It will really be a focal point of cultural synthesis and crucible of intellectual ferment from which will radiate new ideas and new thoughts. On piazzas, Tamilians and Kashmiris, Punjabis and Gujratis, Biharis and Bengalis, will rub shoulders with one another, exchange glances, and make friends; in its coffee houses and restaurants, poets and writers will gather from all parts of India, bubbling with passion and poetry, and engaging in animated discussions; and on its theaters and community halls will appear musicians and artists from all States and regions, presenting different facets of our life and society. The new centre will truly be a confluence of our diversities, cross-roads of our country, harbinger of cultural synthesis and national integration for which Pt. Nehru worked all his life.
>
> (Jagmohan, 1972)

In the event, Nehru Place turned out quite differently from Jagmohan's plans. Soon after its opening, not unlike Palika Bazaar, Nehru Place began to take on the character of a post-planning urban palimpsest, part crumbling, part bazaar, and also home to major companies. After going through a few years of stagnation in the 1980s Nehru Place exploded with the computer boom, in effect becoming the main supply hub of the country. The first years were similar to the video experience, with imports by traders from trips to South East Asia and widespread software piracy. Traders would typically visit Taiwan or Hong Kong to secure supplies, often bypassing customs and the tax authorities. "We would get smuggled parts from Nepal, Taiwan and Singapore," a trader told me in 1998, "often it was cheaper those days to travel and come back with suitcases of parts."[36] By the early 1990s Nehru Place had hardware suppliers, pirate software shops, secondhand computer shops, as well as mainstream distribution outlets for multinational companies. Everyone interested in software or computers at that time visited Nehru Place, and traders built lucrative links with local computer gray market assemblers. Although the computer trade coexisted with specialized shops for export fabrics, banks, and public sector offices, it was the software and hardware that gave Nehru Place its name. In the later years, when customs duty structures dropped, many traders became large legal distributors of hardware imports, while the direct imports through personal visits and secondhand computer shops shifted to smaller towns. The open face of software piracy also became muted due to incessant raids by Microsoft.

All three media markets of the "long" 1980s grew out of planned developments; Palika Bazaar had careful zoning in the initial phase, and Nehru

Figure 2.9 Nehru Place side street. Despite the decaying DDA buildings visible on both sides, a high energy level always marks the market.

Source: Sarai Archive.

Place had a large public plaza. At their best they were expressions of the DDA's blank urbanism, planning's own generic city, a form of bureaucratic escape from the memory of the old city and partition. The infrastructure of the planned markets began crumbling soon after their inception, coterminous with the crisis of the planned city. Nehru Place's public plaza became a bazaar; Palika's zoning system collapsed, and Lajpat Rai market expanded into sidewalks and backyards. In combining consumption, circulation, and urban decay, the markets brought together myth and ruin in a profound constellation. The "virtual chaos of signage" referred to disparagingly by the revitalization plan for Nehru Place, the constantly moving crowds in the market, the periodic bouts of darkness due to power failure, were indicative of the peculiar out-of-joint media urbanism of the long decade.

Figure 2.10 Pirate CDs in a Nehru Place alleyway.
Source: Sarai Archive.

Market, factory, work

By the 1990s markets began asserting their own version of "splintering urbanism," developing internal illegal telephone exchanges to cut costs,[37] and putting in place local control technologies[38] which competed with that of the police, and fighting with enforcement detectives in raids against media pirates. Horizontal networks developed with traders and informal courier systems in the Gulf, East Asia and China. Each market generated backend geographical footprints with local electronic factories and neighborhood shops. For many years Palika Bazaar was the main place for sourcing the latest movies for neighbourhood cable video. When radical piracy further decentralized distribution, the market's large shopkeepers were widely alleged to own pirate media factories in neighboring states. Nehru Place was integral for all gray market and mainstream computer supplies, spare parts, software, and repairs. Lajpat Rai market had the deepest footprint in the city, with links to the electrical market in Bhagirath Place, and electronic factories in Angoori Bagh and Shahadra. Shopkeepers as well as skilled workers from the markets of Lajpat Rai and Bhagirath Place set up media production workshops in Angoori Bagh and Shahadra, developing dynamic links between production and trade. These were mostly areas that were developed through squatting, where home-based production would develop slowly into more sophisticated clusters where informal capital mobilization (chit funds or committees), profitable sharing of raw materials, and technological skills were used along with the cultivation of local political leaders for regularization and infrastructure development. Most of the neighborhood factories emerged in unauthorized areas outside designated industrial estates largely owing to the high costs of legal entry (Benjamin, 2005a). During the 1980 to 1995 boom period, neighborhood factories mushroomed in Delhi, supplying a range of industries all over northern India. It was not just their non-legal and multiple (de facto) tenurial status that marked the neighborhood factories; entry costs were reasonably low, and it was not improbable that the small workshops would be led by a former skilled worker himself (ibid.). In small electronic component workshops, "owners" would even work with their own workmen. Marketing agents or suitcase entrepreneurs connected enterprises with media markets in Delhi and small towns all over India. The small town supply orders that reached Lajpat Rai and Angoori Bagh may well have been lured by suitcase entrepreneurs; in this case they were part of a large and rapidly changing distribution chain of the pirate industry in Delhi.

Angoori Bagh is hidden away outside the western corner of Delhi's Red Fort close to the high security pedestal zone from which the Indian prime minister addresses the country on August 15, Independence Day. Just across the Lajpat Rai market and Bhagirath Place, the neighborhood is perfectly located to supply components and finished electronic products. Small workshops turn out TVs, CD, VCD, and DVD players, audio goods, and surgical components. The small streets are stacked with packaged televisions and DVD players with labels entirely unfamiliar to middle-class buyers used to large brands. There are often local variations of Korean, Japanese, and Chinese brands in the smaller towns and working-class districts of the country. Workshops attach labels to finished products when orders come in – they could be from businessmen in small towns deploying their regional labels, or from dealers in local variants of major brands. When Rakesh Kumar Singh began researching Angooribagh in 2004, the workshop he visited had ready-to-paste "local" labels (Bluebird, Diamond) along with Sony, Samsung, and Indian brands. That particular workshop was assembling TVs; some parts were imports from China, some from neighborhood factories, and other components were even sourced from Delhi's ragpickers and refurbished. When completed, orders would be shipped to parts of northern India or carted by workers across the road to Lajpat Rai market. Rakesh Kumar Singh found out that there were three levels inside the workshops. The highest paid was the most skilled and experienced (an engineer), followed by regular workers with an eight-hour shift. Next were those on contract who followed a daily piece rate, and at the bottom were unpaid interns who graduated to paid employee status once they could demonstrate the necessary skills.[39]

This was a highly efficient form of production; work skills circulated in various workshops outside a restrictive intellectual property regime, and the production cycle was tied very closely to supply almost on a daily basis. In every sense there was the kind of affective relationship present in Braudel's description of "non-capitalist" markets.[40] Fierce competition between workshop-factories existed in a kind of Smithian universe where no monopolistic victors emerged. For many years in the early 1990s, when many products were roughly equal in quality, price competition was fierce; enterprises would desperately scrounge around for recycled and refurbished materials to please customers. Scrap dealers, used parts, cheaper materials, local and imported, were all sourced in the struggle to survive. After one fell back in the competition, "nobody picks up the loser," says Akhtar, summing up the mood at that time (Sharma, 2004).

A section of the profits went to build infrastructure, security, cleaning, paying local officials in the police, DDA, the electricity board and, in the later years, legal battles against eviction. Political patronage was carefully cultivated by local associations in neighborhood annual cultural functions.

This was a form of subaltern industrial production in many ways, violating the law of the planned city, its ecological utopias, and normative entrepreneurship. This was private enterprise without classic capitalists, or classic workers, or legal industrial estates, without brands or legal monetary rents to the state. This was in fact ironically recognized by the Supreme Court judgment of 1995, which in effect legally exiled much of this industry and its workers out of the city, leading to social scars from which the city has not recovered to this day.

3   The pirate kingdom

The body is a thing among things.[1]

(Merleau-Ponty)

In an essay titled "Theatrum Philosphicum," Michel Foucault made one of his now widely cited predictions – that the century may well be known as "Deleuzian." Less is known of the exact occasion of this statement – Foucault's discussion of Deleuze's two books, *Difference and Repetition*, and *The Logic of Sense*. After Deleuze, Foucault suggested that "the philosophy of representation – of the original, the first time, resemblance, imitation, faithfulness is dissolving; the arrow of the simulacrum released by the Epicurians is headed in our direction" (1977, p.172). Since Plato's time, the relationship between the real and the copy has been framed in a manner where the simulacrum has existed almost entirely as a negative mode of comparison, a false claimant to the real. Plato's hierarchy was that of the model, the copy, and the copy of the copy, designated as the simulacrum. In the *Republic*, Plato had displayed his hostility to the "imitator" who as the "creator of the phantom, knows nothing of reality" (*Republic X*, p. 601c). In *The Logic of Sense* Deleuze argues for the equality of representations, in a philosophy that abolishes classical distinctions between essence and appearance, "The simulacra is not a degraded copy. It harbors a positive power which denies the *original and the copy, the model and the reproduction*" (1990, p.262).

Plato's philosophical distinction became significant by the seventeenth century when Western modernity refashioned itself through the lenses of creativity and authorship, both tied to an emerging theory of cultural property. The establishment of a widespread discourse on authorship has by no means been easy. From the seventeenth century mass reproduction techniques inaugurated by print rendered Plato's philosophical distinction increasingly suspect through the proliferation of more versions of the same. This book argues that as more people in the postcolonial world move into media cities, the proliferation of things, urban crises, and productive life enter into a strange, dynamic compact. This experience of the media city produces a complex hyperstimulus; an escalation of the senses along with the increasing speeds of the city, and a relentless circulation of things, images, and people. Proliferation produced a diversity of media experiences, but also unsettled the classic boundaries of consumption and circulation, drawing urban populations into a dynamic but addictive loop.

With globalization, Indian cities saw unending waves of new technological objects entering markets, homes, and offices. Pirate production and circulation was a publicly perceived sphere of this new world of things. This included most consumer products but was particularly significant for media goods whose surfaces spread in every part of the city. These goods took on a life as counterfeits, fakes or copies, or in popular language the "pirated," the "local," or "duplicate." When the new media boom began in India and other parts of Asia around the introduction of the cassette deck, the VCR and the home computer, the old regime of media property and control went into a spin.

By the mid-1980s piracy became technology's cultural kingdom of the many, and the source of mass cultural ambiguity towards the regime of authorship and originality that has been conferred on things. As with early modern print culture, piracy is again at the center of the debate over access and authenticity – low-cost digital reproduction in our time both recalled and radically expanded early modern conflicts over media property. In twentieth-century global terms, the radical "everywhereness" (Govil, 2004, p.2004) of this new reproducibility is not confined to the digital alone, but seems to increasingly allegorize the production of industrial and consumer goods. Counterfeit culture is here to stay. Corporations have sought to defend their markets with brand protection and vast advertising budgets. In a world where Asian factories export vast quantities of consumer goods globally, a commodity sold as an expensive label in Paris could equally appear as a low-cost surplus item from an Asian factory in a street market in Lagos. Piracy affects debates on medicine, biotechnology, international trade disputes, trademarks, youth culture, indigenous knowledge and corporate "bio-piracy," sovereignty, and property. Piracy, along with terrorism, is now the favored language of global fear, with its consequent attractive/destructive semantic overflow. For liberals and old-style Marxists, piracy seems to allegorize an impure transgression, tainted by commerce and an inability to produce a discourse about itself. Pirate production of commodities and media objects fit neither a narrative of resistance nor normative critique, nor does piracy seem to fit received models of creativity or innovation. Piracy today produces a series of anxieties, from states, transnational capital, and media industries and even among some liberal proponents of the public domain. The efflorescence of non-legal media production and circulation exists as a series of publicly articulated facts, constantly referred to in media panics, national security discourses, and everyday conversations.[2]

The pirate zone

In his remarkable book on early modern print culture[3] Adrian Johns suggests that widespread piracy in early Western print culture had both "epistemic" as well as economic implications. Most significantly, piracy localized print reception, and undermined the imagined fixity and unity of print communities. As readers' access to texts vastly increased, so did the experience of uncertainty about the authority of the printed word. Writes Johns,

> Piracy and plagiarism occupied readers' minds. . . . Unauthorized translations, epitomes, imitations and other varieties of "impropriety" were, they believed routine hazards. . . . From Galileo and Tycho to Newton and John Flamstead, no significant learned author seemed to escape the kinds of practices soon colloquially subsumed under the label of piracy.
>
> (Johns, 1998, p.30)

Printed titles with the same "authors" differed from region to region, throwing readers into both confusion and ecstasy.

> Martin Luther's German translation of Scripture was actually beaten into print by its first piracy, and in succeeding years the proportion of unauthorized to authorized was roughly ninety to one. . . . A century later, the first folio of Shakespeare boasted six hundred typefaces, along with nonuniform spelling and punctuation, erratic divisions and arrangement, mispaging and irregular proofing. No two copies were identical.
>
> (Johns, 1998, p.31)

New media geographies of readers, publisher-pirates, and interpretations emerged in a zone where the object itself (the printed book) actually opened up more debate and conflict rather than producing a unity through technological fixity. Johns' main target in *The Nature of the Book* is Elizabeth Eisenstein's hugely influential *The Printing Press as an Agent of Change* (1980). Eisenstein argued that "ancient and medieval scientific traditions were transformed by the capacity of printing to transmit records of observations without any loss of precision and in full detail" (p.470). As a result, new communities of experimental science emerged, communicating across boundaries. For Eisenstein, standardization produced collaborative communities and experimentation. Benedict Anderson's (1991) work on nationalism takes this argument a step further, arguing that common, imaginary print journeys of national elites prefigured the rise of nation-states. In Johns' book, by contrast, the category of "print" is evacuated from the classic story of the serial expansion of Western modernity from Gutenberg to cosmopolitanism.

Among print's many geographies is that of nineteenth-century India that has been recently touched on by a range of writers (e.g. Ghosh, 2006; Stark,

2007). Print exploded after the revolt of 1857, a process that was significantly aided by colonial desire for surveillance and access to local knowledge. Ulrike Stark's exhaustive and pioneering study of the Naval Kishore Press in the nineteenth century tracks book history through the intersection of technology, colonial patronage, and dynamic circulatory networks. Suggesting that "there is a paucity of empirical work on the material, technological aspects of the literary sphere" (2007, p.25), Stark presents us with discussions of lithography and print proliferation in local scripts. Stark also shows radical distribution networks in print where hawkers peddled books in small towns and collected manuscripts from authors. At times manuscripts were an alternative to payment.[4] Anindita Ghosh's recent study (2006) of nineteenth-century print culture in Bengal details the massive rise in print production paralleled by complex publics of Bengali readers, printers, and authors. Around 200,000 titles were registered between 1868 and 1905, something Robert Darnton suggests was "more, by far than the total output of France during the Age of Enlightenment" (cited in Ghosh, 2006, p.15). The center of local print culture in Calcutta was the Battala area, in North Calcutta. Battala's smaller presses produced titles that ranged from mythological dramas, legends, romances, almanacs, and educational material. The print runs also included sensational and scandalous texts particularly popular among readers. Sneered at by highbrow reform elites, Battala books enjoyed a wide readership. Writes Ghosh, "Despite bhadralok disapproval, these small presses did a brisk trade in light pamphlet literature, their publications enjoying a large and popular readership, particularly, but not exclusively, in lower middle class urban and rural homes" (Ghosh, 2006, p.17). The passing of the colonial Copyright Act in 1847 formalized literary property in India. The passing of the Act was motivated partly by colonial governments' need to monitor local print culture, and to anticipate local dissent. Copyright now combined Western-style property ownership with surveillance, as all publications were required to be registered with the local authorities. Copyright was held variously by printers, publishers, individual authors, and commercial proprietors.[5] Larger printers tended to buy copyrights from individual authors and convert them into print runs. The emergence of literary property in Bengal in the context of a commercial capitalist economy exposed the new colonial elites to individual fears about the usurpation of property through piracy and copying. The uneasy combination of property and personhood that stood at the heart of Lockean theory's argument for individualism and appropriation had moved in colonial Bengal from land to print.[6] Copyright presented the colonized elites with the dream of profit and propriety, but it was clearly a vision that was ridden with the anxiety of being overtaken by copiers and pirates. A nineteenth-century woodcut artist's warning on his engraving captures this anxiety well: "This plate has been recently engraved. Whoever steals it will be engulfed by fear and sin."[7]

For most of its modern history media piracy has been legally referenced as the negative other of copyright. Copyright's own pasts are deeply contradictory – the late twentieth-century regime has emerged out of conflicts between authors, publishers, corporations, states, and legal philosophies and statutes. The broad legal consensus is that the "origins" of copyright can be traced back to the Statute of Anne in England in 1710. This statute ended the system of royal privileges and print monopolies that had developed in Europe in the early modern period. In the last few decades of the seventeenth century this system of monopolies was largely held by the Stationers Company, a printer's guild, which combined monopoly with censorship of prohibited works.[8] By the early eighteenth-century this monopoly was under attack and the 1710 Act removed printed monopolies in the name of authors who were now granted rights over their work for a total period not exceeding twenty-eight years.[9] To be sure, authors' rights in a growing capitalist society meant that writers typically assigned their rights to publishers; at best, the statute tried to balance private monopoly with a rough notion of public purpose.[10] Copyright doctrine since the Statute of Anne has seen the confused and often conflictual coming together of three streams:

- The Anglo-American utilitarian legal model that modified the Lockean theory[11] of property into a system of incentives for cultural goods, setting up statutory limits on eternal property rights in print and other media to help authors and creators to contribute to public good. Thus the US constitution argued for the Congress' power of "progress of Science and useful Arts, by securing for limited times to Authors and Inventors the exclusive Right to their respective Writings and Discoveries" (Article I(8)(8)).[12]
- The idea of the moral rights of the author drawing from German idealist and expressivist traditions where the idea of copyright is an expression of the personality of the author. The collusion between the idea of literary property that drew from Anglo-American utilitarianism and a nineteenth-century Romantic notion of creative authorship[13] played a significant role in the rhetorical discourse around copyright law, if not its substance (Woodmansee and Jaszi, 1994; Boyle, 1997).
- The concept of an abstract authored work, which laid the grounds for immaterial control and exploitation irrespective of the media (print, music, image). This was summarized in the Berne convention of 1886 which opened the contemporary discourse on copyright doctrine. The Berne convention was revised many times to accommodate the spread of newer media like photography and the cinema.[14] Abstract authorship, perfected under the TRIPS agreement of the WTO in 1994, has now moved firmly into the global arena, with copyright and patent compliance becoming the legal requirement for membership in the world economy. The post-WTO era has seen a new discourse of globalization emerging worldwide. Intergovernmental organizations joined advocacy and enforcement organizations for the US and regional media industries in the campaign against piracy and the push for compliance.

The best-known organization is the International Intellectual Property Alliance (IIPA) formed in 1984 to represent the US copyright-based industries.[15] The IIPA's members include all the major US media industries, Association of American Publishers (AAP), Business Software Alliance (BSA), Entertainment Software Association (ESA), Independent Film and Television Alliance (IFTA), Motion Picture Association of America (MPAA or MPA), National Music Publishers' Association (NMPA), and Recording Industry Association of America (RIAA). Of these the MPAA, the BSA, and the RIAA have been the most active in the international campaign against piracy, lobbying national governments, conducting workshops for police and judges, and leading punitive raids against pirates. For its part the IIPA issues periodic country reports that detail its version of compliance with the international legal copyright regime; the reports also recommend to the US[16] trade representative (USTR) that various countries be placed on "priority watch lists"[17] for alleged non-compliance. In 2007, the US trade representative put Argentina, Chile, Egypt, India, Israel, Lebanon, China, Russia, Thailand, Turkey, Ukraine, and Venezuela on its priority watch list.[18] The IIPA, the MPA, and the BSA have all been active in India and other parts of Asia, with local offices and advocacy initiatives with local police and the local media and information industries.

The spread of media technologies in the post-digital era has vastly expanded the potential scope of the copyright regime and the ambitions of international media industries. In fact, global media industries have been on the offensive since the 1990s, hammering away at legislators, courts, and national governments to widen the scope of copyright protection. The campaign was also aimed at limiting that bundle of public access rights known as "fair use." Fair use doctrine emerged primarily in US case law, where the use of copyrighted material was allowed without permission for creative purposes.[19] In theory fair use exists as a balance between private ownership of media property and social use. James Boyle points out that fair use is "part of the implicit *quid pro quo* of intellectual property; we will give you this extremely valuable legal monopoly. . . . In return, we will design the contours of your right so as to encourage a variety of socially valuable uses" (Boyle, 1997, p.139). The shrinking fair use regime and the public domain in general has been the focus of the Left liberal critique of the contemporary media property regime (John Frow, James Boyle, Yochai Benkler, Laurence Lessig). Curiously the campaign against piracy has paralleled this transformation of older notions of copyright which still left open the domain of individual use for non-commercial and personal use. As legal scholar Jessica Litman points out, the campaign against piracy has generously incorporated domains that were perfectly legitimate under that label:

They've succeeded in persuading a lot of people that any behavior that has the same effect as piracy must *be* piracy, and must therefore reflect the same moral turpitude we attach to piracy, even if it is the same behavior that we all called legitimate before. Worse, any behavior that *could potentially cause the same effect* as piracy, even if it doesn't, must also be piracy. Because an unauthorized, unencrypted digital copy of something *could* be uploaded to the Internet, where it *could* be downloaded by two million people, even making the digital copy is piracy.

(Litman, 2000, p.8)

High-speed networks of the 1990s have seen the deployment by the media industry of tracking and controlling architectures that dreamed of resolving the historic tension between intangible private property and its material circulation in the Thing – the very tension that has plagued the copyright regime from the outset. This has been paralleled by some of the most draconian laws against piracy, leading to legal cases against individuals[20] and small shops, and violent raids by enforcement agencies against "infringers." The discourse against piracy as both morally reprehensible and illegal is in a large part produced by this campaign. A spectral zone of infringement statistics,[21] pirate P2P networks, the existence of factories in South East Asia, and the supposed link between terrorism and piracy are retailed by the anti-piracy campaign on a global scale. By all accounts the success of this campaign has been mixed. The very expansion of contemporary copyright's power has been challenged at each step – by hackers, who break every digital encryption used by the industry, by peer-to-peer networks who dodge enforcement and provide a platform for users to share media files,[22] and most importantly by hundreds of millions of ordinary buyers of pirated media, who seem not to share the media industry's vision of the world today. I want to suggest that there is more to piracy than its illegality or economic potency, destructiveness, or radical alterity.

The debate around authorship and the shrinking public domain that has emanated from Western critiques of the property regime is an important one, but limited by its axis, the split personality of modern liberal individualism and personhood that modernity inaugurated. In their critique of the current property regime, public domain theorists have variously mobilized the category of the information commons, the right to share and reinterpret cultural material, and a domain of creative authorship through collaborative P2P networks (Boyle, 1997; Lessig, 2004; Benkler, 2007). These are surely important and significant resources for a critique of the current property regime. However, as Lawrence Liang points out in his excellent critique, there is a general silence about piracy in the entire public domain debate.[23]

Piracy's absence in this debate is significant, perhaps because it fundamentally disrupts the categories of the debate of property, capitalism, personhood, and the commons that have moved the debate over the past decade. Postcolonial piracy is typically a post-liberal (if not a post-Marxist) cultural effect. Piracy destabilizes contemporary media property, both disrupting and enabling creativity, and evading issues of the classic commons, while simultaneously radicalizing media access for subaltern groups. Postcolonial piracy has worked more through dense local networks of bazaar exchange and face-to-face contact, rather than individual online downloads.[24] In an earlier essay I termed this phenomenon a pirate or recycled modernity (Sundaram, 1999), unconcerned with modernity's search for originality. More pragmatic and viral than the avant-garde or tactical media pirate culture allowed the entry of vast numbers of poor urban residents into media culture.

The metaphor of the virus suggests parasitic attachments to larger structures, rapid replication, disruption, and transformation of official networks through non-linear communication. "Recycling" is not a process of more of the same (i.e. simple replication), but works as a complex difference engine – each copy is different from its predecessor through variation and recombination. Piracy therefore occupies a field whose edges move all the time, margin to center, international to local. Governments and industry have been publicly repelled and secretly fascinated by media piracy, a sure sign of the latter's corporeal power. This is piracy's great public secret – and the relative ease with which it has withstood severe attacks from industry-sponsored enforcement campaigns.

For urban populations long used to more stable sites like the cinema hall, piracy's decentralized proliferation induced a narcotic disorientation of the senses.[25] Populations conceived by state media policy as an abstract public now entered piracy's landscape of infinite attractions, where images, sounds, objects, moved rapidly through networks of proliferation, small shops, bazaars, video theaters, friends. Piracy escapes the boundaries of space, of particular networks, of form, a before and after, a *limit*. Although it has complex strategies of deployment and movement, piracy is like no other form of expression, respecting no formal barriers. The lines between the surface and the inside, original and copy, which transfixed the Western modernist archive and its postmodern reformulations, are called into question in piracy. What appears is a subjectless subjectivity; there is no being behind doing, or, as Nietzsche said, *the deed is everything.*[26]

Strategies of media piracy approximate Deleuze and Guattari's description of an assemblage in their work *A Thousand Plateaus* (1988). In that work, Deleuze and Guattari move through a variety of assemblages – of capture, of enunciation, and of thought. An assemblage is a multiplicity, and they distinguish between arborescent and rhizomatic assemblages. The former is a unifiable system of clear boundaries – the institutions of modern government. Rhizomatic assemblages lack a central axis, and are defined by Deleuze and Guattari in the early pages of *A Thousand Plateaus* as "by the outside; by the abstract line, the line of flight or deterritorialization according to which they change in nature and connect with other multiplicities" (Deleuze and Guatarri, 1988, p.9). The most attractive aspect of this formulation is that it captures the productivity of pirate economies, expansion, mutation, breakdown, reterritorialization. Following Deleuze and Guattari,[27] rather than initially defining what piracy *is*, we can ask what piracy *does*.

The cassette assemblage

In January, 1984 the journalist Ayesha Kagal traveled around the country to examine the spread of video, which had been introduced in the country on a wide scale barely a year before her journey. Kagal painted a picture of booming makeshift video theaters and thriving cassette libraries in small towns and villages all over the country. Showing the latest releases from Hindi and regional cinema, as well as a reasonable selection of pornography, video drew people from all walks of life – youth, working people, businessmen, women, and children. The landscape of picturesque India – the great cattle fair in Puskhar in Rajasthan, the hill station in Panchgani in central India, Leh in Ladhakh – all bore witness to the turbulence unleashed by video, closing film theaters, bankrupting distributors and a film industry under siege. "We're sunk," film industry producer Gul Anand told Kagal. "Cinema simply can't face the competition. Our prints are bulky, our processing charges are going up while the prices of cassettes are going down and will drop further. . . . I sometimes feel the 35 mm projector is going to be a museum item."[28] The main problem for video was identified as piracy – libraries and theaters sourced the latest movie from an international circuit almost immediately, bypassing local laws and film industry prohibitions. This was then distributed through low-cost VHS cassettes – in local video libraries and makeshift theaters. New parallel infrastructures of distribution came up rapidly – cable networks, video libraries, and small video theaters. A significant expansion of the media public was underway, at the same time as the decline of older cinema theaters and exhibition spaces.

The situation in the audio market was even more dramatic. Audio cassette technology had spread rapidly and easily by the early 1980s, spawning an army of small music producers all over the country. Conservative estimates which tend to privilege the legal industry (including smaller players) show that the turnover of the music business increased *twentyfold* in the decade of the 1980s (Swamy, 1991). The music scholar Peter Manuel hazarded a guess of 250 producers in North India alone based on his research – a figure that *excluded* pirate and unregistered players. Small and medium players ripped through the main monopolies like HMV, and opened a large, hitherto untapped market of regional and local music, and as in the case of video, also set up a low-cost geographically diverse distribution network. The spread of cassettes in the 1980s as a dominant form was rapid. Peter Manuel's standard work on that period summarizes the situation well: "By the mid 1980s cassettes had come to account for 95 percent of the recorded music market. . . . The recording-industry dominance formerly enjoyed by GCI dwindled to less than 15 percent of the market, as over three hundred competitors entered the field" (1991, p.63). The share of film music dropped to a minority position in the market, replaced by a combination of regional, devotional, and non-filmi pop (ibid.). Manuel's still unsurpassed study of that period calls this the cassette "revolution," where a mix of new producers and technologies responding to regional and local genres overturned the classic music monopolies and the star system of singers associated with it. This is what Manuel dramatically summarizes:

> In effect, the cassette revolution had definitively ended the hegemony of GCI, of the corporate music industry in general, of film music, of the Lata-Kishore duo, and of the uniform aesthetic which the Bombay film-producers had superimposed on a few hundred million listeners over the preceding forty years. The crucial factors were the relatively low expense of the cassette technology . . . which enabled small, "cottage" cassette companies to proliferate throughout the country.
>
> (Ibid.)

Small labels, argued Manuel, were responsive to local tastes and now offered their diverse audiences an equally diverse range of musical forms. In ownership, content, and in the circulation of a musical form, argued Manuel, cassettes democratized the audio experience. New artists emerged as a fresh pool of talent came into the business all over the country, some of whom entered the music star system in the 1990s. Despite Manuel's mixed feelings about copy culture, there was no hiding the fact that pirate production was a critical part of the emergent world of audio production. Says Manuel, "Until the late 1980s pirate producers dominated the industry in terms of turnover and profits, and they continue to claim a significant share of the market" (ibid., p.78). Piracy's structure of law-bypassing techniques marked almost all emergent enterprises in audio; in the case of companies like T-series it was central.[29]

Manuel's account of the 1980s complicates the analyses of the global spread of the VCR put out by media scholars of the time. Writing in the Australian media journal *Continuum* in 1991 Tom O'Regan mapped out the three global sites of video: the VCR as part of the personalized home entertainment market of the West, the extra, semi-underground TV service in Eastern Europe and the postcolonial world where national monopolies controlled television content, and a third hybrid which was part pay service and part alternative TV, as in the Gulf. Piracy was identified as a major source all over the world, with lesser effects in the West, where major studios moved to control distribution chains and video outlets.[30] Overall the VCR disturbed national sovereignty and media monopolies. In the long run O'Regan forecast accurately that video would provide lucrative markets for media industries with distribution control and even more integration of media industries.[31] In the non-Western world the 1980s saw video as a mode of *disassembly* – of space and of audiences. The effects were diverse but equally widespread.

In Mexico, Canclini (2001), citing a study by Deborah Holz, reported that video clubs played a significant role in disrupting the older cultural citizenship that had emerged in post-World War II Mexican society. In a report tinged with nostalgia for a disappearing age of the old cinema hall Canclini suggested that video took place in a "present without memory" (Canclini, 2001, p.116). Old arrangements of genre were ignored in video clubs, as was information about directors, in favor of a culture of the instant.[32]

> Immediacy and the value of the instantaneous are reflected in what young videophiles seek. The numbers of images that succeed each other by fraction of a second are the beginning of a challenge to time that does not correspond to time.
>
> (Holz cited in Canclini, 2001, p.116)

In India the early years of video saw viewers engage in a similar play against time, the rush for the latest movie, to beat the circuits of distribution, even obtaining a film before the official release. This limitless desire became a significant part of the pirate assemblage, mutating into networks that spanned global and regional temporal zones.

If the Mexican researchers perceived the emergence of video as disturbing national cultural citizenship, reports from Nigeria underlined a more democratic proliferation of video culture that compared with India[33] in the 1980s.

> Video rental clubs rent (pirated) videos for a very modest [price]; such businesses at the lower end are very informal affairs, run out of someone's room in a compound with no signboard to advertise their presence. There are also one-room video parlors, equipped with ordinary televisions and VCRs, which cater at low prices to a poorer clientele. Cassettes are sold out of modest shops and stalls on the street very much a part of the ubiquitous West African petty trading. Traders and market women are said to be major consumers of video films.
>
> (Haynes and Okome, 1998, p.117)

The video and the audio cassette boom illustrates the rapidity of its expansion in Indian media history. It marked new parasitic media geographies, and a vast spatial expansion of media life. Drawing from a growing infrastructure of small enterprises and an emerging class of entrepreneurs, cassette culture of both audio and video let loose a series of conflicts around piracy, between large and small companies, between pirates and copyright enforcement detectives, and between large and small pirates. As a form that bypassed the law, media piracy was not unique to social and cultural forms in postcolonial India. Nor was piracy new; it had a past since the coming of print. Nevertheless, by shifting the material and spatial registers of copy culture into an uncertain sphere of disturbance, the cassette era opened up a new phase in

Indian media history. Mutation followed reproduction, ensuring a kind of permanent instability for years to come.

Piracy produced a certain novel form of panic in the media industry which had always been accustomed to a certain manageable chaos. Piracy suggested not just a permanent loss of space and markets, but also a model of dispersal where "distribution" took on a productive form. As distributor pirates also produced more media, piracy bred further piracy. It was a breakdown of cultural management that has been impossible for the industry to fathom to this day. Industry panic in the 1980s went through a series of cycles; initially the film industry declared a noisy war on video piracy. No person in the Bombay industry was allowed to sell national video rights by the main association. The implication was that by default, any video cassette sold in the country was illegal. Regular press campaigns, court battles, delegations to Delhi to convince the government to change copyright laws to incorporate video, and an industry-wide strike against piracy marked the first half of the 1980s. Behind all the facades of unity the industry was actually deeply divided, with many producers wanting to break rank and sell video licenses to local distributors.[34] The association was already tearing at the edges and there was a growing demand to move to an adjustment with the new network. By the mid-1980s technologies of cultural management were already emerging in the area. Court judgments and government notifications were slowly putting in place a licensing regime that drew from legal knowledges on publicity and censorship, copyright and taxation. In 1983 the government suddenly realized the spatial dangers of hundreds of thousands of VCRs that had been imported during the Asiad and also smuggled through different channels. It issued a notification drawing from the colonial-era Indian Telegraph Act of 1885, mandating that every VCR had to be registered with the District Magistrate. This order reflected the uneasiness of the regime with new technologies, and also a response to the film industry's clamor for the regulation of video. At any rate, the order proved so impossible to implement that it was withdrawn in 1985, a sign of the growing ineffectivity of older techniques of control after video.[35] Early court judgments mobilized colonial and postcolonial fears of disorder and licentiousness (Hughes, 2000). Alarmed at the spread of video, the Madhya Pradesh High Court pointed out in a 1983 judgment:

> The dangers to which people would be exposed if the petitioners are allowed to run their restaurants as mini cinemas without any regulation are obvious. There would be risk to the safety and health of persons visiting those restaurants. Overcrowding outside and inside the restaurants when a popular movie is being exhibited would create problems of public order. Further, many of the proprietors would be tempted to indulge in exhibiting pirated and blue films.[36]

Legal judgments slowly brought video under the licensing regime of cinematography. Video parlors and video itself came under the State cinema regulation Acts, with licensing, taxation, and censorship requirements.[37]

By the mid-1980s analog cassettes entered the industry's definition of a market segment, with rights management, regional distribution, and a staggered temporal cycle where the cassette would come in after the film had its initial run. The idea was that with adequate management the industry could expand profits and produce a new widening of publicity. The model, if it could be referred to as such, was fraught with immense anxiety about leakage and non-compliance right from the outset. In the event, these were reasonable intimations.

A landscape of people and things

In the summer of 1996, I was travelling on a train in southern India where I met up with Selvam, a young man of 24, who I saw reading used computer magazines in the railway compartment. Our conversation threw up insights into a whole new world that was emerging at that time; Selvam was born in the temple town of Madurai in southern India, the son of a worker in the town court.[38] After ten years in school, Selvam began doing a series of odd jobs; he also learned to type at a night school after which he landed a job at a typists' shop, which also provided phones and computers. It was there that Selvam first encountered the new technoculture of the 1990s.

From the late 1980s, India witnessed a unique communicative transformation – the spread of public telephones in different parts of the country. Typically these were not anonymous card-based instruments as in the West or other parts of the Third World, but run by humans. These were called Public Call Offices (PCOs), a brainchild of Sam Pitroda, the then Prime Minister Rajeev Gandhi's technology advisor. The idea was that in a non-literate society like India the act of telecommunication had to be mediated by human beings.[39] Typically literates and non-literates used PCOs, which often doubled as fax centers, xerox shops and typists' shops. Open through the night, PCOs offered inexpensive, personalized services which spread rapidly all over the country. Selvam's typing shop was such a PCO. Selvam worked on a used 286, running an old version of Wordstar, where he would type out formal letters to state officials for clients, usually peasants and the unemployed. Soon Selvam graduated to a faster 486 and learned programming by devouring used manuals, also by simply asking around. This is the world of informal technological knowledge existing in most parts of India, where those excluded from the upper-caste, English-speaking bastions of the cyber-elite learn their tools.

Selvam told me how the textile town of Coimbatore in Tamil Nadu set up its own electronic Bulletin Board System, by procuring used modems, and connecting them late at night. Used computer equipment is part of a vast commodity chain in India, originating from various centers in India, but one of the main centers is Delhi. The center of Delhi's used computer trade is

Nehru Place market, a rundown cluster of gray concrete blocks, filled with small shops devoted to the computer trade. Present here are the agents of large corporations, as well as software pirates, spare parts dealers, electronic smugglers, and wheeler-dealers of every kind in the computer world. In the 1990s the used computer shops were in the main market, and when I visited them in 1997, they were packed with visitors from all over India – all armed with complicated computer part names, out of service motherboards and complicated repair issues. Outside in the street, surplus from the main shops – scratched CDs with damaged memory, software CDs and floppy disks, computer cables – all drew curious observers. The computer trade in the 1990s followed the circuit of cable television. Just as small town cable operators would come to the cable market in the walled city area of Delhi for equipment, so people from small towns like Selvam would come to Nehru Place to source computer parts, used computers, older black and white monitors, and out of fashion mother-boards. Nehru Place, along with other media markets in the 1980s and 1990s, indicated that the transformed morphology of media was actually initiated by piracy. This was a peculiar in-between morphology – of shops, markets, cable, wiring, cassettes, distributors – which drew tens of thousands of small entrepreneurs, technical DIY kids, and people excluded from older economies of patronage. By the late 1980s and 1990s Indian cities were swarming with small entrepreneurs and migrants who took part in the pirate trade, along with older communities of traders. In Delhi they flocked to the small factories of east Delhi, and the markets of Nehru Place, Lajpat Rai market and Palika Bazaaar. Some became cable operators, others joined the booming music business, and yet others tried their hand in the computer trade. Lamington Road in Bombay, Burmah Bazaar in Chennai, and National Market in Bangalore were other similar media markets that developed at that time. By the 1990s travel to South East Asia by small businessmen in Delhi[40] and other cities to source computer parts and electronic goods was standard; in Delhi's old city a whole business of travel agents grew around ticket booking for Asian travel for small business. In retrospect this map of commodities and people was more fluid than had been assumed at the time.[41] In Delhi, researcher Lokesh Sharma met Shrikant, a working-class migrant and garbage dealer in a squatter settlement in North Delhi, who typified this fluidity. Shrikant arrived in Delhi in 1980 in Shiv Basti and began a cable business in his *jhuggi* (working-class settlement) in 1996. Sensing the *jhuggi* would soon be demolished, Shrikant ran his business part time. When the demolition took place Shrikant bought out the cable business in the nearby area of B.D. estate, where he competed with well-established players in a tough middle-class market.[42] In Mumbai, young researcher Prasad Khanolkar discovered many seasonal entrepreneurs in the pirate business, migrants, working-class and lower-middle-class folks – all attempting to enter the chain of circulation in the commodified city.

CD sellers at Andheri Station, a south Indian from Kerala came to

Mumbai because it's his off season for farming. He comes in summer to earn some money in the city and goes back after rainy season. Bombay it seems is the city of opportunity anyone without money also can come and earn and go. He stays in Dharavi with a number of other guys who also have come here to earn; and his entire community stays there. He came to know of [piracy] through a friend who had come earlier and done this business had gone back. The friend who runs a shop next to him also sells the Duplicated software. This friend [name unknown] introduced Rajat to the main guy and asked him to let Rajat open a shop of his own. Initially since Rajat had no investment the shop was run on a % per CD basis i.e. 30% of every CD sold has to be given to this main guy. But now after earning some money he can afford to buy CDs form that main guy and sell it at a higher rate i.e. RS 150 for software per CD, RS 100 for porn CDs and RS 100 for new movie CDs.

(Khanolkar, 2005)

The shifting cultural landscape of the media networks built in the 1980s and the 1990s was in contrast to the more abstract state-sponsored discourse around computers under the Rajiv Gandhi era which sought to graft new technology on to a modernized nationalist model. Popular knowledges about breakdown, assembly, duplication, hardware, and software hacks dominated conversations in the pirate zone of the late 1980s onward, displaying an almost counter-tactical model – assembly rather than attack, evasion rather than resistance.

In his work on Nigerian video Brian Larkin argues convincingly that pirates produced a vast viral infrastructure of media, generating both the speed of globalization and the noise of postcolonial cultural production, used equipment, assemblages, decentralization. At a time when the world economy has seceded from Africa, piracy has brought a globalization of recycled technological artifacts to Nigeria, and provided media products to a subaltern population of Indian and Hollywood films, Hausa dramas and Islamic religious cassettes. Says Larkin, "Instead of being marginalized by official distribution networks, Nigerian consumers can now participate in the immediacy of an international consumer culture – but only through the mediating capacity of piracy" (2004, p.297).

Post-independence, mass piracy first grew rapidly with print in the early 1980s with the introduction of new photo-offset machines which lowered the costs of reproduction. Then the audio culture arrived, and transformed popular music culture. This was followed by the video also in the 1980s, and cable television and computer expansion in the 1990s. Delhi was a significant site of this transformation as it was the home of T-series, the first major beneficiary of this phase.

In the second chapter of *The Nature of the Book*, Adrian Johns writes that pirates were not a distinguishable social group, but that "each generation did produce its mythically squalid 'pirate king,' as it were, whose exploits were spectacularly infamous" (1998, p.167). Delhi's Gulshan Kumar who set up T-series came closest to this description by Johns. From his near-mythic origins as a juice seller in Daryaganj, Kumar typified the rough-and-tumble media entrepreneurship of the 1980s, importing equipment and tape from East Asia, undercutting competitors and building corrupt networks with politics and government to emerge as a ruthless media magnate by the late 1980s.[43] Today T-series is one of India's largest companies active in film and music production. T-series used an opening in the copyright laws to push version recording, an innovative use of less well-known artists to sing duplicate songs sung by well-known singers under contract with major labels. In doing so, T-series pioneered a media form that developed dynamically all the way to the recent remix culture. T-series also became the "nodal" form for the development of new music companies. As Liang usefully summarizes, the key T-series' success was the mix of the legal and the non-legal:

- Using a provision in the fair use clause of the Indian Copyright Act which allows for version recording, T Series issued thousands of cover versions of GCI's classic film songs, particularly those which HMV itself found to be unfeasible to release. T Series also changed the rues of distribution by moving into neighborhoods, shops, grocery shops, paan wallahs, and teashops to literally convert the cassette into a bazaar product.
- T Series was also involved in straightforward copyright infringement in the form of pirate releases of popular hits relying on the loose enforcement of copyright laws.
- Illegally obtaining film scores even before the release of the film to ensure that their recordings were the first to hit the market.

(Liang, 2005, p.10)

The T-series phenomenon paralleled the development of new media markets in the 1980s and the 1990s: Palika Bazaar in central Delhi for video, Nehru Place for software and hardware, and Lajpat Rai market in the old city for music as well as hardware for the cable industry. Transnational links with South and East Asia were established for hardware supplies. Through the 1980s there was a range of small players in the media markets, developing new networks of distribution and production. Production was concentrated increasingly in the Trans-Yamuna areas and parts of UP and Haryana, while distribution was managed from the media markets linked to neighborhood entrepreneurs. These were early boom years, when entrepreneurs imported blank media and hardware from East Asia, built satellite dishes and hardware ancillaries, and developed local cable distribution. Music companies emerged catering to a range of tastes all over north India.

The early years of piracy in Delhi saw a complex network of production sites in the eastern part of the city that produced low-cost hardware for TV and music networks retailed in the media markets. At the lower level local dealers in the neighborhood would source the media bazaars for pirate goods. The next phase was neighborhood centered where a significant part of copying and distribution was done in the locality with the "master" being sourced from dealers.[44] Today, copying is part of a vast Asian network of procurement. Bombay films are sourced for the pirate market from Dubai and Malaysia, mixed in Pakistan, and sent on the Internet and courier to India. Master disks (from which more copies can be made) are made in factories outside Delhi (safe from enforcement raids). Sales agents then go to neighborhoods on scooters with album covers and pitch to local shops. The shift of production from the neighborhoods back to the small factories has vastly increased the quality of the final product, and to some extent prevented seizure of pirated goods at the neighborhood level. Shopkeepers typically keep only the covers for display, and procure the main item only when trust is established with the customer.

The puzzle of the original

"Is this an original?" asked an article in the Bombay music industry magazine *Playback and Fast Forward* in 1988, referring to the constant confusion among buyers of audio cassettes on the authenticity of products they were buying (Chopra, 1988, p.56). The magazine went on to conduct a test and found that just about all cassettes were in fact produced in India, despite international labels and claims of import. "And whether it's HMV, CBS, MIL or Weston or any of the pirated music available on the streets, all cassettes are 100 percent Indian" (ibid.). *Playback* was in fact addressing the anxieties of a turbulent landscape of media life in the first half of the 1980s when piracy was the dominant form through which populations experienced new media. While the regime had hoped that television would generate a space binding domestic site of consumption and national unity, piracy was an edge that moved to the center of urban life, throwing up semiotic confusions of original/pirated, and branded/local. Televisions and audio systems were smuggled or assembled, as were video and audio cassettes. These were the wild years of the cassette era, when a cluster of piracy, local media production, and neighborhood copyshops set the benchmarks for media culture. For most early users, it mattered little that the cassette was "original"; it simply had to be available.

From the later period of the 1980s companies began rapidly catching up with copy techniques, price cuts, strengthening of distribution, and design changes to mimic pirate aesthetics. Of course, piracy ranged from the straightforward reproduction of mainstream film/audio releases, remix and remake audio/video, local and regional music and video. With the movement to the digital by the mid-1990s this situation became even more fluid, where producers, ship-owners, discerning consumers, and enforcement agents produced complex short-term classifications to distinguish between the original, the pirate, and the local. What emerged was a materiality that disclosed popular ideas of authenticity and surface, within the context of a bazaar economy reasonably integrated in a regional global technological constellation.

In the early 1980s VHS tapes typically had handwritten covers setting up an explicit pirate surface, while popular audio tapes were dominated by the T-series/regional music aesthetic. The T-series innovation of pre-release advance copies of well-known film scores drew liberally from the main title of the film released. In the case of *Hum Aap Ke Hain Kaun*, T-series pre-released its version of the sound tracks before the official release by the Gramophone Company of India. The T-series cover had the titles of the songs, while the inlay cards had *Hum Aap Ke Hain Kaun*'s movie stars from a previous title with T-series, a classic T-series tactic.[45] Widespread version recording perfected this technique across all media registers, forcing companies to join the market themselves by the 1990s, lowering costs by using cheaper media (tapes and then CDs), and then copying the design of version recording releases. While media companies theorized this transition as an effort to move into different market segments, it reflected a certain anxiety as mainstream production sought to enter domains monopolized by pirate production. What was the cultural fault line of propriety, the border between legal and non-legal?

In the 1990s when pirate distribution and reproduction of mainstream film and music releases was localized, the differences between the original and its copy were twofold; the latter typically preceded the original release, and was marked by a modest cover screen printed or even handwritten as in the case of VHS. By 2002 the entry of larger players in the pirate business took mainstream releases away from the locality but the quality of the cover and the disk improved substantially. Digital printing and cardboard designs came in, and camera prints (a phenomenon of early piracy) now declined, with more high-quality reproductions coming in from Dubai and Pakistan. While the hierarchy of master disk and copy has remained in the pirate market, it is something that has been subject to considerable techno-cultural flux after 2000. In the past decade shopkeepers in Palika Bazaar and Lajpat Rai market in the old city prided themselves on classifying the original and the pirate. Pirate CDs were distinguished not just by their early release time and their slim cover, but by a particular holographic sheen emitted by lower quality disks. These identification techniques of pirate media have been seized upon by the enforcement industry, which has on its websites and publicity literature similar divisions between pirate and legal, focusing almost entirely on the surface and the quality of the disk. Anti-piracy websites produce detailed images of pirate and original label covers that verge on the simulacral, marking colors and design types.[46]

For the industry piracy emerged as the perceived culture of the urban edge, inflected with a certain materiality that ranks it different from the brand. This edge space is partly seen as functional with the pirate surface, a reference to the over-informationalized and tacky designs and the lower quality of inlay cards and CD covers. This perception carries over to sections of the media

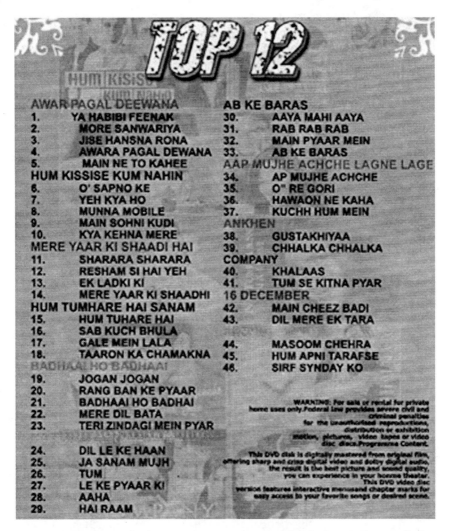

Figure 3.1 The Pirate Surface, version one. A typical label of a music compilation from various Hindi film numbers, sold in a neighborhood store. The quality is basic and functional, suggesting local production and distribution.

Source: Sarai Archive.

industry who actually sell to the pirate market along with legal releases. This happens in the case of a flop or very simply for tax evasion purposes. In an interview with media researcher Ankur Khanna, Megha Ghai of Mukta Arts candidly described this process allegedly followed by a rival company Eros:

So Eros releases limited copies of the official DVD (as per the contract), as well as larger numbers of the pirated version which are priced at one-fourth the cost of the official DVD. Special care is taken to ensure that the pirated DVD possesses all the characteristics of what is perceived to be the prototypical pirated disc. In other words, an attempt is made to deliberately downgrade the packaging of the disc so that it subscribes to a certain notion of a pirated disc cover, soft sleeves (as opposed to a hard case) containing high grade colour printouts of original disc covers. The disc itself is of exactly the same quality as that of the original, but Eros makes huge profits selling these self-pirated discs primarily because they don't pay tax on it; and because they can muscle out other competitors in the piracy market through the quality of the disc, and by the sheer velocity and range of their distribution network.[47]

Media capital, fragile in its domains, also tries to enter the edge through a local aesthetic.

Surfaces and objects

In the well-known opening lines of the *Mass Ornament* Siegfried Kracauer suggested that it was in the surface of things that the secrets of mass culture lay buried. In Kracauer's phenomenology of everyday life in the city, the world of surfaces – shop windows, photographs, movie halls, hotel lobbies, objects of mass culture, advertising, street signs – all disclose the secret consciousness of modern life. Walter Benjamin went even further in his Artwork essay (1969, p.221), suggesting that this encounter of surface, technology and urban life was experienced as an exhilarating and "tremendous shattering," disrupting tradition and the stability of the classical bourgeois subject.

The crowding of surfaces after the arrival of the media city to Delhi may initially suggest a similar exercise to that of Kracauer's. For here too the mass production of images and things grew in the context of urban crisis; the crowded image culture of the post-globalization era mobilized spectacle, advertising, and intensified circulation. While Kracauer and Benjamin had referenced photography and cinema, post-media Indian cities articulated both of those forms in a larger constellation of print forms and technological objects like cassettes, television, and later phones and computers. While this suggests a far more dramatic transformation, there is little evidence to suggest that the change worked through a head-on shattering of traditional forms of image making and reproduction, as Benjamin's essay seemed to indicate.[48] Pirate modernity was a supremely post-binary cultural technology. Here arrangements of images and typefaces evoked a range of emotions – erotic, cultic, ecstatic, fearful, distracted, religious, devotional. Cassette and VCD covers that symbolized this new mode drew from conventions of calendar art, film posters, popular advertising, signage, to feed into the corporeal economy of emotions and things. As surfaces were crowded with new arrangements of image and text, objects (CDs and cassettes, television screens) and built forms (walls, lamp-posts) attracted new transformations of surface.

The cassette and CD covers cover a wide range of what can be heuristically clubbed as a "pirate aesthetic" (Larkin, 2004). I shall take up three of these forms. The first type of covers ranged from the straightforward counterfeits of mainstream film and audio releases, to local productions. In the early period when cover production was somewhat decentralized, the design was fairly basic; the main motive was to get the release to time with the official release. Since 2000 the covers have moved to sophisticated design – a product of the increasing centralization of pirate master CDs along with the packaging. The assembled CD/cover remains a slot below that of the official release deliberately, as the interview with Megha Ghai shows, to mark the object as a pirate, though this is sometimes confused with the original by customers. In another type, Mp3 and VCD compression technologies combined with a host of new singers to produce a collection, where a large number of songs and a cluster of films were bundled into one release. These were lucrative, popular, and were not always subject to the time pressures of the pirate copy of the mainstream release. These collections enjoyed huge popularity and developed their own aesthetic. The audio cover consisted of a basic digital reproduction of the singer's photo in a montage with other elements, and text combined with images. The back cover was an index card of titles available for the perusal of the discriminating customer. VCD collections included disks that combined three film releases in one, videos of film, seasonal music, remixes, and ones with explicit lyrics. In many designs pirate covers carried traces of their regional geography outside India. In the early years a large number of mainstream film releases came from the USA or Dubai, but in recent years the bulk of such releases are attributed in the design to Sadaf Electronics in Pakistan, a well-known firm in Karachi's Rainbow Center.[49]

The third type of CD cover came from regional music genres with a local star system. Here the arrangement of text and image followed a convention where the photos of the singer are placed in a design montage with a heavy emphasis on textual information including the singer's mobile phone number. In 2006, researcher Khadeeja Arif tracked[50] the journey of singers Tasleem and Asif, who specialize in producing a new form of Islamic devotional music (*Muqabla-E-Quawalli*) with a liberal use of remixed tunes. Tasleem first went to Bombay where he tried to make it as a star and failed, but later hit success when he finally returned to Delhi and set up his troupe. The troupe has released numbers from T-series and Rk music. The CDs are distributed in the old city areas of Delhi, and the Muslim pilgrimage sites of northern India. The cover design consists of a montage that carefully balances the photos of the shrine with the signature of the singer.

For Tasleem the VCD exists in broader constellation of fan communion, recognition and access to the singer.

Figure 3.2 The Pirate Surface, version two. A current release Hindi film compilation in a DVD originating from the Pakistani company Sadaf, bought in a Delhi weekly market. Notice the higher quality label, though the DVD quality is often uneven.

Source: Sarai Archive.

In the era of the audio cassettes, when our fans heard us, they liked our music but they could not see us. VHS solved this problem to some extent, but VHS was not available everywhere, so fans could not connect with us easily. The VCD's solved this. Now, when fans see their favorite singer singing they also want to meet them in person and listen to them live. That's why they call us for public performances. And, by publishing our numbers/addresses onto a cover, it is easy for them to write to us and contact us and tell us what they want to hear and what they are not interested in.[51]

In this sense the CD cover is the medium through which the artist and fan imagine and recognize each other. The sensory dimension of this is crucial as the cover is not simply an ocular device; it combines commerce, devotion, and communication in a never-ending loop. The fans do not "write" to Tasleem, they simply call him on his mobile phone.[52]

The pirate surface therefore rested in a particular corporeal economy of emotions and things – assuming a tactile movement of the city dweller between touch, vision and the operation of media objects. In short, the surface of the media object was not simply a window that exposed a broader set of exchanges on subjectivity and representation. The surface "bled" into multiple media objects (CDs, cassettes, video tapes) and screens (TV, computer, mobile phone) deploying its concentration of commerce and information, to produce a space of apperception that paralleled the street signs of the city. The television screen was a significant site of this circulation.

From the late 1980s Indian companies were selling technologies that allowed local cable operators to insert neighborhood advertising in film and video releases. This technology became fairly refined by the 1990s, producing a cluttered viewing screen. Local cable channels run by the operator had running advertisements in pirate film releases, and even TV shows. This informationalized, overcommodified frame of video transgressed the classic rules of disembodied television spectatorship which used to separate the commercial from the main feature. The crowding of the TV screen with moving information and advertising in US and Indian TV networks in the past years was actually introduced through pirate video in India way back in the 1990s. Advertisements[53] are inserted in various layers of the commodities journey from its origin to its final destination. Viewers trained their senses to adjust to the cable video screen cluttered with moving local advertising, the price of partaking in the pirate aesthetic. The claustrophobic space of the screen existed in a force field with crowded urban spaces in the city, producing a periodic warping of the media experience.[54]

The commodified mingling of surfaces and objects recognizes no limits today: paper flyers inserted in local newspapers delivered to homes, television channels that implore their viewers to call in on shows or text their opinion, impossible-to-remove stickers on walls and newspapers, sms and text solicitations. This is a hypermedia zone that presumes an active anthropology of the

Figure 3.3 The Media Surface – a television monitor playing Muslim devotional music at a street corner store near the Nizamuddin shrine in New Delhi in 2001. The clutter of information on this television screen has become the signature of TV in general today.

Source: Sarai Archive.

senses – of readers, consumers, viewers, participants. Piracy was clearly the wild zone of this constellation; sometimes occupying center stage as in the 1980s and then moving at times to the edge, as in recent years when the media corporations moved rapidly to try to discipline and stabilize the arrangements of space and image through authorized sites like malls and multiplexes. Piracy's disruptions ranged from media property, secular cultural arrangements, older image economies, media distribution, stardom, and consumption – the very fabric of urban social life. The a-spectacular nature of the pirate zone is the key to the corporeal constellation. Piracy set up a zone of attractions that drew from the vernacular to the modern, from the regional to the more mainstream cultural fare.

Piracy's law

In 2002 Rakesh Kumar was researching the growth of Palika Bazaar, Delhi's well-known media market. On October 22 Kumar was witness to a remarkable incident – a massive raid by officials of the Delhi Economic Offences Wing (EOW) along with Court-appointed commissioners[55] and private enforcement agents. Palika was well known as Delhi's most significant center for pirate video distribution, dreaded by all enforcement agents as a site of violent conflicts between local shopkeepers and copyright raiders. "No one ever left Palika without getting beaten up," an enforcement agent told me in 2002. Palika was an underground market with crowded, labyrinthine passageways, complex shop morphologies where one legal entity would split up into many sub-shops, and a strong local association of video dealers. All this made an anti-piracy raid into Palika a dreaded experience. On that day in 2002 when Kumar went about his usual fieldwork rounds, he suddenly heard loud shouts – a large, well-organized raiding party had arrived, and proceeded to seize "infringing" material in the market's M block. This is what Kumar wrote in his diary for that day:

> Within few minutes it was completely houseful in the central hall. Barring a few like me the rest were all shopkeepers and their respective staff. Suddenly some one from the hall whistled, which was followed by voices like "maro sale ko, iski bahan . . . [curses] And with this people started moving towards the stairs which was seized by the *dandadharis* [Crime Branch R.S]. They started pushing the police personnel which resulted in a little *lathi* charge. Since the policemen had already cornered the crowd in both the entry points, it was difficult for them to reach at the point of action.
>
> The raiding party then began leaving with the seized materials. . . . Here again the crowd started shouting against the raiding party. It became difficult for them to move out from the crowd (around 300 people). So finally they kept out their revolvers. Though the crowd seemed to disperse for that moment, but within a few seconds they started abusing the raiding party and pelting glasses and bottles on them.
>
> (Kumar, 2002a)

The Palika Bazaar report was by no means unusual in the loud[56] "war against piracy." Incidents like the one in Palika refracted in different parts of the country in media markets and neighborhoods that saw raids[57] against shops, small factories, and roadside stalls for a variety of trademark and copyright infringements. The raid was the significant ingredient in a complex web of anti-piracy campaigns, where the idea of formal resolution in lawcourts was seen as a near impossibility by most in the enforcement business. As we will see, enforcement's law is neither about judgment, nor even about discipline in the classic sense.

On October 4, 2006 the film industry's trade magazine *Screen* carried a rather innocuous story that a sessions court in Mumbai had sentenced two persons for video piracy for six months, and also ordered a fine of Rs 55,000 ($1400) on each of the accused. The conviction was based on information provided by the Motion Pictures Association and the IPR wing of the crime branch. By itself this story was not remarkable; it could stand in for any everyday story from the legal war against piracy. What stood out was the comment by the counsel of the MPA, Mr. Chander Lall of the firm Lall and Sethi, that this was but the third copyright case he had won and this was but the *fifth* conviction in India for piracy of all the cases combined.[58]

Despite India's stringent anti-copyright laws,[59] anti-piracy convictions have been modest. This is also in spite of a growing enforcement regime with easy access to the police, a sympathetic media, and elites publicly committed to intellectual property. The contemporary infrastructure of enforcement rests on *four* interrelated layers. At the apex is a constellation of legal firms including those like Lall and Sethi, which tend to be largely based in Delhi. Along with the media elites and the vast tribe of consultants, the IP law firm occupies the public face of neoliberal globalization in India. Confident and with increasing access to government and corporate power, law firms provide inputs into public policy while simultaneously representing international and local corporate clients. This conflict-of-interest situation is a remarkable shift from the 1950s when public policy was typically framed by elite but independent Nehruvian technocrats and academics. At any rate, the law firms act as advocacy groups for the international IP regime, they lobby bureaucrats, organize workshops for police personnel and judges on IP law, and top lawyers make regular appearances on television news shows. The *second* and probably the crucial layer enforcement is the field detective agency. These are usually small firms with a high turnover of field operatives who may have an army or police background, or in some case even be former pirates themselves. The third layer is the local police, and the specialized Economic Offences Wing (EOW) which is equivalent to the Crime Branch with city-wide jurisdiction. EOW conducts *suo-moto* (on its own) raids as well as on tips provided by detective agencies and law firms. The final layer is the court system which falls into lower or session's court, the High Court, and then the Supreme Court.

Law firms are retained by their clients who may be the overseas MPA with offices in Hong Kong and Delhi or local Indian media companies or distributors, who pool together money to limit piracy of a current release. In addition, detective agencies may be hired by medium distributors, detectives also double up for trademark cases. T-series has a very active and fairly aggressive enforcement wing,[60] as has the Indian Music Association, which hires well-known policemen to run its anti-piracy campaigns. Copyright holders grant power-of-attorney (POA) to enforcement agencies who act on their behalf in prosecuting cases. The spawning of this new breed of professional complainants (who are also private investigators/musclemen),[61] involves a significant move in the way the law conceptualizes the "complainant"/"victim" and has for the most part gone unnoticed in legal discourse.

Simultaneously with the release of a film, the enforcers pick areas and shops and conduct raids on their own if appointed as Special Commissioners by the Court or work with the EOW to conduct raids. They are sometimes witnesses in raids conducted by the police. On occasion, they also

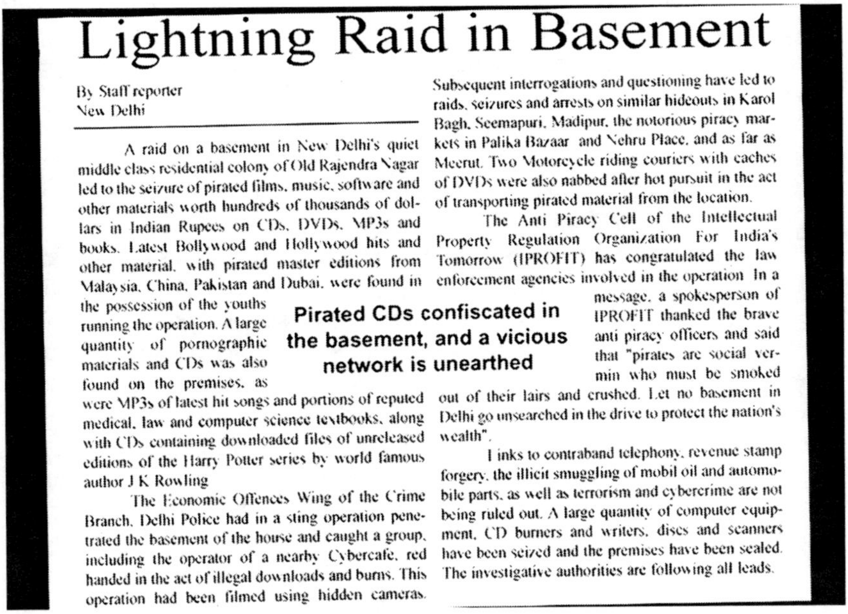

Lightning Raid in Basement

By Staff reporter
New Delhi

A raid on a basement in New Delhi's quiet middle class residential colony of Old Rajendra Nagar led to the seizure of pirated films, music, software and other materials worth hundreds of thousands of dollars in Indian Rupees on CDs, DVDs, MP3s and books. Latest Bollywood and Hollywood hits and other material, with pirated master editions from Malaysia, China, Pakistan and Dubai, were found in the possession of the youths running the operation. A large quantity of pornographic materials and CDs was also found on the premises, as were MP3s of latest hit songs and portions of reputed medical, law and computer science textbooks, along with CDs containing downloaded files of unreleased editions of the Harry Potter series by world famous author J K Rowling

The Economic Offences Wing of the Crime Branch, Delhi Police had in a sting operation penetrated the basement of the house and caught a group, including the operator of a nearby Cybercafe, red handed in the act of illegal downloads and burns. This operation had been filmed using hidden cameras.

Pirated CDs confiscated in the basement, and a vicious network is unearthed

Subsequent interrogations and questioning have led to raids, seizures and arrests on similar hideouts in Karol Bagh, Seemapuri, Madipur, the notorious piracy markets in Palika Bazaar and Nehru Place, and as far as Meerut. Two Motorcycle riding couriers with caches of DVDs were also nabbed after hot pursuit in the act of transporting pirated material from the location.

The Anti Piracy Cell of the Intellectual Property Regulation Organization For India's Tomorrow (IPROFIT) has congratulated the law enforcement agencies involved in the operation In a message, a spokesperson of IPROFIT thanked the brave anti piracy officers and said that "pirates are social vermin who must be smoked out of their lairs and crushed. Let no basement in Delhi go unsearched in the drive to protect the nation's wealth".

Links to contraband telephony, revenue stamp forgery, the illicit smuggling of mobil oil and automobile parts, as well as terrorism and cybercrime are not being ruled out. A large quantity of computer equipment, CD burners and writers, discs and scanners have been seized and the premises have been sealed. The investigative authorities are following all leads.

Figure 3.4 The ubiquitous, repetitive headline of the anti-piracy campaign, creatively transformed into part of an artwork on piracy.

Source: "The Network Of No_des" Sarai Media Lab 2003, ISEA 2003.

perform a vigilante role, conducting "raids" and confiscating articles while masquerading as policemen. Periodically stories surface in the press of extortion rackets involving enforcement agencies, real and counterfeit.[62]

I met my first enforcement agent in 2002, at his office in South Delhi.[63] I had been witness to a raid in Nehru Place in 1998, but at that time the raid was led by the Crime Branch (EOW), the whole place was in complete turbulence with street stallholders running to pack up their wares and shutters closing down. In fact I saw no detective agent at that time in fact; only later did I gather from a shopkeeper that detective agencies worked with the police in raids. In contrast to the smooth discourse of elite IP lawyers, field investigators in enforcement agencies are more open to franker discussions on the state of piracy. The investigator moves in the tense interface zone between the neighborhood/market, the Court, and the media industry. Field investigators are often the derided subaltern foot soldiers of the anti-piracy conflict. They face physical assaults during raids, and are forced to undertake incessant court visits as complainants in cases. In addition, they are saddled with a media industry client base that tends to be parsimonious and erratic with payments. It is a frustrating life, with constant travel and stress in a murky world of hustle, intimidation and payoffs, and the lower investigators leave in an average of two years.

The investigators' role took on an increasing significance after the Nagoti judgment of 1996[64] which made seizures of pirated goods easier even in the absence of the original copyright holder. This enabled a more proactive stance on the part of both the police and the enforcement agencies. The detective agencies worked with IP law firms (and the police) to try and seal all the spots they felt were causing piracy: airports where couriers were thought to arrive, media markets like Palika Bazaar, Nehru Place, Lajpat Rai market in Delhi, National Market in Bangalore, Lamington Road in Bombay, neighborhood factories and local shops. Interviews with investigators reveal incessant travel to large and small towns, even suburban villages. Wherever investigators reached there were conflicts – with shopkeepers, local police, and in some cases local politicians. At every step of the journey the pirates were actually ahead of the enforcers. Shops that were closed down due to raids reappeared in a few weeks, new pirate factories and courier systems emerged, while older ones melted away. Cases kept collapsing, producers lost interest after a few weeks of a film's release and faded away, and police charge sheets were often badly filed, given the confusion between original and duplicate media. It could even be the lack of knowledge of copyright law provisions, which led to technical errors on the part of the police. These narratives are in contrast to the stories of raids every day in the papers and on TV with spectral statistics and seized goods. These reports, put out by enforcement PR agenc.es' evoke nothing but scorn from field investigators. One agent, a veteran with ten years experience, told me in bitter exasperation that "stopping piracy was simply impossible."

From the outset investigators tried to make sense of a media landscape that produced neither classic criminal subjects, nor classic criminal acts. The more investigators entered the pirate zone, the more they were subject to its plasticity and dispersal – the scrambled social landscape of fast-moving technologies, mutating networks, and general public indifference, if not active hostility to ant piracy drives. They had to unpack the cultural puzzles of the original and the fake, and that of legitimate manufacturer and pirate, something that became increasingly difficult over the years, since small CD factories produced for anyone who paid them. Detectives faced hostility from the local neighborhood police (whose revenues anti-piracy undercut), and even sometimes from the central Crime Branch which held the enforcement profession in low esteem.[65] Pirates played a cat-and-mouse game with detectives; at any rate, given the network internationalism of piracy and the national limits of enforcement, copy networks were always ahead in the speed of delivery, almost matching the simultaneous time of high-profile releases. The biggest problem was of course that piracy lacked clear boundaries, spilling into legal factories and shops – something that made detection a nightmare.[66] The detective agencies were also drawn into periodic inter-pirate competition, and counter-tactics against enforcement. A now retired enforcer for the MPA, talked in an interview about the confusing and murky world of "enforcement":

In India there were some guys who from the beginning were doing the authorized reproduction of cassettes and CDs and were also pirates. So by the time we found them out a good amount of damage was done because they had inroads into us and that began some kind of a competition among the pirates, because one pirate would pay our investigators not to have his premises raided, he would allow a raid maybe once in six months but he would give information about his competitors, the other pirates so that firstly the competitor is harmed and this guy gains his business and guy also grows. We tried to put an end to it, by the time we realized it some of our investigators were also double agents getting money from them also as well as from us.[67]

As the raids began to accelerate, the affected parties launched counter cases against investigators for violence and extortion, in some cases the larger pirate operators persuaded the local police to arrest detectives. Consider this story in the *Indian Express*:

The film industry's attempts to stop video piracy have suffered an embarrassing setback after a raid on a suspected pirate ended with members of the raiding party being arrested by local police and charged with trespass and extortion. . . . The story begins with a raid on a house in Jangpura on Sunday morning, where 400 pirated VCDs were recovered. The disclosure pointed to a manufacturing unit in Kundli, Haryana, owned by Mahinder Batla. Owner of a company Lara Music, Batla's two DVD and VCD manufacturing units are worth nearly Rs 10 crores and was set-up three years ago. When a raiding party comprising private investigators of the Motion Pictures Association and the Delhi police reached there, they searched the premises for nearly three hours before the local police arrived on the scene. They accused the team of "planting the pirated tapes" and arrested seven people on grounds of trespass and extortion. Six people were released the next morning; one of the investigators, Vikram Singh, is still under arrest.

(Jain, 2001)

Neighborhood hostility has been a major impediment for raids. When cable operators were raided for showing current film releases, detectives usually first targeted the local control room of the cable operator, only to find it locked. The operators began ingeniously using either a person's home or a moving vehicle to relay current film broadcasts on the local channel. Here is the same retired detective again; this long excerpt gives a sense of the tactics employed at the neighborhood level:

Cable operators always have one or two of their own channels in which as they say that the demand is very strong from our clients show the latest films. So we try and raid them but it is very difficult because we have to try and raid them in those 2–3 hours that the movie is being shown; in that time to know yes they are showing it, then to get the police, then to reach there it is tough. Then you have to reach that place where it is being aired from you know that particular place where the DVD is kept, the control room, then the cable operators have become very smart, they have started broadcasting not from the control room they will do it from a location away from there what is called the reverse something (signaling) which meant that they had one cable running from the control room along with the hundreds of wires running to several houses, one of them was running to room lets say 100 to 200 meters away where a DVD player is there and through this cable actually feed was coming in, from there input would come in and go again to all other outputs. But we couldn't make out which cable it was! Sometimes they would do it in a moving vehicle, and it's got a DVD player connected and if the raiding party comes they have just got to disconnect the cable and flee. This was very difficult to catch unless we had insider information; there was no way to know where this Reverse Signal was coming from.[68]

A typical raid cycle on a small shop or factory took the following journey. The raid would be conducted by the EOW either by themselves or with lawyers and detectives. If suspicious material was found it would be seized and taken to the police station. The seizures would be recorded, and an FIR would be filed. The arrested parties got bail in a few days or weeks, and were soon back in business. The next stage in the case would be for the defense to demand return of the seized material. As the case dragged further, media industry representatives would lose interest or stop paying the lawyers; some of the complainants (i.e. detectives no longer on the rolls of the company) would drop out; the case would become part of the huge backlog of the system.

Very soon the legal firms realized that more important than winning a judgment was preventing the copy network from releasing films in the cable/neighborhood market at the time of a major release. This led to the strategy of persuading courts to give temporary injunctions, ex-parte, an injunction issued as an interim measure, without the presence of the other side of the dispute. Given the rapid depreciation in value of the media commodity over time, winning a temporary injunction in copyright matters is often the most crucial part of the battle. Law firms have preferred to approach more sympathetic High Courts for such injunctions. In contrast, courts subordinate to the Delhi High Court (i.e. the District Courts and the Courts of the Civil Judges below the District Courts) have been more circumspect in granting such injunctions. As a general rule, lower courts have fewer discretionary powers than the High Court. While this is not the case in the granting of temporary Injunctions, lower courts tend to apply the requirements of the law more stringently, and allow ex-parte ad-interim injunctions only in rare cases.

Once parties have secured the protection of an interim injunction, the strategy is merely to exploit the delays in the system, to extend the injunction for as long as possible. By the time the cases come to trial, the material often has little financial value to either party.[69] With some minor exceptions, the trend has been out-of-court settlements, as lawyers and industry clients are worn out by the proliferation of cases.[70]

The lawyer Chander Lall once suggested that Indian piracy, unlike Chinese piracy, was akin to a cottage industry – it was small scale, and dispersed among shops and neighborhoods. Although this proposition has been contested by most field investigators,[71] Lall's suggestion highlights the inherent problem of collapsing pirate practices on to a particular space or practice. Piracy as an economic network is inherently dispersed, with procurement, production, packaging, and distribution redistributed at different points in the chain. Give this, it became impossible to produce piracy's criminality in court, despite a strong public campaign in the media.

In the event, the encounter of "enforcement" with piracy produced contradictory results. On the one hand, players like T-series enforce an informal licensing regime on shops carrying their media, through a mixture of intimidation and threat,[72] while loss-making media companies sell to the pirate distribution market after a few months.

The parasitic, adaptive mode that piracy set up made it difficult to produce it as a clear "outside." The emergence of the raid was an acknowledgment of the viral nature of piracy. The raid attempted to manage the swarm-through tactics that were like filters and temporary firewalls, slowing down the endless circulation of pirate media through pincer-like violence, and securing temporary injunctions in court. As I have shown, these actions were limited and temporary, giving way to new pirates and new raids. *Piracy was a profound infection machine*, taking on a life in heterogeneous spaces, and overcoming all firewalls.

For the media industry the dominant strategy seems to be that of a dream-escape from the pirate city to secure zones of authorized consumption – malls, multiplexes and online stores. Direct-to-air (DTH) is now promoted for more elite customers as part of this strategy of escape from the pirate city. Piracy's non-linear architectures and radical distribution strategy rendered space as a bad object; the media industry's yearning for secure consumption ghettos is in many ways an impossible return to the old post-Fordist days.

Imitation, dispersal and the fear of the many

Twentieth-century movements of proliferation and urban circulation combine the movements of modern capitalist commodities, money, and media. In the first response to this phenomenon in Europe in the 1920s money was seen as performing a dual role with "massification," the destruction of classical bourgeois autonomy while bringing millions into the circuit of exchange and monetization. In its desire to proliferate endlessly, money drew even more

Raid Map 2002

Delhi Raid Map 2003

Figure 3.5 The expansion of anti-piracy raids in Delhi's neighborhoods, 2002 and 2003.

Source: Bhagwati Prasad, Sarai Archive.

commodities into the circuit of exchange, while destroying the free "exchange of things and people" (Marx). Seriality or the doctrine of the similar was seen as emerging from this language of money. The community of the many became subordinate to the logic of the same. This, dialectic of money, massification, and crisis of the classical bourgeois individual roughly summarizes the early commentaries on the urban subject that emerged from German modernism, Simmel, Adorno, and even Kraceauer. In the work of Elias Canneti's brilliant *Crowds and Power*, this doctrine of the senses is complicated further in times of capitalist crisis. Massified by money, but impoverished by capitalist crisis, the many became the one in the figure of the crowd. The loss of autonomy is reversed in the expansion of the power of the crowd, as that which was the same becomes the many, a potential force threatens the order of the capitalist city.

Piracy is that practice of proliferation following the demise of the classic crowd mythic of modernism. Piracy exists in commodified circuits of exchange, only here the same disperses into the many. Dispersal into viral swarms is the basis of pirate proliferation, disappearance into the hidden abodes of circulation is the secret of its success and the distribution of profits in various points of the network. Piracy works within a circuit of production, circulation, and commerce that also simultaneously suggests many time zones – Virlio's near-instantaneous time of light, the industrial cycle of imitation and innovation, the retreat of the commodity from circulation and its re-entry as a newer version. Media piracy's proximity to the market aligns it to both the speed of the global (particularly in copies of mainstream releases) and also the dispersed multiplicities of vernacular and regional exchange.

In her work on copying in early cinema Jane Gaines writes,

> Copying literally followed the first logic of the motion picture apparatus itself, which is, "to produce is to reproduce." Stories crossed national boundaries shipped in cans, duplication factories were hooked up to the beginnings of distribution routes, only barely imagined as the global networks they would become.
>
> (2006, pp.237–238)

Gaines' story is remarkably similar to many techniques of copying in India which follow the logic of the formal economy, in print, in music, and in film. In cinema the pirate market follows the journey of the film closely; if a film does well at the box-office, the more likely are the pirate editions and supplements. Like in Gaines' 100-year-old story, speed is central to the race between distributor and pirate. Just as distributors now plaster the market with many prints produced in simultaneous time, so pirates release camera print prequels, and high-quality sequels. The race between industry and copier is a small part of piracy's trajectory. The larger story is one of endless imitative frenzy, media companies copying each other, and remixed versions in local music and cinema. While media companies fight it out in court, outside copyright a vast cultural universe of regional cinemas, recensions, re-releases and remixes are produced. "True copies" of the original are filtered through the "noise of the real" (Gaines), pirates cut longer films, insert advertisements, and sometimes add censored scenes. Each version becomes a new one, with camera print⁻ in the first release, advertisements in the next, and hundreds of versions of popular film and audio hits.[73] This proliferation of near-copies, remastered versions, and revisions refract across a range of time–space shifts, moving between core and periphery of the media city phenomenologically, rather than spatially. Versions of popular numbers are produced by the pirate market, fade from the big city and return in devotional music, local videos from Bihar, Haryana, and Western UP – and back to the city, brought by migrants and travelers. Piracy does not dwell only in objects or spaces, it enacts them momentarily. Its materiality consists in its mix of place, time, and thing, a mix that dissolves and reconstitutes itself regularly. Piracy *an sich* seems to have no end, just as it had no particular point of beginning.[74] Piracy therefore produces a surplus of cultural code, which fractures the surfaces of media spectacle through a tactic of dispersal.

As a phenomenon that works on a combination of speed, recirculation, and dispersal, pirate products are consumed by the possibility of their disappearance – by more imitations and versions. This is a constant anxiety in small electronic enterprises; the first past the post stays there for only a few months. New copies follow, from rivals and former collaborators.[75] The doctrine of the many is haunted by its own demise – all the time. Just as Marx once wrote that the only limit to capital is capital itself, so piracy is the only agent that can abolish piracy.[76]

4   Death and the accident

Daily life is becoming a kaleidoscope of incidents and accidents, catastrophes and cataclysms, in which we are endlessly running up against the unexpected, which occurs out of the blue, so to speak.

(Paul Virilio, Foreword to the *Museum of Accidents* (2002))

[The] motor car with its retinue of wounded and dead, its trail of blood, is all that remains of everyday life, its paltry ration of excitement and hazard.

(Henri Lefebvre in *Every Day Life in the Modern World* (1971, p.101))

In the early days of globalization, the Hindi writer and poet Uday Prakash wrote a short story titled *Paul Gomra ka Scooter* (2002),[1] which was a bleak prognosis on the coming years in Delhi. In Prakash's story, we enter the world of Ram Gopal Saxena, a subeditor and hopeful poet in a newspaper office whose life is overturned by the new commodity world circulating through media images. This was an experience common to many city dwellers in the early 1990s. Late at night Saxena watched a television commercial of a scooter with a jungle theme, where a tribal boy discovers a scooter in the jungle and rides off with it in wonder. At this moment Saxena goes into a dream state, where primitivist fantasy merges with the technological, and he wakes up with the decision to change his name to Paul Gomra so that he can stand out in the crowd ("the opposite of Gregor Samsa in Kafka's story"). Reborn as Paul Gomra, and exhausted by long journeys on the public bus, he decides to go in for a private vehicle, a Bajaj scooter. The new scooter arrives and is immediately seen as possessing fetishistic powers of Nature itself:

the green color, very light, like the brand new shoots of a tree. Newborn innate, natural. . . . The scooter was an extension of nature itself. . . . Every piece of it, each and every part, was made from the metal that had been pulled out of the womb of the earth in the form of iron ore. The rubber used in making it came from the resin that trickled day and night from trees in Udipi. . . . The fuel that gave this scooter its motion was what else if not petroleum, a carbonized, liquid form of trees that had

transformed over thousands of years in the natural fire and geothermal
heat of the earth's womb.

(Prakash, 2002, p.155)

It is significant that Gomra chose a Bajaj scooter, a nationalist technological
icon. Almost like a modern shaman, Gomra summons the magical powers
of Nature in the scooter to lead the fight against globalization and "con-
sumerism." The main reason soon emerges; it is to escape the daily commute
from his office to the Delhi suburb of Ghaziabad, where Gomra lives. That
journey is a cruel one:

> Over the past six or seven years the number of dudhwalas, sabziwalas,
> babus, workers and labourers who commuted between Ghaziabad and
> Delhi had grown so much that, instead of inside those morning buses,
> most of the passengers hung from outside its doors, roof, footboards,
> rear end and bumper. The unsuccessful, unrecognized and marginalized
> poet Paul Gomra was being dragged day by day from middle to old age,
> and his poor body, full of weariness, age, memories, worries found the
> long bus ride more and more unbearable.
>
> Behind his decision to buy a scooter also lay the time factor, which,
> when applied to his life, frightened Paul Gomra. To go from Ghaziabad
> to ITO Bridge took two hours. To go back took the same amount of
> time. Meaning that, out of every twenty-four hour day, he spent four
> hours in a State Transport bus cheek by jowl with strangers, barely able
> to stand their sweat and gas. . . . If he were to calculate for an entire year,
> he spent fifty two days, that is one month and fifty two days in that bus.
>
> (Prakash, 2002, p.148)

Having bought the scooter Paul Gomra is unable to acquire driving skills;
the Bajaj gathers dust at home. An abortive attempt to learn to drive the
scooter fails, as it turns out that the teacher and local playwright does not
know the skill himself. Then, unable to bear the taunts of his neighbors,
Gomra meets up with a friend, Rajiv Menon, who offers to drive the scooter
for him to his office in central Delhi. Gomra rides as a pillion passenger. In
the event, Gomra's effort to save travel time fails as he has to wait for Menon
to get off work late at night. Gomra spends the time in his office writing
poetry. One day, when returning from a function at the India International
Center where he had denounced the cultural elite of the city, Gomra and
Rajeev Menon meet with an accident on the road. The scooter is smashed,
Rajiv Menon dies, and Gomra is declared insane, spending his time wander-
ing the highway, denouncing the elite.

Throughout the story Prakash provides us with a vivid *mise-en-scène* of
Delhi in the 1990s, the spread of commodity culture, media events, political
scandals, massacres of peasants, and the opportunism of the new elites. At
one level Prakash's use of misogynist images of the commodity as well as the

muted left-nationalist rhetoric in *Paul Gomra* reflect the deep discomfort and trepidation of some of the Hindi cultural elites with globalization and the new commodified city. While *Paul Gomra ka Scooter* does not fully escape this imaginary, Prakash's tale manages to capture a powerful sensibility of everyday life in the 1990s when the city became increasingly organized around the world of travel. In this emerging landscape, the road was the site of traumatic injury as also the dreams of the new: witness the escape of many of Delhi's middle-class citizens towards private transportation from the late 1980s. Danger and life, machine and human, merged in an experience where death on the road, particularly for travelers like Gomra, was a real possibility. Some time from the late 1980s the experience of the road transformed fundamentally: becoming the reference point of constant dread, and everyday stress. Road culture also mobilized new discourses on speed, machines and, an unending flow of images of death, of broken human bodies and crushed machines. The road was equally a site of conflict, between passengers and drivers, bystanders and motor vehicles, between the new urban design of a city of speed and efforts to desperately manage a world of motor-machines that seemed to have lifelike effects: contingency, unpredictability, and excess. Courts, experts, and newspaper editorials all produced new forms of governmental knowledge about safety, flyovers, lane management, bus-drivers, and speed. The road provides a useful allegory of urban life in the 1990s caught between the dream of the new commodity world and the fear of death while circulating in the city.

Travel, a familiar, repetitive experience of the everyday, was now inflected with the feeling of the uncanny. This claustrophobic space was felt most by Delhi's working-class and lower-middle-class population, but fear of the road was generalized in the city. This was what Freud had called the unhomely, which was the "fundamental propensity of the familiar to turn on its owners, to suddenly become defamilarized, derealized, as if in a dream"(cited in Vidler, 1994, p.7). It is its very familiarity that makes the urban uncanny so disturbing. The most troubling part of this in globalizing Delhi was the fear of the road crash.

I remember the first accident I saw in Delhi, in 1983, barely four years after I moved to the city. A friend and I were standing near the All India Radio Building at night, waiting for a bus. This was the 1980s and Delhi became eerily silent at night, reflecting an era before the mass production of private cars. Suddenly, a familiar green and yellow Delhi Transport Corporation (DTC) bus raced towards us ignoring the red traffic light. There was a sickening thud; a cyclist who was crossing the road fell under the bus. I remember blood everywhere when we rushed to the accident, the blue and white rubber slippers of the victim, his blue-and-white pyjamas now sticky-red with blood. The bicycle was twisted beyond recognition. The entire bus had emptied, and from nowhere a small street crowd had gathered, grabbing the driver and marching him to the police station. The bus passengers, mostly middle-class office staff, were concerned with getting home, "not the driver's fault, one of them said." It was to no avail; the driver was dragged away to the police station. My friend and I took the victim to the nearby Willingdon Hospital in an auto-rickshaw, but he was already dead. When we returned still dazed after filling out the complicated forms at the police post in the hospital, the bus was still in the middle of the road. I can still remember that night, and the dead worker-cyclist, the terror of the contingent irrupting upon the calm of the night. In contrast, my memories of the dead on Delhi's roads in the 1990s are imagistic, like a blurred series of discontinuous movie frames. The road memories come as a series of discontinuous shock-images: a dead scooterist on the road, a solitary helmet in a pool of blood, a body with its face covered by a white sheet near the ITO Bridge across the Yamuna River. Almost every day we were assaulted by scenes of death and tragedy on the road. And every time at night when I crossed the Nizamuddin Bridge to east Delhi to return home, there were sights of broken or stalled machines on the highway. It could be a truck with a broken axle, or a goods vehicle with its contents spilled obscenely across the road. Every friend seemed to have lost someone in a road accident: families of two-wheelers and cyclists waited anxiously for their return home in the evening. It was a feeling of generalized anxiety and dread, a schizophrenic disturbance at a time when the city was experiencing an economic boom. In his work on schizophrenia, Roger Caillois spoke of a fear of being eaten up by space. "To these dispossessed souls," writes Caillois,

> space seems to be a devouring force. Space pursues them, encircles them, digests them in a gigantic phagocytosis. It ends by replacing them. Then the body separates itself from thought, the individual breaks the boundary of his skin and occupies the other side of his senses. . . . And he invents space of which he is "the convulsive possession."
>
> (cited in Vidler, 1994, p.174)

It is this convulsive desire to possess space that may account for the rapid migration of vast numbers of Delhi's middle class to the motor car. Spurred by cheaper car prices, and easier financial credit access, Delhi soon became the city with more cars than all the major metros put together. The city's vehicles had expanded from half a million in 1980, to 1.8 million in 1990 to 1991, and 4.1 million in 2003 to 2004.[2] The car boom was centered on the Maruti-Suzuki 800 "family" car, but later diversified into a range of other models as the market differentiated. Along with the growth of private cars came all the features of "automobility": legal and non-legal repair infrastructures, specialized advertising, and road networks (Urry, 2004). Car ownership went hand in hand with modern notions of economic success, sexualized images of consumption and desire, and an abstract ideal of freedom from the road. At one level the commute was, as Henri Lefebvre (1971) pointed out, "constrained time" that throttled the vibrancy of the everyday, but it allowed the driver/owner to consume space outside in the relative comfort of the car. In her excellent book on postwar France, Kristin Ross points to how the Renault 4CV (not unlike the Maruti 800) became the emblem of a domesticated French middle-class drive to consumption. Yet the car was both domesticated space as well as an anti-domestic one – a home away from home. It was a place of imaginary freedom. "With the actual decline in mobility brought about by mass car consumption, the inviolate shell of the car can still provide, though in a weakened form, the liberty from social constraint that speed once promised to provide" (Ross, 1996, p.55). This promise of freedom remained fragile for the car drivers of Delhi for most of the 1990s.[3] Unlike Europe where the system of automobility was well rationalized by the postwar epoch, Delhi in the early 1990s had a diverse range of vehicles: public and chartered buses, lorries, private cars, scooters and motorcycles, auto-rickshaws, motor-cycle taxis called *phat-phatiyas*, cycle-rickshaws in the MCD areas, and larger tempos and some tempo taxis called *vikrams*. All forms of transport went through expansion and/or convulsion in the 1990s, with crowded roads, and middle-class campaigns in the Court to regulate and standardize this diversity. Private cars have had to contend with low average speeds, traffic breakdowns, and stoppages due to accidents.

"A city made for speed is made for success," wrote Le Corbusier in *The City of Tomorrow* (1978, p.375). Le Corbusier's appeal to organize the modern city around the logic of speed had a profound influence on postwar urban design. The Athens Charter had linked the demand for strict zoning with easy traffic circulation.[4] The idea of a city whose health depends on circulation goes back to early Enlightenment urban design in Europe. Says Richard Sennett,

> Enlightenment planners wanted the city in its very design to function like a healthy body, freely flowing as well as possessed of clean skin. Since the beginning of the Baroque era, urban planners had thought of making cities in terms of efficient circulation of people on the city's main streets. . . . The medical imagery of life-giving circulation gave new meaning to the Baroque emphasis on motion. Instead of planning streets for the sake of ceremonies of moving towards an object, as did the Baroque planner, the Enlightenment planner made motion an end in itself.
>
> (Sennett, 1996, pp.264–265)

In the *Grundrisse* Marx drew links between transportation and the commodification of social life; the circulation of commodities in capitalism produces transformations in systems of accumulation and communication. Endless accumulation is the motor of the system, and as such it opens up the logic of endless *mobility*. The French Revolution, says Paul Virilio (1986), produced "an obligation to mobility." This compulsory mobility, which was the calling of the cosmopolitan individual in the West, also set in motion the logic of violence and displacement in cities, as urban settlements were razed to the ground to make way for roads and highways.

Delhi's transport system had a history that stretched back to the pre-colonial period. The Mughals had set up a road transport system that connected the system to the market towns of the empire, and within the design of Shahjehanabad the road axis connecting the fort revolved around Chandni Cowk and the city gates. In the colonial period after 1857, when Delhi came under direct control of the British, the city began to slowly reorganize by setting up a municipal authority, and new forms of urban governance. A part of this was an urban transportation network that began by widening existing roads and introducing new forms of public transport. While motor cars made their way into the city by the early twentieth century, in 1902 an electric tram system was set up in the walled city, replacing the earlier horse-drawn system.[5] By the time of independence in 1947, Delhi had a motor bus service run by the Gwalior and Northern India Transport Company Ltd. This was taken over by the post-independence government and the Delhi Transport Authority was set up, which became the Delhi Transport Corporation in 1971. For many years the DTC's yellow, silver, and green buses were ubiquitous with public transport. In 1988, faced with a strike by the DTC union, the government opened up the transport sector to private operators, and in 1992 this was formalized under the Redline scheme. Three thousand permits were given to private operators owning fewer than five buses each. This was a well-honored strategy of ensuring the political support of small transport operators in the city; the end result was fragmentation of the fleet and a nightmare for the Transport Department to administer.[6] The shift in Delhi's urban discourse prompted constant changes in the bus system, with a city government fending off criticism from the media and the courts. First, the Redline private bus system was renamed the Blueline to deal with public outrage over road deaths. Following this the entire kilometer scheme under which the private buses operated was abolished in 2002 after the courts insisted that all public transport shift to compressed natural gas (CNG). The Bluelines continued but as "stage carriages." (TERI, 2002). Finally in 2006 the Delhi transport minister announced a move from the small operator-based Blueline system to a model where the bus network would be divided among corporate operators.

From the outset, the Redline/Blueline buses became a reference point for public anger and debate in Delhi as part of the larger discourse on the city in the 1990s. The landscape of the road was set up through images of a permanent state of emergency where both subjects and machines seemed out of control. Traffic breakdowns and deaths opened up the first salvo in the breakdown narrative of the city that reached fever pitch by the early years of the twenty-first century.

One of Paul Virilio's insights has been to show the link between vehicular travel media culture. Virilio argues that mobility is actually suspended with the spread of new media: in this catastrophist reading, the "speed of light" is the *end* of all travel (2005). However, the link made by Virilio between optics, urban life, and transportation helps us understand this side of Delhi's technological culture in the 1990s. Here, debates on speed and road-machines were embedded in a series of profound media effects that moved between everyday events and representation. The growth of machine mobility paralleled urban crisis, and the ecstasies of private vehicle ownership went hand in hand with perceived death-effects of road-machines. From the early 1990s the average number of people killed in traffic accidents in the city every year remained at 2000, and thousands more are injured – the bulk of them the working poor. It is possible to look at the experience of this time through different, some-times conflicting vantage points: the shock of contact with an accelerated technological culture and the traumatic repetitive viewing of public road death, mangled bodies, and media representations of the accident. Most importantly, there emerged a destabilizing confusion of distinctions between the inner psychic world and the public "social," between media "truths" and the urban experience.

The senses on fire

In the summer of 1993, when most of political India was dealing with the fallout from the demolition of the Babri Mosque, Edward Gargan, cor-respondent of the *New York Times in India*, informed his readers of a sense of urban crisis facing the country's capital.

> For the first time, there is a feeling of collapse here, the sense that this capital city – once a way station for Mogul armies, later an exhibition of British town planning by Sir Edwin Lutyens – is finally being over-whelmed by people and traffic and the final crumbling of fragile and inadequate public services.[7]

The report went on to quote Malavika Singh, who was then editor of *Business India*. The city was breaking apart, said Singh: "It's tearing at the seams. There's no power and water. The phones don't work. The bus drivers are mauling human beings as they go by. It is grim."[8] Gargan went on to set up a picture of electricity breakdowns and resultant neighborhood riots and gar-bage everywhere. Most significantly, he reported the presence of widespread "carnage" on the roads with the arrival of the private Redline buses, widely blamed for the deaths. " 'Killer Buses' and 'Killers on the Loose' headlines screamed," wrote Gargan.

The Redline bus scheme which was started as a solution to the public's transport woes soon became the main component of a breakdown narrative that moved across all the new material forms that emerged during the 1990s. The buses became the "Bloodline" in the media, complaints against them filled letters to the editor, and television and print stories. In the same month that the *New York Times* reporter came out with his story Krishan Guruswamy reported,

> [M]any of New Delhi's 11 million residents are beginning to feel that greedy bus owners, reckless drivers and corrupt officials have created a

lethal monster. "Burn them, burn the buses," one woman wailed on television after her child was run over by a bus. The buses bulldoze through
traffic blasting horns that sound like express trains, pushing aside cars
and motor scooters.[9]

From the outset the death rate was high, and fed rapidly into a sense of the
city descending into chaos. At the core of this was the *accident*. Here are two
typical stories from the local reporters of *The Times of India*. The first took
place in October, 2000, almost seven years after the *New York Times* report.
The Redline had now become the Blueline.

> Sunday turned bloody red for Delhi-ites as its killer roads were witness
> to several gruesome accidents. A four-year-old boy and his 29-year-old
> mother were crushed under the wheels of a speeding truck in Welcome
> colony, north-east Delhi. The boy's father, a ministry of home affairs
> staffer, escaped with leg injuries. An angry mob gathered in no time and
> set the truck on fire. The driver fled. The traffic police later caught up
> with his helper. At about 11.30 am on Sunday, the couple, Anil and Saroj
> Kumar, and their child Mukul, were going on a scooter from their
> Dilshad Garden home towards the Inter-state bus terminus. A speeding
> truck hit the scooter from behind and the Kumar family was thrown off.
> Saroj and Mukul Kumar were catapulted towards the back wheels of the
> truck and were run over. They died on the spot. . . . At the accident spot,
> the deaths were followed by violence as an irate mob vent its anger by
> setting the truck bearing number DL 1G 3957 on fire. "It was a large
> crowd," said a policemen.[10]

Barely a month before, *The Times of India* reported that an accident had
sparked off a mini "riot" in East Delhi. Mohammad Hassan was returning
home with a friend when a bus hit him. "But as soon as the news of Hasan's
death reached his Jaffrabad neighborhood, hundreds of angry relatives and
friends gathered at the spot and began stoning passing vehicles, demanding
the arrest of the bus driver,"[11] the paper reported. The driver, like in the
earlier incident, was "absconding." In the same report, the paper quoted
the police about the relationship between reckless driving and the absence
of street lights at night in many parts of the city. Darkness and urban fear,
an old motif in the history of modern life, seemed to overlap with stories of
speed and unanticipated death.

Barely four days before this story, *The Hindu* newspaper reported a "rampage" by high school students in South Delhi protesting against the death
of their colleague.

> More than 100 students of Sarvodaya Bal Vidyalaya gathered in front
> of 12-year-old Virender Kumar's house in Bhavishya Nidhi Complex
> at Malviya Nagar this afternoon, shouting slogans. The protest turned

violent when a few among them hurled stones at passing buses. Soon, the students rushed on to the main road and blocked traffic. While two and four-wheelers were allowed to pass through, buses were forced to stop and passengers made to get down before they smashed the windows and the windscreens. The incident which triggered the violence a day later, occurred after 5-30 p.m. on Tuesday. Virender Kumar, son of Ramesh Kumar and resident of Bhavishya Nidhi Enclave, was a student of class VI at the school, located near Shivalik in Malviya Nagar. As he came out to board a bus, a Blueline bus, plying on route No. 500 between Saket and Super Bazar, came, Virender ran towards the front entry with a heavy bag on his shoulder. He was on to the first step, when the driver abruptly started the vehicle, throwing him off balance. Virender fell on the road and did not have any time to move away from under the bus. Virender was rushed to All-India Institute of Medical Sciences where he was admitted at the Intensive Care Unit. He died this morning.[12]

These stories (all within the space of a month) reflected a typical snapshot of the compression of untimely death experiences produced by bus accidents in the 1990s. The vividness of the detail went into a "model" of the accident – the out-of-control bus or driver, resultant social disorder, missing drivers, the tragic death of innocent people. The victims were mostly bystanders, bus passengers, cyclists, and scooter drivers. The prominence of accident stories reflected a new form of writing and reporting about the city that emerged in the 1990s. *The Indian Express*, *The Hindustan Times*, and *The Pioneer* all developed strong city reporting; later entrants were *The Hindu* and *The Times of India*. The Hindi papers with quality city reporting included *Jansatta* and *Rashtriya Sahara*, and the evening paper *Sandhya Times*. By the late 1990s Hindi news television channels began broadcasting Delhi-specific slots, which offered instant coverage of accidents. In print, local news began to gradually move to the front pages by the end of the decade; and by 2005 city news took on the same weight as national news. This reflected the growing predomin-ance of an urban discourse in the city. Here narratives of consumption and spectacle coexisted with stories of death and disorder, sharpening the sensory experience of the growing metropolis. The accident reporting coexisted with increasing stories of brutal murders of old couples and families, infrastructure breakdowns, and traffic chaos. The urban reporting also presented a deliber-ate archival strategy – careful detailing, character types (victims, heroes, and villains), an effort to move through diverse viewpoints, perhaps a diminishing quality in national journalism. While the reporting technique was almost surgical, it created a heightening of sensations through its sharp headlines and allegories of a dark city.

The breakdown narrative is central to the discourse on Delhi in the 1990s. Perceptions of urban disorder and untimely deaths increased as millions came into contact with a rapidly changing city. As George Simmel pointed out in the early twentieth century, the bombardment of shocks, crowded images, and unexpected rush of sensations was typical of the metropolitan experience. The city became an active stimulus, where individuals experienced an intensified nervousness, vigilance, and avoidance of injury. Urban populations developed habitual forms that set up regular rhythms in the midst of perceived chaos. Walter Benjamin pointed out that the cinema responded to "a new and urgent need for stimuli" (1969, p.175). The breakdown narratives of the 1990s operated within this rapid traffic of urban crisis, shock, and media forms that re-enacted them. Although the context is vastly different, urban media reporting in Delhi was not unlike the 1920s European avant-garde who embraced the shock-effects of cinema in its early years. Benjamin wrote that both Dada artists and cinema had a common quality, hitting the spectator "like bullets." Unlike the avant-garde, whose professed purpose was the defamiliarization of rationalized life, Delhi's news reporting operated within a "reality" effect, producing an uncanny archive of the city.

Stories about accident deaths moved between reportage, the debates on urban planning, and email discussions. The death of the student Abhishek Rawat was a typical one, and *The Indian Express* reporter's story placed the tragedy within the compression of urban space, collapsed roads, and a callous city. A Blueline bus driver killed Rawat on May 20, 2004 just outside the private Rai University, in the congested Badarpur border area. In that area alone, the *Express* reported that five people had died in fifteen accidents over the past five months. The area's traffic, said the *Express*, was "chaotic," full of buses trying to overtake each other and pick up passengers, and no zebra crossings or traffic police. At any rate, when Rawat was hit, his friends tried desperately to persuade the auto-drivers to take him to hospital. Ankit Sikka was there when his friend breathed his last atop the Apollo flyover. "It took us 15 minutes to force an autodriver to take us there. And through the jam of buses at the terminal, it took another 25 to reach the hospital," he said. "The hospital is barely 2.5 km from the bus stand."[13] The following day, predictably, students stopped and stoned buses at the Badarpur crossing.[14]

A perpetual unease and heightened stress during travel developed in the 1990s among diverse residents of the city, which fed its way into newspaper columns and everyday recallings. In her column in *The Sunday Pioneer* in 2001, Latika Padgaonkar recounted an ordinary travel story:

> The mid-afternoon traffic crawls to a stop at a crossing as the light shifts to red. Ahead of me, hefty truck, some twenty feet tall, bulbous with overstuffed grain, and ten times overweight. Best stand apart, I warn myself, just in case the cargo decides mischievously to snap its ropes, burst its scams and spill their clouds of wheat and chaff on my little bonnet.
>
> We wait, I can't see the lights. They are blocked by the truck's immense bulk. But must have moved to green. A chorus of horns and honks and toots fills the air. I press my horn and add hastily to the cacophony. Get moving, get moving, I yell. To no avail. The traffic has stilled. There is not a hint of movement, no sound, not even a whisper. And then the axe falls.

Figure 4.1 "The Accident" made its way into popular renderings of the road. A Delhi bus shown running amok in a local comic series.

Source: Raj Comics, 2006.

A thud. A bump. The heart sickens. An accident, one more, on the streets of Delhi, I am sure. And this time, curse it, I am nearly a witness.[15]

It turns out that this is not an accident, but cattle blocking the road. Padgaonkar's column was written in dark humor, but incorporates the nagging anxiety felt by many during travel in Delhi. Congested space, disruption of speed, possible death, and the role of reluctant witness were ever-present.

This stress was felt across different classes of the city; and in many cases accounts were troubled. Shahana Qureshi, a young woman from the LNJP working-class settlement in central Delhi, recalls a typical journey with her family to Zafrabad. Shahana and her family were traveling by bus, when the traffic suddenly halted close to her destination.

> We peeped out of the bus window and saw three dead bodies lying on the road. A two-wheeler was standing near the bodies. . . . A truck had rammed into them. Seeing three dead people, I started wondering about them. Who are they? Where must they have been coming from?[16]

In this state of shock, Shahana realized that her relative's house was closer than she thought.

> The house was just two minutes away from the scene of the accident. But the two minutes seemed endless. What if I die this way? My body shivered with the thought. We couldn't sit in Khala's house for long. My younger *Khala(aunt)* also kept mentioning the accident over and over again during our conversations.

Shahana returned home and there was no end to the stress:

> When we were returning home, our bus stopped again at the red light and the scene flashed before my eyes. When we got off at Dilli Gate and took a rickshaw to go home, we saw there had been another accident near LNJP Hospital. This time it was a rickshaw-*wala*. But there were no dead bodies. The rickshaw was broken, and glass from the bus standing next to it was scattered on the road, near the rickshaw. I turned to my aunt and said, "Another accident?" Then our rickshaw-*wala* told us there had been an accident in which the rickshaw-*wala* had died.
> I had seen two accidents in the span of a few hours.[17]

This is precisely the sense of being overwhelmed by space that Caillois spoke about in his writing. These stories of compressed space and a stream of death images invading the space of the home were the ones mobilized by popular newspapers at that time.

The mix of impacted reporting of accidents, broken bodies, and machines in the context of a heightened sensory environment of the city has an earlier parallel in urban history. Ben Singer (1995) talks of the experience of "hyper-stimulus" in early New York city, as sensational newspapers, cartoons, and popular media presented a lurid account of urban life, adding to and heightening the urban delirium. Playing on the fears of modern metropolitan life among migrants, this experience existed in an environment of both revulsion and attractions enhanced by the commodity form. The fear of possible death and the shock of the new commercial visual culture went hand in hand, magnified by reporting. Singer's account is one that is nevertheless centred on the early history of Western urban modernity, where the collision between "two orders of experience – modern and premodern" played itself out through self-representation (1995, pp.72–99).

In 1999 *The Times of India* local edition asked if Delhi was a "Killer Metro," placing accident deaths within a montage of sensational violence produced in the city:

- The conductor of a Blue-Line bus is accused of stealing Rs 200 by his employer. The same night, he recovers consciousness to find both his hands chopped off. He holds his employer responsible for this.
- A three-year-old playing outside his home is attacked with red chilli powder and castrated. A 16-year-old transvestite too is castrated by the very eunuchs he used to perform with at weddings.
- A bank officer and her elderly mother commit suicide because of financial hardships caused by her husband's desertion. Although the mother-daughter duo poisons the granddaughter too, the child survives.

These recent tales of gore are not the only ones tainting the spirit of Delhi. The International Day of the Older on October 1 has not seen a sudden spurt of respect for senior citizens; attacks on them continue. Even in the week of the zero-tolerance drive by the Delhi Traffic Police, gruesome accidents – scooterists being crushed by errant bus-drivers and the like – added to Delhi's abysmally high rate of road accidents. Incidents of robberies abound; the Kacha Banyan tribe's bloody activities in the North-West district and Faridabad hogged the headlines last week.

So, is Delhi a Killer Metro?[18]

The image of a killing machine in the shape of the Redline/Blueline bus was now inserted into a *mise-en-scène* of sensational death, which intruded into domestic and public space. "Killing" which had been attributed to the machine now became an image of the urban personality out of control. As death became inherently contingent, and unmarked, the effort was to reorganize the unpredictability of violence itself. Foucault talks about how the category of the dangerous individual meant a shift from the act itself to the "nature" or character of the individual. This involved, says Foucault, a technology that was "capable of characterizing a criminal individual in him-self and in a sense beneath his acts" (1988, p.144). Psychological profiling of individuals was central to crime detection in the early modern city, whose conditions increased anonymity and circulation. Marking an individual type with a propensity to violence from the urban crowd is an old technology of modern crime detection. The second strategy is statistics. Both were used increasingly in popular writing on road accidents in Delhi. Local psychologists gave advice and analysis in advice columns and interviews about road rage, and speculated about the profile of "killer drivers." These columns were often part of the style/entertainment supplements that became the driver of profits in the 1990s. The personal stories of stress, sexual crises, violent acts, and new-age solutions blended uncannily with lifestyle stories.

Statistical images

Statistical charts took pride of place in the reporting on accidents. Often bundled with the main story, these became a regular feature, drawing from databases on pollution, traffic, and road deaths. They sought to explain the

Figure 4.2 Montage of accident headlines, Mrityunjay Chatterjee.

Source: Sarai Media Lab.

contingency of death, often narrated graphically in the accompanying stories. The explanation by numbers took a radical step in the 1980s itself when the magazine *India Today* used desktop publishing software to produce 3-D images of numbers to great effect. With the spread of cheap computers and design software in the 1990s the statistical image became ubiquitous, standing in as an explanation for the contingencies of elections, the weather, crime, and public opinion in general. The more unpredictable, dangerous, and contingent the urban experience became, the more widespread was the use of the statistical image as a knowledge form. Multimedia design rendered an abstract knowledge form "readable" for a larger audience used to moving between different media environments. Allied with the idea of expert knowledge, and popularized by the digital interface, there is little doubt that statistics offers a significant response to the widespread anxiety and unpredictability of life in the postmodern era. Statistics, as Ian Hacking (1990) has shown us, was the nineteenth century's most powerful legacy. The "avalanche of numbers" that Hacking says began in that century also assumed a certain marking of subjects. Those who conformed to the boundaries of statistical laws were "normal," while those on the periphery were seen as "pathological" (ibid., p.2). In her book *The Emergence of Cinematic Time*, which makes an argument for the relationship of contingency and early cinema, Mary Anne Doane says the following about statistics:

> Not only did it acknowledge the intractability of the contingent, the unknowablity of the individual; it was based on and depended on these affirmations. The uniqueness and aberration of individual events, their domination by chance, was assured by the displacement of knowledge to the mass. This was both an acknowledgement of and an attempt to control the anxiety of contingency.
>
> (Doane, 2002, p.18)

The statistical explanations of the contingent in 1990s Delhi went far beyond the classic nineteenth-century epistemology. As Lev Manovich has pointed out, the digital database is a cultural artifact; the use of graphic multimedia techniques has produced a variable product that can be transformed, manipulated graphically, and circulated endlessly (2002). Statistics as graphical *objects* were present in accident reports in the newspapers, television coverage, and massive digital signboards on the main traffic signals that gave the numbers of those killed in traffic accidents as well as air pollution figures. The newspaper image-graph followed a filmic sequence of a ticking time bomb, assaulting viewers with alarming statistical graphs. This went outside classic governmental concerns for defining personality types. Statistical objects as media pursued and penetrated the urban traveler in a never-ending delirious media barrage, transforming the original optics of statistical epistemology. At one level the ubiquity of numbers in graphical interfaces attempted to naturalize the accident. At another level the sensational statistical graph fed an image of an out-of-control city. Its very structure of hyper-sensation-producing effects made the statistical media object's utility as important knowledge form limited. Statistics as media was further compromised by an excessive circulation and a contradictory relationship with crash photographs in newspapers. Most importantly, the statistical explanation drew attention unintentionally to an injured public body, wounded by the contingency of death or gradual ecological decay.

Machines and subjects

From the 1990s Delhi was swept into a bloody drama around road culture that entangled buses, passengers, drivers, bystanders, and almost everyone in the city. Although buses never exceeded more than 1 percent of Delhi's motor vehicles, they were at the center of a public violence that moved between broken machines and human bodies, and the enactment of an uncontrollable subjective force that sometimes seemed to emanate from machines, at other times from actions of human beings. This discourse refracted through media stories, personal narratives, technical reports, and court judgments. As such, the road stories of the 1990s rehearsed the early turmoils of technological life in Delhi at the turn of the century.

The bus fleet in Delhi represented a distinctive human–machine ensemble. Like its counterparts in the rest of India, the Delhi public transport "bus" in the 1990s was actually the converted chassis of a truck. It was a *bricolage* of the original truck chassis supplied by companies like Tata and Ashok Leyland and a local metal body built by regional contractors. Passengers braved an unusually high bus entrance, modest shock absorbers, and basic seating. The DTC bus had a frugal interior and a stricter control of passenger flow, entry was only from the rear of the bus, and there was a two-person conductor-driver crew. Signage in the DTC system was somewhat standardized and by the 1980s the bus route followed a color-coded route system. In contrast the private Redline/Blueline's exterior and interior was heterotopic. The external body of the bus was a riot of information about the bus route, the owner's name and mobile number, stenciled alphabets indicating the bus license ("stage carriage") and later, the letters CNG were added after the buses moved to a natural gas regime. The passengers often entered from both doors of the bus, where they would be confronted by an interior occupied by a driver and cronies in the front area, a minimum of two energetic ushers and conductors, whose job was to ensure the bus picked up passengers. Religious pictures and incense, and music blaring from an inexpensive casette/CD player, marked the driver's area. This front section was a strictly male space and often reserved for the driver and his friends; in rare cases older women could move into this area if the bus was crowded.

Another category of transport was the chartered bus, meant for white-collar office workers who could not deal with the stress of traveling by public transport. The chartered bus was a more domesticated space, with a set route and a reasonably stable clientele. In contrast to the more fleeting experience of public transport travel, chartered buses encouraged bonhomie and inter-passenger association in order to keep a stable membership. Sweets would be distributed on special dates, and the membership fees were usually collected on a monthly basis. The departure times of the buses were stable, in line with the needs of the passengers. For many middle-class women with regular schedules this was also a safer environment compared to that of public transport.

Bus travel in the 1990s began to be increasingly perceived as a stressful experience, where passengers, while relatively safe from the mayhem on the road, began to experience the combination of fear and shock so distinctive of modern mass travel. The assemblage technology of the Indian bus set up an experience of "exposed" travel where passengers were subjected to shocks at the sudden application of breaks, the wild turns around Delhi's roundabouts, and an internal sensory experience of smell and claustrophobia due to over-crowding. It was not uncommon to see recent migrants leaning out of Delhi's bus windows to relieve road sickness. The body moved and adjusted with the rhythm of the bus, suffering wear and tear, along with the machine. For many travelers the fear of the accident was never far away. Nasreen, another young woman from the LNJP settlement, writes about her journey to a suburb of Delhi:

> We caught a bus to Loni from the Inter State Bus Terminus. Buses to Loni were very infrequent then. We were half way to our destination. It was very hot. And the bus was moving in fits and starts, jerking. Whenever the bus would turn, I would think the bus was going to topple over. The bus was very crowded; there was no room for anyone to get on. My brother was standing at the door. Frankly, it was quite scary. Many people were trying to get on. But because the bus was crowded, the driver was speed-ing, halting at the stops very briefly. One man, who was trying to get on, was clutching on to the handle on the door. He was trying to put one foot on the steps of the bus. But unfortunately, he slipped, and along with that, his hand also lost its grip on the handle. He fell. The driver drove on.[19]

In Nasreen's narrative the man dies "his skull split wide open"; the driver runs off, and the police chase everyone away. In Delhi's public buses the psychic distance between the passenger and the road as well as the passenger and the driver/conductor was a slim one. Passenger conflicts with driver and conductors were perennial, periodically breaking into violence. Manjeet Kr Singh of Mansoraver Hostel in Delhi University wrote about a typical incident in a letter to *The Times of India:*

> I boarded a blue line bus on May 6 near ITO together with five of my friends. The bus route no was 423 and license plate no was DL1PA 3974. The bus conductor refused to accept DTC passes and told us to get down from the bus. When we refused, the bus conductor with the help of the

driver and two others physically shoved us out of the bus. When we resisted, they started beating us. My friends suffered bruises on the face and I was inflicted with a nose injury. Since then, I have been running from pillar to post to lodge a FIR, but till date neither the FIR has been lodged nor any action taken against the culprits.[20]

Violent conflicts between drivers and passengers sometimes ended tragically. In May, 2005, *The Indian Express'* city edition reported another story.

An argument with a bus conductor led to the death of 26-year-old Santosh Upadhyay last night. Dharambir, the conductor, threw a stone at Upadhyay, injuring him in the head. Upadhyay died on the way to hospital. The incident took place in Janakpuri, west Delhi, on a Blueline on route 879.[21]

Often the driver–machine assemblage would mock passengers sadistically by racing into bus stops, and moving the vehicle on before all the passengers had embarked. Yashoda, also from the LNJP camp, talks about how she once got into a bus

but my heart was jumping up to the height of a yard. The next stop was ours. The driver stopped at the bus stop, and all my friends got off. I had reached the steps to get off. I was about to put my foot down on the ground, when the driver moved the bus with a jerk, and I froze right there on the steps.

Other passengers protested, and then, says Yashoda, "I turned around to look at the driver. That mustachioed monkey was looking at me and smiling. His gaze at me was deep. I started feeling scared of him. I got off the bus immediately."[22]

This everyday proximity to the driver *and* the road outside was in contrast to many accounts of travel culture in Europe and the United States. Modern travel after the speed coach and the train has tended to separate the passenger from the driver and the outside environment. Hurled on the track and the road, passengers became "living packets," one among many. In Wolfgang Schivelbush's work The *Railway Journey* (1986), passengers go through a process of double commodification: losing their distinctiveness in travel and contemplating a rapidly moving outer landscape from the inner world of the carriage (1986). Jeffery Schnapp talks of the logic of this experience:

Missing from the picture, however, is the perception of danger, eliminated by a battery of technologies that detach passenger from landscape, passenger from passenger, and passenger from engine: soundproofing, upholstery, sealed windows, enclosed compartments, suspension systems, smoothed out rail beds, specialization of function among railway cars.

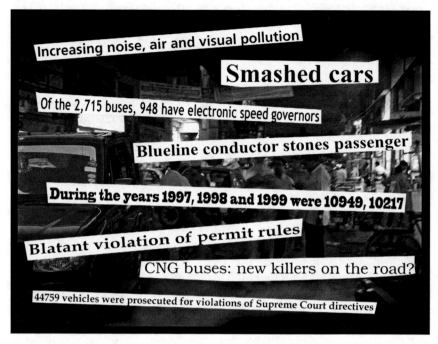

Figure 4.3 Montage of accident headlines, Mrityunjay Chatterjee.
Source: Sarai Media Lab.

All are devices that foster a feeling of safety and its subjective correlative:
a sensation of tedium that can be alleviated only by means of the reading, sleep or awkward conversation.

(Schnapp, 1999, p.25)

This was not always the case. In the 1880s the journal the *Lancet* talked
about the "fatigue" of travel. "The eyes are strained, the ears are dinned, the
muscles are jostled hither and thither, and the nerves are worried by the
attempt to maintain order, and so comes weariness" (Schivelbusch, 1986,
p.18). In Delhi media effects further inflamed and reproduced the experience
of travel. Death stories of crushed bodies, exploding buses, overturned
vehicles made public transport an edgy experience. The bus moved in *"fits
and starts,"* Nasreen from LNJP colony writes; her reference to the "wild"
swing of the bus when it turned on Delhi's roads draws our attention to a
particular experience of speed, an old trope in the language of modern life.[23]

Speed

In his column in the *Midday*, the then Commissioner of Police Maxwell
Perreira reflected on the "problem" of Delhi's drivers. "[T]he most common

driver faults among Delhi's motorists are," wrote Maxwell, "their utter lack of knowledge as to the basic rules of the 'right of way', and an aggressive lack of consideration towards the other road user leading to bulldozing and cutting into another's path." He continued,

> All this invariably leads to wrong overtaking, misplaced sense of one's own right on the road, a wanton disregard for traffic signals. Indiscriminate honking, obstructive/unauthorized parking, disregard to the prescribed norms in display of registration number plates, driving without a helmet and hazardous triple riding on two wheelers.[24]

Among the many reasons given by Maxwell for this sorry scenario were Delhi's "wide roads" and a comfortable surface, which encouraged drivers to speed.

The relationship of asphalt to speed is an old one. "Asphalt," says Jeffrey Schnapp, "erupts on the scene of modernity to redeem the world of industry from the banes of friction and dust" (2003, p.7). The innovations in surfaces by English engineer McAdam in the 19th century radically transformed the experience of road travel. Cheap, frictionless travel now emerged in the modern travel imaginary, with parallel innovations in vehicle suspension design, sidewalks, traffic management, and social divisions between the motorized and the pedestrian classes. With this, says Schnapp, asphalt became part of the modern imaginary as the substance of frictionless travel.

> If, from an economic standpoint, modernity's dream is the unimpeded circulation of commodities and persons, and, from a phenomenological standpoint, the experience of unimpeded psychic and somatic flow, then asphalt asserts itself as the era's invisible but ubiquitous support.
>
> (Ibid.)

Asphalt or "metalled" roads as they were called in Indian engineering technology was the perfect aid to the peculiar human/machine ensemble that was the Delhi bus. In Delhi speed culture first came with the public bus. I remember, even in the 1980s when the DTC was a monopoly, public buses used to race into the crowds at bus stops. Crowds at bus stops learnt the familiar and dangerous ritual of rapidly stepping back when buses would rush in. The tragic enactments of the culture of speed – racing machines, accidents, untimely deaths – were all overwhelmingly part of an experience of public transport, which increased in the Redline/Blueline era. This contrasts with the Western experience where the individual driver subject played out the drama of speed culture: the erotics of the machine, celebrity deaths on the road from James Dean to Princess Diana. Motor culture in 1990s Delhi intimated a new *kinetic subjectivity*,[25] where speed was part of an accelerating city, where time for both passengers and drivers became meaningful in powerfully new ways. Combined with the competitive, calculating world of the new commodity explosion, drivers and passengers were caught in a loop where buses raced against each other, and broke every formal-rational rule of an ordered transportation system. And this process was always marked by the shadow of death. Public bus travel thus allegorized the new acceleration of urban life, but did so in "exposed" forms where technological life was best described in Paul Gomra's bus journey every day to Ghaziabad. It was a cycle of circulation, speed, shock, more speed, and violence, adding to the rapidly expanding catalog of new urban sensations and stimuli. Schnapp talks of speed being the drug of modern circulation, where

> the driver ... as the *kinematic subject*, once reshaped by repeated experiences of this stimulant, finds himself caught in an addiction loop, threatened, on the one hand, by monotony, and, on the other, by the need for ever new stimuli in order to maintain the same level of intensity.
> (Schnapp, 1999, p.4)

At the end of this addiction loop is the crash. This kinematic subject was an important part of the public sensibility of Delhi's roads in the 1990s. As drivers of buses, trucks, and cars were caught in this cycle of speed, they imitated each other's acts, and courted death. As the population of drivers and machines grew in leaps and bounds, so did the risks. In the emerging urban order where everything accelerated and reaching destinations on time became critical, the private contractors who owned the Redline/Blueline buses became increasingly vulnerable. A complex system of daily quotas was imposed by bus owners on their staff along with the insistence that a minimum number of trips be completed. Buses fought to get passengers, with each other, and with routes and time schedules. One west Delhi resident summed up the scenario to a reporter:

> Since the second bus does not get enough passengers, it tries to overtake the first one so as to reach the next bus stop earlier and pick up passengers. Driver of the first bus does everything to prevent the driver of the second bus from overtaking him, ensuring they get into a race, press accelerator, cut lanes while constantly keeping a hand on the high decibel banned pressure horns to clear the traffic ahead of them, constantly posing a threat to other road users.[26]

Buses were also accused of suddenly changing routes in order to cruise bus stops with more passengers.[27] Along with speeding, buses were also accused of standing overtime at stops in order to fulfill passenger quotas. A journalist of *The Pioneer* reported significant passenger anger over stationary buses.

> Prem Das, a passenger of a Blueline plying on route number 501, asks angrily, "Why can't they pick up passengers as they go along? Why

wait?" He and the bus conductor nearly got into a fist fight at AIIMS a
few minutes before the conversation this reporter had with him.[28]

Bus drivers pointed out those empty buses would mean low commissions
for them. Low daily wages for private bus staff gave an added urgency to
commissions on tickets sold. To evade the eyes of the traffic police, buses
would keep "moving the bus every few minutes" at stops.[29] Private buses were
attacked both ways: for speeding up *and* bypassing stops to make more trips,
and for stopping excessively to fill the bus with passengers.[30] This became the
commodity form of speed in Delhi's public buses: endless circulation, disruption of any "rational" mapping of the transportation grid, and "suspending"
circulation in order to realize passengers and profit. This dialectic of speed
and disorder did not even spare the bus stop. The disorderly rush of passengers towards the bus doors matched the familiar rhythm of the bus speeding
into the stop. Orderly lines of passengers that were common in Mumbai were
out of the question in Delhi. A city reporter of *The Pioneer* wrote in exasperation, "Today, if a person asks his fellow commuters to stand in a line and
wait, he will be considered a raving lunatic."[31] A recent migrant from Mumbai
told the reporter, "The bus stop scene in Delhi was a culture shock. On my
first day here, I tried to get people into a line, but when the bus arrived, they
all rushed."[32] In Delhi, passengers and buses rushed into the frenzy of circulation, pushing away anything that stood in their way. When it fully arrived
in the 1990s, speed became a cultural force that exceeded all structural limits
of regulation in Delhi. Cars, auto-rickshaws, and two-wheelers often ignored
signals when they could, and took opposite lanes to break traffic jams. Trucks
would race through residential areas to ensure they bypassed the limits set
on their daytime travel by the Supreme Court and reach toll points at the
earliest time possible.

Benjamin once wrote that moving through dangerous traffic generates nervous impulses that flow through individuals like "the energy from a battery"
(1969, p.175). All stationary movement on the road (traffic jams, red lights)
became implicated in a specific human–machine *sensory* environment that
combined sound, tactile perception, and impatience with other machines.
At the time of the change of lights from red to green, a crescendo of horns
would start, beginning seconds before the visible green signal. Drivers
developed an instinctive and highly conflictual relationship to traffic signals.
The easy resort to horns in Delhi never ceased to amaze, and horrified travelers from out of town. Speed culture accelerated the affective register of the
new urban soundscapes.

By the late 1990s speeding machines generated a capillary form of bypass
and insubordination affecting every part of road culture. At one level, in its
disregard for all clean visual architectures of traffic plans and routes, Delhi's
speed culture recalled Michel De Certeau's famous evocation of "everyday"
tactics. Praising inventive moments of practice for its "tactile apprehension
and kinesic appropriation," De Certeau suggests that the urban tactic is both

mobile and often unreadable. (1984, p.105) De Certeau is of course not talking of machines; he detested machine travel of trains and buses. "Only a rationalized cell travels," wrote De Certeau, calling such mobility "traveling incarceration," stationary passengers locked in moving machines (ibid., p.111). In Delhi's road culture where the distinctions between machines and humans was often blurred, De Certeau's powerful image of the "ordinary man" squeezed by the larger forces of rationality is difficult to hold on to. The "evasive tactics" that De Certeau celebrated were deployed all the time on Delhi's roads by speeding human–machine ensembles – with terrifying effects. The figure of alterity was in fact grounded in a dark anthropology of death.

The rule of experts

The idea of the road as a dangerous, polluting, and debilitating sensory environment exposed an image of a damaged urban order under threat from untamed machines and driver-subjects. By the later 1990s newer explanations of the urban crisis surrounding the road emerged, centered variously around environmental advocacy groups, traffic management and safety experts, and public interest litigation in courts. These portrayed the mess on Delhi's roads as a civic crisis of knowledge and regulation. The problem of the road was "unregulated": polluting buses that were faulty and accident-prone and Redline/Blueline drivers who routinely drove recklessly. Scientific knowledge of the road, control of deviant machines and subjects through regulation, and driver/bystander education were the main keywords in the discourse of experts. These sets of discourses radically changed the language of urban governance towards one centered on spectacular techniques, media campaigns, and the classic deployment of numbers as an objective explanation for the crisis. Numbers were now transformed as media interfaces accompanied expert reports and pronouncements. Numbers were produced every day in newspapers and on television in accidents, pollution levels, respiratory diseases, sourced from a wide plane of governmentality: NGOs, hospitals, specialist reports, and new databases. Writing in 2002 on cleanliness campaigns Awadhendra Sharan noted the shift from the language of political society where the dignitary with the broom cleaned the streets.

> Instead, we find a new vocabulary on offer – pH levels, clean fuels, suspended particulate matter, common effluent treatment plants – these are the terms that increasingly saturate the media and public spaces around us, from billboards that provide information on SO_2 levels, to weather reports that report on pollution across cities, to the legal discourse that relies on expert committees to guide them on technical matters. Objective science rather than an ambiguous political rhetoric, we argue, signals an important shift in our conceptual apparatus regarding environmental issues.
>
> (Sharan, 2002, p.34)

The accident was the golden age of civic liberalism which, as argued in the Introduction of this book, set out a domain of intervention outside the older formations of political society. What was remarkable about Delhi's discourse on road safety, and the debate on air pollution before it, was the relative paralysis of the political elites. Civic liberalism successfully evacuated the debate on justice away from urban populations, focusing on dramaturgies of court, new experts, and media-technical discourse.

In his book *War and Cinema*, Paul Virilio talks about how the speed of information relay increasingly begins to consume its meaning. This information *velocity* was set up by technologies of war; thus in World War II, "reports lost their value within a few hours, or even a few minutes" (1989, p.75). The accelerated nature of modern information after the telegraph is aimed at mobile travelers reducing history to a dizzying landscape of events destroying perception (*"now you see it, now you don't"*), and the event itself. Accelerated time and information consume themselves. Civic liberalism operated in this context. Almost self-reflexively, the mode of the campaign was that of info-war: the bombardment of media outlets with massive amounts of information during the process.[33]

The language of statistics and scientific rhetoric was produced in civic liberal public campaigns and media events. These event-scenes were run by organizations adept at the new technologies of publicity. The campaign event was also produced around public interest litigation in the Supreme and High Courts, and a barrage of interviews and reports in the media. The new discourse enacted and affirmed the idea of a civic subject that needed to be protected from a diseased political order, while seeking to restore to governmentality its true path: the idea of a rights-bearing liberal citizen. It was as if a failed citizenship, consumed by the ruin of political society in the "lost" decades after independence, could be reborn in the liberal civic order after globalization. The media campaigns around the road deployed typical global technologies of the civic: public release of all urban reports, cultivation of media personalities who represented "middle-class citizens," mailing lists and newsletters. In the case of road transport the effort was twofold: to explain the contingency of death due to faulty machines and ill-trained drivers. Transport knowledge set up a detached space of observation from the accident itself, which became scientifically analyzable and preventable with correct machines and well-designed roads.

The writer V.J. Thomas underscored the relationship between bad design and road safety in a disaster report:

> Only recently have Indian car manufacturers started placing fuel tanks towards the middle, reducing the chances of rupture and explosion during rear impacts. Seat belts are a belated addition, mostly for drivers and front co-passengers. Airbags are unknown, rigid monocoque design almost absent. Anti-roll bars are aftermarket additions. Speed governors in buses are extracted, tires are re-treaded so often that they explode at

highway speeds, or lose their grip. Floorboards are rusted and seats loosely welded. There are no luggage restraints, side indicators, and headrests to arrest whiplash.

(Thomas, 2000, p.342)

Road reformers campaigned for special lanes for cyclists, speed flow design, new management techniques, and better public transport in general.[34] While the pollution debate set up the image of a vulnerable body under threat from emissions the transport debate highlighted the contingency and reversibility of accidental deaths. Accidents could be prevented through lane driving ("sane" driving as the police billboards said), the implementation of speed governors in buses, and speed limits in general, and intelligent management of traffic. Bus-drivers who were widely reported to be "uneducated" and often without a license were sent to driving school, asked to wear uniforms, and penalized for offences. The breakdown narrative of the city thus paralleled the rise of a liberal civic consciousness among the city's middle and upper classes for whom the courts emerged as a crucial reference point. This intervention showed a secular movement in the 1990s, but was dynamized by a major accident in November, 1997 which led to the deaths of twenty-eight schoolchildren. A private bus filled with schoolchildren from the Shaheed Amar Chand Sarvodya Vidyalya fell into the Yamuna River after the driver[35] was believed to have "lost control" and smashed into the barriers on the bridge. The ensuing days and months saw a crescendo of public criticism leveled against the school and public authorities, bus-drivers, and speeding machines. The following months saw every ingredient of 1990s road culture mobilized on to the public stage: frenzied media discussions and expert opinions, the gradual invisibility of the dead in the tragedy, and the vulnerability of the city dweller in a speed culture.

The significant intervention was an order of the Supreme Court immediately after the incident in November, 1997. The judgment delivered by V.N. Khare and B.N. Kirpal was an example of the type of court order that refashioned the city from the 1990s. Responding to an ongoing public interest litigation by the campaigner M.C. Mehta, the court mobilized graphic images of urban disorder and suggested immediate intervention. The wide-ranging order made speed governors compulsory in medium and heavy city vehicles, limiting speed to 40 km per hour, transport vehicles were forbidden from overtaking others, roads were segregated and buses confined to lanes. Buses could stop only at bus stops, buses could be driven only by authorized drivers with photo-IDs, school buses could only employ drivers with five years experience and without a history of traffic offences, and uniforms were made compulsory for drivers. Practices that were ordinarily part of the pastoral power of government were suddenly rendered visible through dramatic civic judgments. A few months later the Court followed up with another dramatic judgment in response to yet another petition by M.C. Mehta. Among its recommendations were to make compressed natural gas compulsory for all buses (public and private) by April 1, 2001. Leaded petrol was abolished, two-stroke vehicles (autos and scooters) had their fuel regulated, all auto-rickshaws and taxis made before 1990 were pushed to adopt "clean fuels," and new bus terminals were to be built at the borders to ensure that polluting buses of other states did not enter. In these judgments the Court re-dramatized the image of killing and polluting road-machines, already in circulation in the hyper-stimulus of the city. Judgments typically mobilized expert knowledge, and addressed campaigns by groups who combined research with media advocacy. The Court was clear that it worked in a dense media environment, and implicated its judgments in a culture of circulation. In a judgment delivered on December 1, 1998 where it specified that buses should run on segregated lanes, the justices also said the following:

> We also direct that the Union of India shall ensure that the directions given by this Court on twentieth November, 1997: 16th December 1997 and 28th July, 1998 are suitably publicized in the print as well as in the electronic media so that everybody is made aware of the directions contained in our various orders. Publicity on the electronic media should be, to begin with, carried *on every alternate day, for at least six weeks.*[36]

Operating with a regularity that would naturalize them as part of urban life, court judgments such as these enacted a liberal civic citizenship, staged through a visible plane of expert knowledge, crisis management, rights discourses, and media events. The phantom civic subject was a responsible private citizen, and while all vehicles were subject to some pollution controls, commercial ones were doubly so as they had to use natural gas.[37] By regulating drivers of public vehicles, the Court drew on resources of rage and public anger refracted through the mediascapes of the city. By incorporating particular expert knowledges on regulation, safety and congestion, and conferring recognition on a distinct form of middle-class environmental civic subject, judgments marked a space for liberal governmental practice that could stand "above" politics. It is not surprising that the court judgment and media campaigns of the 1990s gave a fillip to specific modernizing leaders in Delhi like Sheila Dikhsit, who attempted to incorporate the new middle-class subjectivity in the language of governance.

The main thrust now was a technocratic system of controls through a disciplining of the bus–human ensemble. If the machine was specified carefully, the subject who was part of its actions was strictly regulated: through newspaper campaigns and education,[38] monitoring, and increasing police and governmental surveillance. In line with the new mood the traffic police issued a steady stream of enforcement statistics to the media, while the Department of Road Transports dreamed of controlling drivers through a GPS system that would link all buses.[39] In *The Civilizing Process* (1993), Norbert Elias had argued that a system of internal controls would gradually replace external restraints (manners, civilité). Although the rhetoric of civic campaigns in

Delhi pushed for that very system of internal disciplining, the road remains a difficult challenge compared to short-term issues like firecracker noise during the Diwali festival. In a remarkable admission in an internal circular, the Department of Road Transports admitted that the public was less than willing to help the injured during road accidents:

> It has come to notice that on many occasions, the victims of roadside accidents remain unattended for a longer time without medical aid or any help from the members of public till the arrival of police at the spot. The members of the public though basically have got an indifferent attitude in such situations, but due to the unnecessary involvement in the accidental cases, they in turn hesitate to remove the injured to the hospitals to which results in the loss of human life and the image of the police fades in the eyes of the public.[40]

The category of the "public" that is mobilized here is one of failed civic duty, compounded by legal hassles and paperwork. The circular goes on to request police stations to treat people who bring accident victims to hospitals "with courtesy" and under no circumstances should such people be "detained." As for drivers, the circular pointed out that the Motor Vehicles Act made it duty-bound on them to take the victim to hospital "unless it is not practicable to do so, *on account of mob fury or any other reason beyond his control*" (ibid.; emphasis added) Beyond the more abstract techniques of accident statistics and utopias of technological control we witness a tacit admission of failure. The liberal civic subject did not exist; yet he/she had to be enticed towards solidarity.

The disciplining of machines had contradictory effects. The installation of manual speed governers in buses led to persistent reports of their being removed by bus-drivers; this was followed by court orders to use electronic speed governors which were seen as resistant to misuse. While buses tended to stay within speed limits in the main intersections of the city that were heavily policed, the slowing down was a source of constant complaints among passengers wanting to get to destinations on time. In the conflict between speed culture and the discourses of safety, there are no clear winners as yet. In addition, just when CNG buses were introduced as technologically and environmentally safe options after considerable debate and upheaval, there were immediate reports of them "exploding." In a headline "CNG Buses: New Killers on the Road?" *The Pioneer*'s city edition reported such explosions in a new CNG bus soon after their introduction.[41] This was followed by persistent reports about CNG buses exploding, much to the exasperation of environmental activists. Virilio has pointed out prophetically, "Every time that a new technology has been invented, a new energy harnessed, a new product made, one also invents a new negativity, a new accident."[42]

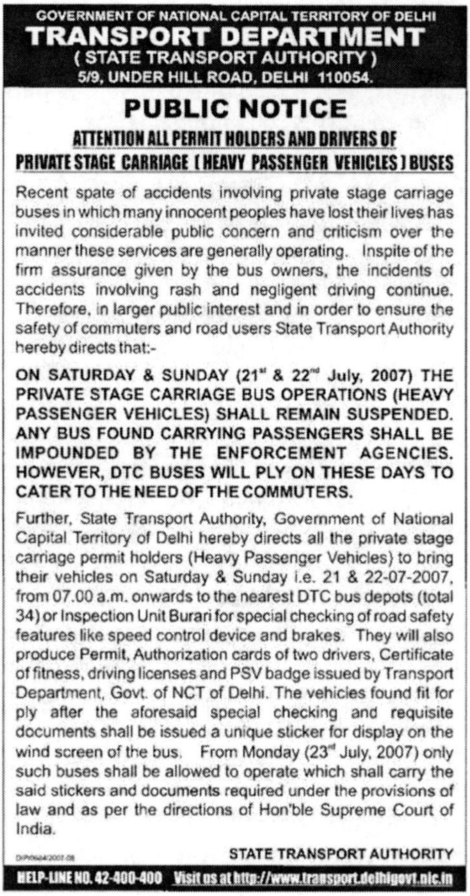

GOVERNMENT OF NATIONAL CAPITAL TERRITORY OF DELHI

TRANSPORT DEPARTMENT
(STATE TRANSPORT AUTHORITY)
5/9, UNDER HILL ROAD, DELHI 110054.

PUBLIC NOTICE

**ATTENTION ALL PERMIT HOLDERS AND DRIVERS OF
PRIVATE STAGE CARRIAGE (HEAVY PASSENGER VEHICLES) BUSES**

Recent spate of accidents involving private stage carriage buses in which many innocent peoples have lost their lives has invited considerable public concern and criticism over the manner these services are generally operating. Inspite of the firm assurance given by the bus owners, the incidents of accidents involving rash and negligent driving continue. Therefore, in larger public interest and in order to ensure the safety of commuters and road users State Transport Authority hereby directs that:-

ON SATURDAY & SUNDAY (21ˢᵗ & 22ⁿᵈ July, 2007) THE PRIVATE STAGE CARRIAGE BUS OPERATIONS (HEAVY PASSENGER VEHICLES) SHALL REMAIN SUSPENDED. ANY BUS FOUND CARRYING PASSENGERS SHALL BE IMPOUNDED BY THE ENFORCEMENT AGENCIES. HOWEVER, DTC BUSES WILL PLY ON THESE DAYS TO CATER TO THE NEED OF THE COMMUTERS.

Further, State Transport Authority, Government of National Capital Territory of Delhi hereby directs all the private stage carriage permit holders (Heavy Passenger Vehicles) to bring their vehicles on Saturday & Sunday i.e. 21 & 22-07-2007, from 07.00 a.m. onwards to the nearest DTC bus depots (total 34) or Inspection Unit Burari for special checking of road safety features like speed control device and brakes. They will also produce Permit, Authorization cards of two drivers, Certificate of fitness, driving licenses and PSV badge issued by Transport Department, Govt. of NCT of Delhi. The vehicles found fit for ply after the aforesaid special checking and requisite documents shall be issued a unique sticker for display on the wind screen of the bus.   From Monday (23ʳᵈ July, 2007) only such buses shall be allowed to operate which shall carry the said stickers and documents required under the provisions of law and as per the directions of Hon'ble Supreme Court of India.

DIP/9644/2007-08   **STATE TRANSPORT AUTHORITY**

HELP-LINE NO. 42-400-400   Visit us at http://www.transport.delhigovt.nic.in

Figure 4.4 A Delhi State Transport Department notice temporarily suspending private bus operators. This token measure was taken in the context of media uproar over transport deaths.

Source: Transport Department, 2007.

Death and the accident

> The human organism is an atrocity exhibition at which he is a willing spectator.
> (J.G. Ballard, 1973)

Towards the end of Uday Prakash's tale, we find that the "mangled remains" of Gomra's scooter are still to be found behind the Daryaganj police station.[43] "On its broken fenders and twisted wheels are drops of the blood of the deceased Rajiv Menon and the insane Paul Gomra. Having dried out, they are now black" (2003, p.185). As machine and human traces are consigned to a junk yard, so Prakash offers his dark commentary on the decade of the 1990s, where commodity and media desires end in the destruction of the machines that propelled those very desires. The accident is the logical conclusion of Gomra's wasted dream of speed. Like Manto's Toba Tek Singh, Gomra's subsequent insanity is the only resource in a world gone astray.

In his experimental novel *Life of the Automobile* published in 1928, the Russian writer Ilya Ehrenburg *begins* with the car accident. In Ehrenberg's story, Charles Bernard, an introvert and a man of letters, becomes a lover of cinema and speed travel depicted in films of that time. He buys a car, learns how to drive and is on his first motor trip to the countryside when the car took over; it "had gone crazy." The inevitable happened. "The linnets warbled and the lavender was sweet and fragrant. Car No. 180-74 – iron splinters, glass shards, a lump of warm flesh – lay unstirring beneath the solemn midday sun" (1999, p.6). The oppositions are stark: between human and machine, cold metal and warm flesh, commodity and life. Ehrenberg's novel stands between two worlds, an indictment of commodity culture and the world of machines it produced on the one hand, and the lost romantic dreams of childhood and the countryside on the other. It is at the crossroads of the passing of the "childhood dream" (Benjamin) of European modernity, and the terrifying exhilaration of the new era of mass commodities. The industrial transformation of Europe and the rise of automobiles in the twentieth century set up a series of encounters of Western modernism with speed culture. In the central origin myth of Italian Futurism, Marinetti and his colleagues get into a speeding automobile in 1909 and crash on the outskirts of the city, an accident that generated the *Futurist Manifesto*. In Futurist re-creation human and machine merge as the poet races through the city, and the subsequent accident generates a new technological identity and celebration of speed. The *Futurist Manifesto* proclaims, "Time and Space died yesterday. We are already living in the absolute, since we have already created eternal, omnipresent speed."[44] In Futurism the technological becomes a prosthetic enhancement to the human body, a shield against shock, all complicit in the drive for war and the interiority of the bourgeois personality. The cleansing acts of the technological drove Marinetti and the futurists to fascism. It is a world of speed that is machinic and misogynist, and convulsed by the death drive: "our nerves demand war and despise women" (cited in Foster, 2006, p.123).

Marinetti's elevation of the technological sublime[45] as a self-destructive yet pleasurable drive intimates many of the discussions on speed culture. Futurism's embrace of speed machines immediately marked it out from older critiques of modernity that saw machines as an assault on the body and nature. However, Marinetti's embrace of the machine to set up the body as an aggressive weapon-projectile presents him with a problem. As Hal Foster points out, there is little guarantee that this embrace "will either subsume the body, or blow it to smithereens, or both" (2006, p.124). In this sense Futurists anticipated the contradictions of speed culture in the dark city of modernity.

As speeding machines were embraced as desiring objects that would become prosthetic shields/weapons in the shock culture of urban life, the subject stood in danger of annihilation through the accident and destruction of the body.

This dialectic of the machine as demon and as also a demonic *supplement* to the body refracted through much of twentieth-century European modernism. The Futurist origin myth of the accident combined speed, thrills, and the fusing of flesh and machine leading to a rebirth. This thematic was inverted in J.G. Ballard's radical underground novel *Crash* (1973), where the themes of sexual desire, death, and technology are brought together. The car is desirable not because of its looks, but in the fusing of metal and flesh. In Ballard's novel Marinetti's terrible wager with the machine has come to fruition: the automobile has consumed the organic body. Human flesh in *Crash* merges with chrome and leather, sexual fluids with machine emissions; we are witness to de-realized bodies, and a world of surfaces, where old distinctions between outer "reality" and inner dreams have evaporated.[46] The body becomes the supplement to the machine rather than its reversal, as in the original Futurist dream.

The memory of the dead

The persistence of images of death on Delhi's roads as late as 2006, despite the large-scale governmental management of humans and machines, became worrisome for the local authorities who have campaigned energetically for a positive image of an emerging global city. One response has been to generate a familiar statistical flood of numbers; the Police Commissioner's report for 2005 stated proudly:

> In the current year, a major achievement of the Traffic Police was in fatal accidents, which showed a decline of 5%, which comes to about 80 accidents. This has been brought about by enhanced vigilance on the roads by improving the quality of prosecution and road safety education. Significantly, prosecutions for over speeding increased by 54%, drunken driving by 49%, tinted glasses by 280%, plying of HTVs for driving without speed governors by 75%. Action against blueline buses was stepped up to 1,65,481 from the earlier 1,48,643. 44759 vehicles were prosecuted for violations of Supreme Court directives as against 40,350 of the previous year.[47]

The point here is not that road deaths were coming down (which they were not) but that it was important to show that rational management techniques were being put in place. This was the new language of governmentality set in motion by the court interventions of the late 1990s. The ability of government to manage technological life has been an open question after globalization; the generation of statistics as an "image-flood" is but one attempt to convince itself that such a process is underway.

Barely two weeks after the Police Commissioner's report was released to the press, the city edition of *The Indian Express* reported an accident on Ring Road on January 25, 2006 the day before the Republic Day holiday.

In a fatal accident on Ring Road today evening, a Blueline bus hit a cyclist, killing him on the spot, besides injuring a scooterist and a passenger in the bus. Twenty-six-year-old Ram Biraji Ram, a labourer, was returning to Naraina village when the Blueline bus (route 891) from Jahangirpuri to Harinagar hit him, killing him on the spot. The laborer was carrying a packet of nails used for fixing shoes, which got scattered all over on the road. A scooterist Kishore Nagpal, 25, was also hit by the bus. A passenger, Prem (32), who was getting down from the bus, came under the wheels of the bus and was injured. Both have been admitted to Deen Dyal Upadhyaya Hospital and are stated to be critical. Nagpal has an ankle fracture and an injury on the head while Prem had a deep thigh injury. The bus driver, however, fled the spot. Meanwhile, for the next one hour, commuters on the Naraina-Dhaula Kuan stretch had a hard time as the nails dropped from the victim's packet flattened tyres. "I was astonished to see at least 35 cars stranded on both sides of the road on my way back from office. People were wondering why everyone was having a flat tyre. For a while, even I got scared," said Nisha Sharma, who was going to Pitampura. "It took us at least half-an-hour to clear the road, only after which traffic regained smooth movement," said police.[48]

I have taken the liberty to cite this news report in full, since it is not a spectacular story, but one tucked away in the local section of the paper. This tragic account of a worker's death on the road is almost cinematic, with all the recurring elements of Delhi's accidents: there is an uncontrolled velocity when the machine goes out of control, the bus-driver flees the scene, and the nails in the worker's bag puncture the tyres of scores of cars, leading to mayhem and chaos, a story so ordinary and dramatic and fear-inducing as the woman witness points out. If there is a kind of ghostly everydayness to the report, it also moves in a plane of urban distraction: it disturbs and also numbs the reader. The preponderance of accident stories repeated themselves every day relentlessly in a merciless mix of reportage and crash photographs.[49] The writing up of the disaster in an age where the urban sensorium is flush with images; the "experience" of the accident is not prior to the technological.

Along with accident stories were the hundreds of news photographs – of crashed vehicles, of accident death victims, sometimes inserted in a ghostly montage in the body of the photograph. Kracauer saw photography as mortification, a ghostly death document of unredeemed lives, a distancing of experience and representation, an afterlife where a person lives on as a thing (1995). For Kracauer, photography as a technological form is the removal of subject from experience. Do other technological media then also block the shock-effects of traumatic events, screening them, allowing them to be viewed from a distance? In her essay "Information, Crisis, Catastrophe" (1990), Mary Ann Doane suggests that television promises us the chance encounter with the "reality" of catastrophe. "Television shocks, and then repeatedly assures, a comforting presence in an insecure world." "Televisual catastrophe is thus characterized by everything which it is said not to be – it is expected, predictable, its presence crucial to television's operation" (1990, p.238). In the idea that the technological media produce distance, "concealing" and containing bodily violence, Doane is in line with a strand of thinking from Kracauer to Debord. While the rush of violent death images in the media has accompanied the removal of death from public visibility in Western modernity,[50] this process has been seen as a progressive loss of the body to spectacle. Disembodiment, the argument goes, encloses the fascination with spectacular violence[51] within the framework of a "mass subject"; thus disaster stories are a way "of making mass subjectivity available" (Warner, 1993, p.248). However, the bulk of what Mark Seltzer calls the "containment thesis" reduces "mimesis or simulation or mediation to a distancing and loss of the real, and reduces the contagious relations between bodies and technologies of representation to distanced or voyeuristic representation" (Seltzer, 1998, p.37). Thus a *dualism* is preserved, between natural and artificial, between the everyday and the spectacular.

Among the many photographs of accidents in Delhi that appeared regularly in the local papers, one comes to mind. I had initially forgotten where I saw it.[52] It is a picture of a crashed bus with the ID photograph of a boy who died in the accident inserted in a grotesque montage. The boy's photograph looks like any other identification photograph: unsmiling, staring nervously at the camera. As an uncanny, terrifying afterlife, this photograph takes the form of a haunting. Kracauer wrote in his essay on photography, "The image wanders ghostlike through the present. . . . Spooky apparitions occur only in places where a terrible deed has been committed" (1995, p.56). Looking at this photograph I felt *I was there*, torn between the role of a witness and a survivor of possible accident deaths. This was a photograph touched by death, of life and the machine, both intertwined in a montage that was disorienting, and refused to go away. In his *Camera Lucida*, Barthes talks of certain photographs having a detail (*punctum*) "which rises from the scene, shoots out of it like an arrow, and pierces me" (1984, p.26).

Road culture of the 1990s dramatized the emerging constellation of technological life in urban Delhi. Narrated through accident stories, statistics, tales of terrible deaths by uncontrolled machines and cruel driver subjects, the story of the accident drew attention to the human machine entanglement as a traumatic site of the city. These were everyday scenes of a "wound culture,"[53] where smashed and dented automobiles, fallen bodies, and the endless cycle of death revealed scars of this encounter. The divisions between private trauma and public tragedy blurred, suggesting a traumatic

Figure 4.5 Accident montage. Smashed bus and passport photograph of the dead
victim, a common sight in local news sections of Delhi papers.

Source: Sarai Archive.

collapse between inner worlds and the shock of public encounters. As populations developed techniques of parrying shock of urban sensations, they
became more and more complicit in a technological world, contemplating
a threatening collapse of the boundary between Nature and artifice. Such
were the "atrocity exhibitions" of urban life in Delhi, ever visible in image,
text, numbers, and the screams of the dying as they met their untimely end.

5   Conclusion

An information city?

In his famous section on fetishism[1] in Volume 1 of *Capital*, Marx wrote, "A commodity appears, at first sight, a very trivial thing, and easily understood. Its analysis shows that it is, in reality, a very strange thing, abounding in metaphysical subtleties and theological niceties" (1976, p.163). A simple table made of wood, said Marx, transcends its "sensuous" nature once it becomes a commodity. "It not only stands with its feet on the ground, but, in relation to all other commodities, it stands on its head, and evolves out of its wooden brain grotesque ideas, far more wonderful than if it were to begin dancing on its own feet" (ibid., pp.163–164).

In a well-known Hindi short story by Sanjay Khati called *Pinti Ka Sabun* (Pinti's Soap, 1990) a village encounters a modern bar of soap for the first time through a child. In Khati's tale, the modern commodity appears as a desiring though dangerous force, destroying the village community and the innocence of childhood. In the event, the lure of commodity culture is broken, the bar of soap goes away, and modernity's spell is broken. For Khati, and so many writers of the post-independence generation, the commodity held out the debilitating threat of the loss of control. For Jainendra Kumar (2000b), another well-known Hindi writer of the post-1947 generation, the bazaar's "magic" could not be denied, but was carefully filtered through an economy of basic exchange. In Kumar's story, the figure of Bhagatji, a frugal shopkeeper who elided the "satiric power" of the market, emerges as the only unthreatening figure of commerce. In Khati's tale, the commodity represented social catastrophe, while in Jainendra Kumar the "metaphysical subtleties" of the commodity could be managed through careful self-control.[2]

These stories reflected a larger cluster of elite cultural fears that were distilled from a combination of nationalism, half-baked Marxism, and Brahmin condescension for small commerce. This became the lens through which many literary elites, urban planners, and bureaucrats saw the world. These views could not survive the 1980s. For many residents of India's cities and towns, the moral of Khati's story has not held, nor has Jainendra Kumar's advice for self-control been fully followed. Technological urbanism opened the way for both spectacular and informal circulation of commodities which magnified the enchanting but "grotesque" powers of the commodity that Marx had spoken about. In Uday Prakash's narration of that time, "Reality had gone past the machine age into the electronics age and beyond. Children now played *gilli danda* and baseball with magic spells, fairy tales and pre-historic dinosaurs. To *Hanumanji, Bhishma Pitamah* and *Krishnaji* they fed Cadbury chocolates and Mcdowell sodas" (2003, pp.135–136).

For many members of Delhi's cultural classes who had genuinely hoped for a liberal cosmopolis, the transformations after the 1980s were nothing short of catastrophic. For these writers the city had lost its ability to signal a better way of life (Singh and Dhamija, 1989, p.198). In 1996, at a time when the urban crisis of Delhi was entering its white-hot phase, the Delhi journal *Seminar* put out a special issue titled "The Other City," edited by Gautam Bhatia, architect and writer. In his editorial statement Bhatia went on to describe the urban present:

> [T]he signs of the city in which I now live are no longer related to the vastness of imagination. They belong instead to dimension. The city of tenements overwhelms, swallowing the past in an uncontrollable spasm, stretching its bounds into unreclaimed countryside. Wheat fields sprout low cost apartments; garbage appears on yet unfinished roads; electricity and phone lines are tapped in unofficial connections. Hotel facades rise up in finely proportioned compositions of tiles and terracotta; in parks behind them . . . village life continues: early morning defecators line up behind the bushes, smoke from suburban factories settles on the gladioli blossoms carefully tended on the city's roundabouts. Raw sewage snakes its way into parkland.
>
> (Bhatia, 1996, p.13)

What Bhatia presented in this expressionist canvas of urban decline was a tombstone for the liberal city. It was also an admission of failure on the "part of professions that had supposedly created the city" (ibid., p.13). It was also a definitive end to the modernist planning dreams of the 1950s which were based on the careful orchestration of rational order and abstract justice for urban populations. Those dreams had ended in the Fall.

This suggests a significant difference between the trajectory of modernist death narratives in the West and the postcolony. Situationism, and then archi-tectural postmodernism began the debate on the modernist city's irrelevance in the West, with iconic moments like Guy Debord's "Naked City" and Robert Venturi, Steven Izenour, and Denise Scott Brown's *Learning from Las Vegas* (1972). Urban modernism's non-Western version had its roots in colonialism and nationalism, and was more clearly affected by the erosion of the regime's urban power on which planning's success was predicated. A year before the special issue of *Seminar*, Achille Mbembe and Janet Roitman were describing a different but comparable situation in urban Cameroon during the crisis:

> Fraudulent identity cards; fake policemen dressed in official uniform . . .
> forged enrollment for exams; illegal withdrawal of money orders; fake
> banknotes; the circulation and sale of falsified school reports, medical
> certificates and damaged commodities: all of this is not only an expres-
> sion of frenetic trafficking and "arranging." It is also a manifestation of
> the fact that, here, things no longer exist without their parallel. Every law
> enacted is submerged by an ensemble of techniques of avoidance, cir-
> cumvention and envelopment which, in the end, neutralize and invert the
> legislation. There is hardly a reality here without its double.
>
> (Mbembe and Roitman, 1995, p.340)

This image of a "doubling" reality in the context of regime decline was part
of a larger postcolonial urban transformation from the 1970s, clearly more
pronounced in African cities than in Asian ones. For Mbembe and Roitman,
the African urban crisis demanded not Western liberal horror narratives, but
a bold search for openings for the figure of the subject in crisis.

In Delhi too, as in many other parts of the postcolonial world the decline
of liberal urban imaginary was not a paralyzing descent into disaster. The
resulting situation offered subaltern urban populations the ability to attach
themselves virally to existing infrastructures, and create new spaces of urban
living. In Delhi the end of the state's technological monopoly opened up
a dynamic space where the existing networks of "political society" and
expanding informal media production quickly moved from a model of parasitic attachment to a vitalistic transformation of the urban fabric. Most of
this was outside legal structures, an urban bypass.

The catastrophist image of the decaying liberal city of the long 1980s draws
from the familiar binarism of nineteenth-century social theory: progress
versus reaction, development versus backwardness/decay, new versus old,
secular versus religious. "Waste, decay, elimination," Nietzsche once wrote,
"need not be condemned: they are necessary consequences of life, of the
growth of life" (1967, p.25). The pirate media city mixed debris, recycled
structures, and hyper-modern technologies in its appropriation of media
infrastructures, refusing the progressive determination of its actions. It
reproduced itself less through representational models of alterity (resistance),
but offered the greatest of challenges to capital, insubordination, and a
refusal of the legal regime pushed by the globalizing elites.

The postcolonial hope on rational planning as a model for the legal city
came apart decisively with globalization. Endless proliferation was unleashed
with globalization rather than from non-modern pasts, as had been feared
during the 1950s. The language of civic liberalism took the urban crisis of the
1990s as a productive space for discursive intervention and enactment of an
information zone of expertise. It was a rescripting of a new language for
liberalism, in a general climate of rising globalizing elites and a capitalist
boom cycle. The civic liberal enterprise represented the most innovative
project for creating a new language of urban life for globalizing elites. Civic

liberalism drew selectively from old liberal models: rights theory, the public domain, a "livable city," and linked it to legal strategies, and media campaigns and events. Not identifiable with any particular group, civic liberalism used the urban crisis to suggest regular court intervention in the city, bypassing traditional political parties except for those sections which were willing to join the new platform. Borrowing from viral media urbanism, civic liberalism initiated a proliferation of court-case media events that created turmoil and terror in the city: the displacement of river front working-class settlements, closure of small industries, and sealing of small shops.

The information war

In initiating the dramaturgy of Delhi's urbanism, civic liberalism's most significant legacy was to magnify the problematic of the information zone, almost in contrast to the planning era. "We have no real information," Albert Mayer had complained after the Masterplan was launched (1962, p.408). In the planning era, information helped to produce the city as a visible, rational entity within a hierarchy of parts. This was done for the public, but particularly for the postcolonial elites who were able to access the city using the authorized language of planning. All this changed with the simultaneous decline of planning and the emergence of globalization and technological networks in the city. Uday Prakash writes ironically of the new age in his *Paul Gomra ka Scooter*: "No reality exists anywhere. There is only information." (2003, p.170).

Pirate urbanism's tactics avoided visibility, except in local political mobilizations or financial arrangements with lower officials. The lack of visibility helped pirate media urbanism exploit the expanse of Delhi, connecting through mobile telecom infrastructures. Invisibility, once the preserve of the urban crowd, now extended to dispersed urban space.

Civic liberalism's tactics shouldered the task of rendering visible the informal city. Modernism assumed that transparency would come through revealing techniques of a Masterplan and architectural interventions. With civic liberalism and technologies of risk, transparency lacked a permanent model of revelation, but was enacted in a series of information events and new technologies of visibility. The court case became an important site for constituting this information zone, reassembling the Illegal city and its infringements. This was supported by television shows, endless statistical surveys, and special columns.

Today information culture remains the overarching cultural attractor of power in the public realm. Governments and corporations rush into biometric technologies as a magic wand for all its problems: reigning office slackers, plugging welfare systems, a paranoid national ID card already deployed in the "border areas" may even one day arrive in Delhi. Muslim and Kashmiri tenants face a double burden: the now compulsory tenant verification procedures, and regular police terror. Displaced populations are forced

Figure 5.1 Information society: the governmental drive.

Source: Transport Department, 2007.

to produce objects of visibility to qualify for possible compensation: ration cards with particular cut-off dates, voter ID cards indicating entry into the city. PAN (tax) numbers filter entry into financial realms. The list is endless: CCTVs all over the city, brain mapping in court cases, GIS maps to catch squatters and bad bus-drivers, all hoping to render transparent a world that is more opaque day by day.[3] Information activists hope that "transparency" will solve the problems of democracy, the RTI (Right to Information Act) the modernized tool of a post-media population.[4]

New urban control technologies copied the model of info-war, and pincer strikes.

In particular, the police have been quick to modernize the urban "encounter" following the model of info-war. The terrorist is now the socio-logical specimen of the urban information war, replacing the slum dweller of the 1950s. A bombardment of copious and useless information, the social profile and intricate life histories of the dead, now accompany encounter killings, ensuring a temporary capture of media space. This model of "capture" was once used by Deleuze and Guattari (1988) in their notion of capitalism as a non-territorial, axiomatic model of flows. This seems to have

Figure 5.2 Information society: "The computer scanner".

Source: Raj Comics.

metamorphosed into an urban media technology *par excellence.*[5] Television "sting" operations allow the media to temporarily capture its own space, a grotesque implosion of the society of the spectacle. If there is any reassurance in the information zone it is in its lack of permanence; most captures are temporary, allowing lines of exit and entry. Activists, media pirates, working-class migrants, ordinary city dwellers, all keep looking and sometimes finding exit (or entry) tactics in the information zone.[6] If pirate modernity imaged informal urban media practices in the long decade of the 1980s, the information war-zone adds another, if disturbing layer for the first decade of this century.

The problem of designation: the image of the city

Writing just two years after the Paris events of 1968, Henri Lefebvre came up with a bold hypothesis: "that society has been completely urbanized" (1971, p.1). By this Lefebvre meant that the "urban condition" had replaced the questions of "the city," and its "secret script" – the map and the plan. The designative oppositions of twentieth-century urbanism – urban versus rural,

Figure 5.3 Information society: The new ID card.

Source: Raj Comics.

industry versus agriculture, order versus chaos – were all up in the air after the urban condition. For Lefebvre, new, uncharted urban practices would replace the language of clear designation.

The US planners who helped make the Delhi Masterplan sought to insure the city against the very possibility that Lefebvre proclaimed was inevitable. The Masterplan's design attempted to deflect migration flows into suburban nodes, while at the same time displacing forms of life that were not considered sufficiently urban from the core. In doing so the Masterplan sought to build a defensible urban core, cemented by law, and a highly centralized command structure, to address the demand of the political regime for control over Delhi. It was the model of the city as an urban machine, with neighborhoods as cellular units, linked by a technocratic hierarchy of functions and power. It was also a machine that was premised on a city of *legal subjects*, demarcated from the rest by diffused centralized power. When both components were fundamentally eroded after the Emergency, the plan's control model became slowly irrelevant.

This was a model of the machine city drawn from US urbanism, whose debates had nurtured the 1962 Masterplan's international consultants. In 1932, Frank Lloyd Wright (1958) distinguished between centrifugal and centripetal space to conceptually separate the older centralized, dense urban core, and a new decentralized urban form. The latter was centrifugal space, decentralized urbanism, increasingly held together mainly by infrastructures of motor transport and communication. The decentralized centrifugal city as the new machine model for urbanism became the modernizing slogan of planners for the coming decades, Delhi included. It was the perfect model of escape from the old city form, condemned as congested and unlivable.

Edward Dimmenberg summarizes the immediate problem of centrifugal space: "its *nonarchitectural* character" (2004, p.178). If concentrated, centripetal space of the older urban core laid a premium of recognizable public spaces and monuments balanced with the anonymity of the urban crowd, centrifugal space dissolved into the urban sprawl. The Delhi Masterplan was part of this larger moment of modern urbanism, where a carefully managed decentralization would solve the problem of the postcolonial city. With one stroke, the festering problems of the old city as well as the dangers of unmanaged urban sprawl could be resolved.[7] As a variant of modernist planning, the Masterplan saw better infrastructure as designating the form of the city. In the 1990s, new liberalism as modernism's *soi disant* successor did not depart from this. But less imaginatively, the "junkspace" architectures of Shanghai and Singapore were hailed as the allegorical model for Delhi's future. The problem of the "image of the city" becomes more pressing as Delhi's elites look for a language to represent the capital to the rest of the world (Gupta, 2006).

More than most Indian cities, Delhi owes an unredeemed debt to its dead. The city has witnessed massacres of its residents in the eighteenth century during the invasion of the Persian ruler Nadir Shah. Delhi was overrun and partially destroyed by vengeful British soldiers in 1857. In the twentieth century, the Partition of 1947 led to large-scale killings of Muslims in the city. In 1984 Congress workers organized a massacre of Sikhs following the assassination of Indira Gandhi. Along with this was the erasure of innumerable ways of living in the city, incomprehensible to colonial officials, modern planners, and postcolonial bureaucrats. If in 1857 dynamite solved the problem of Delhi for the East India Company, urban policy since then has carried out a more far-reaching erasure. The memories of the dead survive in fugitive ways: stray literary reflections, personal stories handed down by old residents, a ghostly archive that leaves its traces in the various ruins, and displaced settlements that dot the city. For the most part, the new planned city that emerged after the 1950s turned its back on the dead, the affective world of the urban pasts found little place in the anti-historical language of the Masterplan.[8] It was the urban crisis of the 1990s that reinstated the problem of the form of the Delhi's urbanism back on the agenda.

There are two parallel archives that mark the contemporary life of Delhi. One archive is that of the detritus rendered illegitimate by the modern period after 1857. This detritus lies in exile in the walls of the old city, ruined monuments of the *Sultanat* and *Moghul* eras, the refugee camps of every major building project in modern Delhi, artisan communities displaced by planning. It is also a Muslim counter-memory of the present, materialized in the production of fugitive, non-historical pasts. The other archive, the subject of this book, is that of the technological kingdom that emerged from the urban expansion and crisis in the long 1980s that has permanently changed the life of Delhi. The two archives are not from *separate* worlds, as is clear from this book, but different points from where urban memories emerged.

The subaltern migrant populations occupied a schizophrenic zone between the two archives. When public discourse rendered them visible in the urban crisis and subjected them to a permanent state of displacement, they entered the archive of the undead, those without a name.[9] At the same time they were among the significant producer/narrators of the subaltern technological kingdom, which spread a universe outside that of formal space and law.[10]

In the second volume of *The Practice of Everyday Life* Michel De Certeau wrote, "The debris of shipwrecked histories still today raise up the ruins of an unknown, strange city. They burst forth within the modernist, massive homogenous city like slips of the tongue from an unknown, perhaps unknown language" (1998a, p.133). Any answer to the form of the city must engage in what Benjamin called "a historical apocatastasis" where both the illegitimate past and present are brought from the archive of the dead into the streams of the living.[11] Only then can urbanism reassert its potential as a critical reflection on the present, the legacy of the twentieth century that still makes sense today.

Notes

Introduction: after media

1 My use of the term "postcolonial" is completely pragmatic – to indicate a successor to the anti-colonial nationalist enterprise. The terms "Third World" and "South" make no sense today in their original formulation.

2 Kittler (1999, p.xxxix). Updating Marshall McLuhan's premise of a new expanded universe after the coming of "electric technologies," Kittler went on to argue that Mcluhan's project was out of date. "Understanding Media – despite Mcluhan's title – remains an impossibility precisely because the dominant information technologies of the day control all understanding and its illusions" (ibid., p.xl). Kittler's pessimism may be due to his reliance on a formal understanding of media in general. See Mark Hansen (2004) for a useful discussion.

3 This was recognized by a range of scholars (see Khilnani, 1998. Nair, 2005. For a good popular account see Sharma, 2000). See also the proceedings of the *City One, First South Asian Cities Conference* at http://www.sarai.net/resources/event-proceedings/2003/city-one. Accessed January 1, 2006.

4 In Gyan Prakash (2002, p.3). See Prakash's article for a wider discussion on nationalism and the city.

5 For a survey of this transformation see Menon and Nigam (2007).

6 For a select literature see Crary (1992), Charney and Schwartz (1995). For an Indian context see Mazumdar (2007). For sound cultures see Thompson (2002).

7 A state-produced educational documentary was made mandatory in all commercial film screenings. For a discussion of the politics of state-produced documentary see Roy (2002). For cinema see the *Film Enquiry Committee Report of 1951.*

8 Ministry of Information and Broadcasting, *Report of the Committee on Broadcasting and Information Media.* New Delhi (1966, p.13); see also Kanchan Kumar (2003).

9 Radio broadcasting in the 1950s carefully avoided any film and popular music, promoting "classical" music and a Sanskritized version of Hindi. It was only after its listeners began deserting the national radio network for Radio Ceylon's broadcasts of Hindi film music that popular music was allowed on the national network of All India Radio (see Lelyveld, 2005).

10 This refuge has proved illusory for many. In recent years upscale apartment complexes in Gurgaon have suffered periodic flooding and infrastructure problems. For a large coverage see http://www.gurgaonscoop.com/, a portal catering to Gurgaon residents.

11 In Kracauer, this hope existed only during a small period of his Weimar years. Kracauer developed Georg Simmel's phenomenology of external forms in the city to indicate that the surface expressions of media technology were hieroglyphs of urban life. Even when he attacked the "mechanization" of the film spectator in

new contexts, Kracauer was constantly drawn to the film experience himself (Frisby, 1986).

12 Benjamin borrowed "innervation" mostly from Freud, and transformed it into a larger, more radical two-way technological physics, where humans engaged with technology through a collective neuro-physiology. This dissolved inner and outer boundaries and the human–nature distinction, opening up the possibility of a new subjectivity. See "The Work of Art in the Age of its Technological Reproducibility" (2nd version) (2002).

13 See Miriam Bratu Hansen (2004). This is what Benjamin says in *One-Way Street*: "Only when in technology body and image space so interpenetrate that all revolutionary tension becomes bodily collective innervation, and all the bodily innervations of the collective become revolutionary discharge, has reality transcended itself to the extent demanded by the *Communist Manifesto*" (Benjamin, 1999, pp.217–218).

14 For a critique of Manovich see Mark Hansen (2004). Hansen argues that Manovich's burden on cinema as a cultural interface of new media serves to produce a formalist model, bounded by the cinematic and hostile to materiality. For Hansen, "digital data is at heart polymorphous, lacking any inherent form or enframing, data can be materialized in any inherent form or enframing, data can be materialized in an almost limitless array of framings" (ibid, p.34).

15 Among these see Ward (2001). Ward contrasts the Weimar era's street-specific spectacle to what she sees as the contemporary erosion of everyday life under digital media.

16 See the discussions on NICNET and Doordarshan in Chapter 2.

17 This "sharing" of the social with non-human elements was pioneering posed by Bruno Latour, who spoke of "complex hybrids" of humans and non-humans. Latour moves the human–technology relationship from the subject–object model to his actor-network theory (see Latour, 1987, 1993). For a recent update of the debate see Lash (2002).

18 International media pirate networks have also attracted organized crime, though this remains a small part of the local and regional story.

19 Gupta (1998). For the colonial stabilization of post-1857 Lucknow see Oldenburg (1985). For Delhi during the revolt see Dalrymple (2007) and Farooqui (2006)

20 The Coronoation Durbar of December 1911 in Delhi was held to announce the coronation of King George V and Queen Mary as Emperor and Empress of India. Crucially, the Durbar announce the shift of the colonial capital from Calcutta to Delhi.

21 For an examination of the postcolonial elites' eagerness to use the Lutyens model for a nationalist architectural discourse for Delhi through the 1980s see Chattopadhyay (2000).

22 Although modern buildings were built in the colonial era, modernism as an expression of the international movement spread only in the postcolonial period. For a longer discussion see Chapter 1.

23 Some architects who worked in Chandigarh set up practice in Delhi. These included J. K. Choudhary's design for the IIT Delhi and Rajinder Kumar's ISBT. Shivnath Prasad, who had worked with the Masterplan, was notable in his distinctive style. Prasad built the Shriram Center in Delhi along with other projects.

24 For a comprehensive survey see Mark Wigley (2001). Wigley shows the range of intellectual energies that flowed into the cybernetic model – Buckminster Fuller, Norbert Weiner, Marshall Mcluhan, Siegfried Gideon, Margaret Mead, Doxiadis.

25 Albert Mayer, head of the Delhi Masterplan team, also participated in the US debates, calling for a "safety of space" to secure cities. See the fascinating discussion in Dimmendberg (2004, pp.249–250).

26 Fredrich Kittler once complained that Foucault's notion of the archive was limited to the alphabet, i.e. the library. Kittler went on to extend the archeological technique to a larger discourse network, the alphabet, after the transmission of the book on to a larger medial plane. Similarly, "political society" can be displaced from its political-explanatory moorings on to a larger plane of non-legal contestation.
27 Beck (1992). My own reading aligns risk technologies more closely with new liberalism, rather than a generalized technology of late modernity.
28 For the development of this argument in the context of Delhi's environmental debate see Sharan (2002).
29 Political support in Delhi came from Sheila Dixit, who reached out to the civic liberal discourse through her *Bhagidari* Scheme.
30 Prevention of Environment and Sound Pollution vs. Union of India (UOI) and Anr. CA 3735/2005, Judgment on July 18, 2005 by R.C. Lahoti, C.J. and Ashok Bhan. The Court mobilized a host of cultural and historical arguments, as well as colonial and postcolonial legal statutes for its judgment. For a good example of civic liberal noise pollution campaigns see the Mumbai NGO Karmyog's list of resources and campaign material at http://www.karmayog.org/noisepollution/ (accessed on May 5, 2007).
31 It is possible that a combination of modernized governmental technologies and models of bourgeois individuation may emerge following the stabilization of the current phase of capitalism in South Asia.
32 *Control and Becoming*, Gilles Deleuze in conversation with Antonio Negri, at http://www.generation-online.org/p/fpdeleuze3.htm (accessed July 10, 2006).

1 A city of order: the Masterplan

1 M.C. Mehta's cases date back to the 1980s. Among the notable cases that had a bearing on the Court's discourse on Delhi was the Oleum gas leak case, when oleum gas leaked from the Shriram factory in Delhi (M.C. Mehta v. Union of India WP 12739/1985 (Oleum Gas Leak Case)). For an argument linking this case with later developments see Awadhendar Sharan, " 'New' Delhi" Fashioning an Urban Environment through Science and Law," *Bare Acts*, Sarai Reader 05, Delhi, CSDS, 2005, pp.69–77.
2 M.C. Mehta v. Union of India and Others. Writ Petn. (C) No. 4677 of 1985. The Court's order was merciless "The closure order with effect from November 30, 1996 shall be unconditional. Even if the relocation of industries is not complete they shall stop functioning in Delhi with effect from November 30, 1996."
3 The Janvadi Adhikar manch estimated that 50,000 workers lost their jobs in the first phase of closures. See *How many errors does time have patience for?* (Mimeo), Delhi 2001. Also online at http://www.safhr.org/docuement_2.htm, accessed July 23, 2005.
4 *MARG* included on its first editorial board architects and art critics like Otto Koenigsberger (a German exile who was later involved in the design of Bhubaneswar) as well as Herman Goetz (also a German émigré, director of the Baroda Art Museum).
5 For a summary of the development of housing in the decade after Partition see pp.185–192. As such the focus on congestion and sanitation also prepare a *raison d'être* for the Masterplan's idea of social housing. For other discussions on the post-Partition years in Delhi see Kaur, 2007.
6 *Report on the Relief of Congestion in Delhi*, Vols I and II, Government of India Press, Simla, 1936. The relationship between social space, congestion, and caste community practices is made forcefully in letters written between colonial officials at that time. Sohan Lal, "Improving the Delhi City," Delhi Archives (DA) DA/CC/

Home/1930/29B. For detailed discussions on the Delhi Improvement Trust see Hosagrahar, 2005; Legg, 2007.

7 A comprehensive critique of the DIT was undertaken by the post-independence G.D. Birla Committee, which suggested the need to move on to a "real" plan. See the *Report of the Delhi Improvement Trust Enquiry Committee*, Government of India, Delhi, 1951.

8 *Report of the Delhi Municipal Organization Enquiry Committee*, Government of India Press, New Delhi, 1948.

9 Ibid., p.3.

10 Delhi Improvement Trust, *Annual Administration Report 1950–1*. New Delhi, 1951, p.21.

11 *Report of the Delhi Improvement Trust Enquiry Committee*, Government of India, Delhi, 1951. See particularly pp.1–31.

12 Ibid. See p.28. It was possible to conceive of the important role of private enterprise in a public document before the "socialist turn" in the mid-1950s.

13 Ibid., p.15.

14 "Letter to Douglas Ensminger," January 14, 1956, Ford Foundation Archives (FFA) New York. The Ford Foundation Archives have virtually all the correspondence and documents going through the Ford office in Delhi relating to the Masterplan (boxes of Ford Foundation project nos 57–108, 57–205 and 57–206).

15 *Hindustan Times* (Delhi) January 4, 1956.

16 "More Jaundice Cases Reported in Delhi," ibid.

17 This led to sewage water from the Najafgarh drain flowing into the drinking-water supply. See "Jaundice Caused by Polluted Water," *Hindustan Times*, January 4, 1956.

18 *Hindustan Times*, January 7, 1956.

19 "Jaundice Cases in Delhi, Inquiry Committee Appointed." *Hindustan Times*, January 11, 1956.

20 Ibid., p.12.

21 "Delhi's Sanitation Problem," *Hindustan Times*, January 18, 1956. Flies from open food venders were seen as a persistent problem, and the health services and the municipality carried out periodic though unsuccessful campaigns against hawkers.

22 "Report of Committee investigating epidemic of jaundice (infectious hepatitis) in New Delhi, India, December 1955–January 1956," Ministry of Health, Government of India. For a newspaper report see the exhaustive story in the *Hindustan Times*, February 18, 1956. The committee itself was considerably controversial, holding its meetings in camera, reflecting the government's nervousness over the public uproar. Political parties like the Praja Socialist Party carried out counter-surveys and produced an alternative report. See *Hindustan Times*, ibid.

23 Report of Committee investigating the epidemic of jaundice, p.6.

24 Report of Committee investigating the epidemic of jaundice, p.31.

25 Report of Committee investigating the epidemic of jaundice, p.2.

26 See Lok Sabha Debates, 1955, Vol. 13, part 2, Debate on Control of Building Operations Bill, Delhi, December 7, 1955. The MP was Dr. Suresh Chandra.

27 For the entire text of the 1949 report see *Gaither Report*, Report of the Study for the Ford Foundation on Policy and Program, online at http://www.fordfound.org/archives/item/0113. See also Sutton, 1997.

28 In the 1951 budget of the Foundation $12 million out of a total of 28 million was allocated to "the relief of tension in underdeveloped areas." Sutton, 1997, p.66. For a detailed examination of the Ford Foundation in this period see Raynor, 2000.

29 The literature on modernization theory is voluminous. For standard critical

accounts see Escobar (1995), and for a long-term perspective see Wallerstein (1983).

30 The combined outlay of projects from 1951 to 1958 totaled almost $28 million of which rural projects comprised $10.5 million. For the list of Ford projects in this period see *The Ford Foundation and Foundation-supported Projects in India*, Ford Foundation New Delhi, 1959 (Mimeo).

31 Ibid. Ensminger's own lengthy accounts of this tenure are contained in Douglas Ensminger, *Oral History, 1972*, Ford Foundation Archives. For urban planning see Oral History B17.

32 FFA, 57–205, 3832/4.

33 Health Minister Rajkumari Amrit Kaur to Douglas Ensminger, Ford Foundation representative in India, January 14, 1956. FFA, 57–205/3832/Corr.

34 For Mayer's early days see Ravi Kalia, 1999 pp.21–26.

35 Kalia 1999, also AM Papers, Box 18, Folders 27–33. Mayer's (critical) assessment of Corbusier's design is contained in his second newsletter from India, June 11, 1958, AM Papers, Box 36, Folder 10.

36 Letter to Albert C. Wolf, February 27, 1956. FFA/57–205/3832/Corr. The regional emphasis is also contained in a letter to Nehru: Albert Mayer to Jawaharlal Nehru, April 22, 1957, AM Papers, Box 22/5.

37 Ibid.

38 Breese, who had to return to Princeton after a year, coordinated the project until August, 1958, and was succeeded by Edward Echeverria.

39 The existence of the Ford team is known mostly to urban specialists.

40 Douglas Ensminger, "The Ford Foundation's Role in the Field of Urbanization," FFA/Oral History/B17, p.7.

41 George Goetschius, "T.P.O. [Town Planning Organization] History and Current Affairs," ms., n.d. AM Papers, Box 23, Folder 3. In all probability, this was written after the first few months of the team's arrival.

42 Ibid. The tension over the US consultants was addressed in a sarcasm-tinged letter to Raj Kumari Amrit Kaur from Ensminger: "The foreign specialists will be people well-trained and experienced in a particular discipline or disciplines. . . . Obviously, if there were economists, socialists, architects etc., in India who already had this experience, the outside experts would not be needed in the first place" (Letter dated March 1, 1957. AM Papers, Box 21, Folder 18).

43 Mayer and Ensminger met Nehru in May, 1957. Ensminger reported to New York: "We are all working on a common thought wave, and the PM. is taking the very keenest interest in this project which affects the national capital" (Douglas Ensminger to Albert C. Wolf, May 13, 1957, FFA/57–05/3832/1).

44 Some of the writers at the TPO had in fact been trained at US architecture schools.

45 Ibid.

46 The reception in the newspapers at that time was unusually sympathetic. The Delhi papers mostly reported protests from towns outside Delhi, reflecting anxieties about the regional focus of the plan.

47 Masterplan of Delhi, DDA, 1962, p.7.

48 Ibid.

49 Major discussions took place among the team over linking the old city to the new through Ram Lila grounds. See Masterplan, p.12, and Albert Mayer to Edward Echeverria (No. 166), February 8, 1960, AM Papers, 21/6.

50 The listing and hierarchy is in Masterplan of Delhi, pp.76–85.

51 The ratios are in Masterplan of Delhi, pp.66–67. For the listing of commerce types see p.50.

52 A public notification was issued by the Delhi administration under section 4 of the Act in the *Government of India Gazette* on November 13, 1959. The public purpose was stated blandly as the "planned development of Delhi." Existing built-up

areas, and a host of others like graveyards, tombs and so on were excluded from the notification. See also *Land Values in Delhi*, TCPO, Delhi, May, 1970.

53 In parliamentary debates MPs were quick to attribute hidden speculative designs to the DIT's demolition drives. See *Lok Sabha Debates*, Vol. VII, Part II, August 24, 1956, 4270–74.

54 For a selection see *Review of Master Plan for Delhi*. Government of India, Town and Country Planning Organization, February, 1973; Singh and Dhamija, 1989; Ravindran, 1996; Dewan-Verma, 1993; Roy, 2004. Of these, Dewan-Verma's book remains the most sympathetic to the 1962 document.

55 "Why a Master Plan for Delhi", *Hindustan Times*, Sunday Magazine, August 21, 1960, pp.1–6, emphasis added.

56 *Slum Clearance and Urban Renewal in Delhi*, Ministry of Health, 1958.

57 Ibid., p.4.

58 Ibid., p.6.

59 *Masterplan of Delhi Work Studies*, Vol. 1, pp.205–243.

60 Cited in Bopegamage, 1957, p.92.

61 See *Hindustan Times*, April 2, 1956. Ensminger claims that Nehru was so upset by the slum conditions after this visit that he ordered "immediate" solutions by the planners, only to be persuaded about the value of a long-term approach after discussions. FFA/Oral History/A8 p.14.

62 *Slums of Old Delhi*, A Survey by the Bharat Sevak Samaj, Atma Ram and Sons, Delhi, 1958, p.217.

63 Ibid., p.217. It is curious that in the Samaj's own survey, slum residents did not see congestion as a significant concern.

64 Ibid., p.220.

65 Albert Mayer, "Ch. 8 Slums and Congestion Rehabilitation Development (Urban Renewal) Preservation, Destruction, Re-creation," AM Papers, 21/11.

66 *Masterplan of Delhi Workstudies*, Vol. 1, p.375.

67 "Why a Master Plan for Delhi", *Hindustan Times*, August 21, 1960.

68 *Roots of Change*, Ford Foundation in India, Ford Foundation, New York, 1961.

69 "India's First Experiment in Urban Community Development." Ford Foundation Program Letter, no.106, February 10, 1959, p.3, FFA.

70 Ibid.

71 Ibid., p.3.

72 Ibid., p.5.

73 The relevant documents are in Box 31, Folders 9, 11, and 13 of the Albert Mayer Papers. The same language also shows up in a note on the subject issued by the Delhi Municipal Corporation, Department of Urban Community Development, in all probability drafted by the US team members; copy in Box 31, Folder 13, AM Papers.

74 Ibid., p.11

75 *Workstudies*, Vol. I, p.201. These are clearly Mayer's own words. See also Albert Mayer to E.G. Echevarria, 22 January, 1960, AM Papers, 21/10.

76 See *Masterplan Workstudies*, Vol. 1, p.202.

77 Ibid., p.203.

78 See the accounts in *Evaluation Study of the Formation and Working of Vikas Mandals*, Department of Urban Community Development, Municipal Corporation of Delhi, 1962; Clinard, 1966.

79 Clinard, ibid., p.152.

80 Paper presented at seminar on Urban Community Development, Hyderabad, December 24 to 30, 1959. FFA/0033322/Reports.

81 Ford Foundation India, report no. 130, "The Delhi Urban Community Project" by B. Chatterjee, Director, Department of Urban Community Development, Municipal Corporation of Delhi, p.14.

82 Ibid., p.13.
83 See *Masterplan Workstudies*, Vol. 2. The influence of the local TPO researchers is even evident in the South Asian syntax errors that are visible in this document, in contrast to the clearer prose in the main Masterplan and the first volume of the work studies.
84 Ibid.
85 See the excellent analysis in Alice O'Connor (2001, p.135). O'Connor suggests that there was an unspoken "racial embargo" imposed by the trustees of the Ford Foundation.
86 *Masterplan of Delhi, Workstudies*, Vol. 1, p.204. The liberal model of the desegregated neighborhood was confronted with murmurs of local discontent in a section of Volume 2 of the *Workstudies*, written up by Indian researchers. The neighborhood study of Daryaganj warned that while mixed areas were all right, "care should be taken to see that this objective is not defeated by a wanton mixture of elements that have nothing in common, resulting in community dissension." *Master Plan Workstudies*, part 2, p.77.
87 This was before the 1961 census which showed in fact that a lower than expected rate of urbanization was underway. See Bose, 1978, pp.1–42.
88 For both Memos see AM Papers, 22/7.
89 There were officially three categories of "urban renewal": conservation, rehabilitation, and redevelopment. On slums see *Master Plan of Delhi*, p.27, and also *MasterPlan Workstudies*, Vol. 1, pp.205–243.
90 Parliamentarians were uniformly sympathetic to slum dwellers and hostile to any form of demolition. The removal of the Jamuna Bazaar squatters near Nigambodh Ghat caused outrage in Parliament when MPs angrily questioned the hapless Rajkumari Amrit Kaur. See Lok Sabha Debates 1956, Vol. III, part II, 4052–4274.
91 A report by the elected Delhi Municipal Corporation wrote of squatters on public land that "it was not considered desirable to resort to such extreme measures on humanitarian considerations." *Three Years of the Municipal Corporation of Delhi, 1958–61*, Delhi, 1962. See also *Report of the Advisory Committee on Slum Clearance*, New Delhi, July 18, 1958.
92 *Masterplan Workstudies*, Vol. 1, p.198.
93 Ibid., p.218.
94 Edward G. Echeverria, Memo, AM Papers 23/7.
95 The hapless TPO researchers of the Masterplan would be not infrequently confronted with the popularity of "mixed use" among residents in their surveys. The planners' answer was to suggest a local version of false consciousness. "This shows people are oblivious to their surroundings, the incompatible uses, and their undesirable influences on the environment of the area." *Masterplan, Workstudies*, Vol. 2, p.113.
96 *Review of the Masterplan of Delhi*, TCPO, Ministry of Urban Affairs and Employment, February, 1973.
97 Ibid., p.41.
98 Ibid., p.27.
99 Ibid., p.11; the Pusa Road district center is mentioned on p.27.
100 Ibid., p.51.
101 *Land Values in Delhi*, TCPO, p.13.
102 For an excellent analysis of land values in Delhi in the 1960s see Bose 1978, pp.167–196.
103 *Masterplan for Delhi, Workstudies*, Vol. 1, p.xxiii.
104 This was first suggested in Ghosh (1968). Ghosh, the future director of the School of Planning and Architecture, accurately perceived the segregationist land-use policy of the plan and its inability to break with the Lutyens model.

105 The nod to "national" historical building was done through state patronage in the 1950s. See Menon 2000, p.148.

2 Media urbanism

1 The reference is to a well-known interview by Delueze and Guattari, "Capitalism, A Very Special Delirium," http://www.generation-online.org/p/fpdeleuze7.htm. The "long" 1980s can be dated from the late 1970s to the beginning of this century, the years including and preceding the period commonly called globalization, which is formally dated in India from the early 1990s.

2 In 1972 the ILO used the term in its report on Kenya, while the economic anthropologist Keith Hart had pioneered the idea in 1971 at a conference in Sussex. Hart provides a concise summary in a recent reflection:

> The "formal sector" consisted of regulated economic activities and the "informal sector" of all those, both legal and illegal, lying beyond the scope of regulation. I did not identify the informal economy with a place, a class, a type of business or even whole persons. Informal opportunities ranged from market gardening and brewing through every kind of trade to gambling, theft and political corruption. My analysis had its roots in what people generate out of the circumstances of their everyday lives. The laws and offices of state bureaucracy only made their search for self-preservation and improvement more difficult.

See the archive of Hart's writings at http://www.thememorybank.co.uk.

3 For a useful survey of the debates see Razzaz, 1994. Sally Moore talks of a semi-autonomous social field (SASF). "The semi-autonomous social field has rule making capacities, and the means to induce or coerce compliance; but it is simultaneously set in a larger social matrix which can, and does, affect and invade it, sometimes at the invitation of persons inside it, sometimes at its own instance" (1973, p.55). Despite the somewhat structuralist language of this formulation, it anticipated the viral urbanism of the 1980s.

4 Mike Davis combines World Bank reports, planner documents, and Marxist writings to call these new areas "pirate urbanization" where slum lords, speculators, and other sundry elements encourage privatized squatting over fallow or unproductive zones. Peri-urban and pirate urbanization is a part of the morphology of urban hell in Davis' image of the "slum."

5 The statistics on Delhi are voluminous. For a useful introduction, see Government of NCT of Delhi (2006) and also Dupont (2000).

6 The special committees consisted of non-elected "experts" and judicial officials appointed by the Court to advice it. The often bizarre extent of these orders is detailed in a later opinion by the Supreme Court itself: "SC loud and clear, activism hurts us." See *Indian Express*, Delhi edition, December 11, 2007.

7 Among the long list of changes suggested by Jagmohan was the removal of Bhagirath Place and Lajpat Rai market that had come up in the old Moghul garden, Begum-ka-Bagh. Both Bhagirath Place and Lajpat Rai market survived Jagmohan's plans and developed in the 1980s as major centers for electrical and electronics distribution all over north India.

8 See *Techno-economic Survey of Delhi*, NCAER, Delhi, 1973, particularly the section on Urban Housing (pp. 85–98).

9 The 1981 figure comes from the Delhi Human Development Report (Government of NCT of Delhi, 2006, p.38). A 1996 survey by the Delhi Pollution Control Committee showed that of 137,000 existing units in the city only about 25,000 were located in designated industrial areas. The rest were in "non-conforming areas."

10 From a *Hindustan Times* report during the Emergency showing the scale of the operation:

> Some 350,000 residents of 27 clusters of jhuggi-jhonpris in Greater Delhi comprising some 85,000 families, mainly construction labour, have been resettled in new colonies in the trans-Yamuna area and in the outskirts of West and South Delhi.... In all, about 600,000 people from 50 jhuggi-jhonpri clusters are planned to be resettled under a project considered to be the world's largest resettlement scheme.... The project was conceived as a slum clearance drive.... The administration was asked to take advantage of the Emergency.... Shopping centres, community centres, parks, play-grounds, health centres, family planning centres and welfare centres have been provided in these localities. The community centres have been fitted with TV and Radio sets for entertainment of residents.

(May 3, 1976. Headline: "3 Lakh Jhuggi Dwellers Resettled in New Areas")

11 See Research and Training Division, Town and Country Planning Organisation (TCPO), Ministry of Urban Affairs and Employment, September, 1995. See also Figure 11 in the same report for the geographical spread of the resettlement colonies.

12 The TCPO report calculates that squatter camps increased to 414 in 1983 to 1984 (from a blank figure for the Emergency period), and to 652 in 1988 to 1989.

13 Olga Tellis v. Union of India, 1986 (AIR SC 180). While affirming the right to livelihood, the judgment also mobilized images of poverty and moral decay:

> Numerous hazards of health and safety arise if action is not taken to remove such encroachments. Since no civic amenities can be provided on the pavements, the pavement dwellers use pavements or adjoining streets for eas-ing themselves. Apart from this, some of the pavement dwellers indulge in anti-social acts like chain-snatching illicit distillation of liquor and prostitu-tion. The lack of proper environment leads to increased criminal tendencies, resulting in more crime in the cities.

14 It could be argued that similar urban explosions also followed the crisis of authoritarian regimes in Latin America.

15 See Circular no. 81/13/1982/A/2/1364, Vigilance Dept, MCD, February 23, 1981. Similar warnings were issued in circulars by the Planning and Monitoring Dept. A typical one is Circular No. PA/Dir.P&M/83/197 dated March 26, 1983.

16 Circular No. 2596/RK/L&E/1220 dated June 27, 1983, MCD, Land and Estate Dept.

17 See ch. 2 of the *Human Development Report for Delhi* (2006) for a useful bundle of statistics including informal patterns of work and industry.

18 Political leaders, led by the then Prime Minister Rajiv Gandhi, would insist on posing beside a desktop; most advertisements after the early 1980s were sure to include images of computers as part of their sales pitch.

19 Early efforts were focused on developing a local telecommunications production base. These efforts were centered on the Center for Development and Communica-tion (C-DoT). Led by the charismatic Sam Pitroda, C-DoT's efforts were later subverted by a section of the bureaucracy sympathetic to transnational capital.

20 Scores of interviewees in the Sarai Archive refer to the Asian Games as the defin-ing shift in the history of the city, along with urban reports, MCD documents, and popular journalism. Disturbingly, very few interviewees referenced the pogrom against the Sikhs in 1984. The interviews were between 2000 and 2006.

21 The government told Parliament in January, 1983 that about 50,000 color TV sets were imported under this gift scheme. *See UNI Backgrounders*, March 3, 1984.

22 This became completely clear with the TRAI (Telecom Regulatory Authority of

India) rulings after 2000. The TRAI made it clear that carriage (its purview) had to be separated from content (the field of film experts). See "TRAI for Laws to Enable Early Convergence," Hindu Business Line, March 21, 2006. http://www.thehindubusinessline.com/2006/03/21/stories/2006032102660400. Accessed on May 1, 2006. For TRAI rulings see http://www.trai.gov.in/Default.asp.

23 See the early sections of *Speed and Politics* for the entire discussion. For a useful discussion on these concepts see also Wark (1988).

24 *Teh Bazaari* tax was the main form of control over trade in public places. This was typically collected on a daily basis. In some cases (e.g. Lajpat Rai market) the shops were first allotted on the basis of *Teh Bazaari*, and then moved into regularization.

25 Fifty-four markets were transferred to occupants on a leasehold basis, five markets went to the Directorate of Estate, two to the MCD, and one was demolished. See "Facts of Lajpat Rai Market" Document, Land and Estate Dept MCD Delhi, n.d. (probably 2001), Sarai Archive/markets/07.

26 Unknown to me at that time, Lajpat Rai market played a significant part in the radio and cassette recorder boom in the 1970s and 1980s itself. For a good sense of Lajpat Rai's move from cloth to radio see the fascinating interview with Bhagatji, tea stall owner in the market and priest of the Shiv Shakti temple, on February 17, 2003, by Rakesh, Sarai Archive, PPHP. See also Akhtar's memoir in Sharma (2004).

27 In total there are 890 pukka shops, constructed in two phases, first in 1958 and later in 1965. The market began in 1948 and consisted of tents.

28 "Facts on Old Lajpat Rai Market." This unpublished survey was submitted to the Ministry of Home Affairs.

29 A sense of the evolving official position on ownership rights is available in the detailed minutes of the meeting on Lajpat Rai market held at the office of Addl. Secretary (Home) on June 6, 1997. Copy, Sarai Archive/markets/02. For an early appeal for ownership rights see letter to Indira Gandhi from the Lajpat Rai Market Welfare Association, October 10, 1970. Sarai Archive/markets/05. Given Lajpat Rai's reputation, for many years the MCD was hesitant to take over the market from the Rehabilitation Department.

30 "Heat on Lajpat Rai Market," *Hindustan Times*, May 2, 2006.

31 "MCD Squad Faces Stiff Resistance from Traders," *The Hindu*, May 10, 2006. http://www.hindu.com/2006/05/10/stories/2006051026080300. Accessed June 1, 2006.

32 Coffee House was seen as a hub of anti-Emergency discussions in 1975 to 1976, and was subsequently demolished.

33 See "Palika Looks Tired at Twenty Three," n.d. PPHP Archive, Sarai. Available at http://www.sarai.net/research/media-city/field-notes/media-markets/palika-story/. Accessed February 1, 2005.

34 For detailed discussions of piracy see Chapter 3.

35 Revitalization of Nehru Place District Center, by Kuldip Singh and Associates, submitted to the Delhi Urban Arts Commission, 2001.

36 Anil Gupta, a local trader and assembler, who later became part of Paramount Computers in Nehru Place. Interview, April, 1998.

37 These were EAPBX networks that ran in Nehru Place, Lajpat Rai, and Bhagirath Place.

38 Lajpat Rai market had multiple ID cards for head load workers, one issued by local shopkeepers, another by the workers' union, and yet another by the police when policewoman Kiran Bedi was in charge of the area. See Rakesh Kumar Singh's paper, "Shiv Sagar and the Delhi Porter's Union," http://www.sarai.net/research/media-city/field-notes/media-markets/shiv-sagar/.

39 See Rakesh Kumar Singh, "Work Relationship in a Factory," n.d. PPHP Archives.

This is now available online at http://www.sarai.net/research/media-city/field-notes/media-markets/work-relationship/. Accessed May 3, 2006

40 Inside Angoori Bagh's small workshops, workers reported that owners could have close relationships with workers, bearing their medical expenses if accidents occurred. When Singh visited the workers' *basti*, he found out that caste identities were often subsumed under strong regional Bhojpuri identities. It is difficult however to generalize about the working conditions of Angoori bagh electronic component factories to other small enterprises in Delhi.

3 The pirate kingdom

1 *The Visible and the Invisible* (1969, p.137).

2 This paragraph is part of an abstract of a joint presentation with Lawrence Liang and Jeebesh Bagchi at the Trespassing Commons Conference, Delhi, 2005.

3 *The Nature of the Book* (1998). See also Chartier (1994), Darnton (1982), and Eisenstein (1980) for the various debates on early modern print culture in the West.

4 Stark also shows that north Indian printers did not rush to register copyrights; even in the late nineteenth century barely 6 percent of all printed documents were officially registered in the Avadh. Registration involved a fee of Rs 2 (p. 90).

5 Ghosh shows that popular printing was dominated by lower caste men, which had significant implications for print culture (2006, p.123).

6 Ghosh's study deals with copyright only in passing, focusing on the print publics of that time. The emergence of literary property in Bengal still awaits a study that can match the depth of Ranajit Guha's Rule of Property for Bengal.

7 Cited in Ghosh (2006, p.141).

8 The literature on this period is vast. For lucid summaries see Rose (1993), particularly chs 2 and 3, and for a comprehensive account see Johns (1998).

9 This act was followed by a long struggle in England (expressed in court cases) between the idea of the authors' perpetual right (i.e. the publishers to whom it was assigned) in common law, and the more limited right that was set up in the Statute of Anne. The matter was finally resolved in the celebrated case of Donaldson v. Becket in 1774, where the statute of limitations was upheld in a majority decision of the House of Lords.

10 Peter Jaszi argues that the Statute had nothing to do with working writers: "The Statute of Anne of 1710 was the result of lobbying by London-based publishers and booksellers seeking new legal weapons against down-market competition spawned by the proliferation of print technology" (Woodmansee and Jaszi, 1994, p.32). Mark Rose (1993) presents a more complex story of debates on property and personhood involving among others personalities like John Locke and Daniel Defoe that led to the Statute of Anne.

11 Locke's "labor" theory of property argued that "everyman has a property in his person," and man had a right to that which he mixed with their labor, converted into a "private dominion." See his *Two Treatises of Government* (2003). In this theory of appropriation, Locke argued that one can appropriate, but also "leave enough for others." If this was followed, property was a natural right, but based on physical possession of property. Lockean theory had to be significantly amended for modern copyright doctrine, but the rhetoric of natural rights and protections has often crept into contemporary enforcement.

12 The Federal Copyright Act of 1790 went further: it opened the door for the piracy of materials of non-US origin. "Nothing in this act shall be construed to extend to prohibit the importation or vending, reprinting, or publishing within the United States, of any map, chart, book or books, written, printed, or published by any person not a citizen of the United States, in foreign parts without the jurisdiction

of the United States" (cited in Frith and Marshall, 2004, p.30). For a fascinating history of nineteenth-century US government encouragement of piracy see Ben Atar. (2004). For over a century the USA refused to sign the Berne Convention of 1886. All this changed in the 1990s with the rise of the digital industries and the move to an information economy.

13 Rose argues that the "the romantic elaborations of such expressions as originality, organics form, and the work of art as the expression of the unique personality of the artist was in a sense the necessary completion of the legal and economic transformation that occurred during the copyright struggle" (cited in Woodmansee and Jaszi, 1994, p.31).

14 The USA refused to be a signatory to the Berne Convention for more than a hundred years.

15 See its website www.iipa.com. Along with the IIPA's industry advocacy model, the WIPO (World Intellectual Property Organization) is a significant intergovernmental body established by the United Nations.

16 For over a century the USA refused to sign the Berne Convention of 1884. All this changed in the 1990s with the rise of the information industries. In 1998 the industry-friendly Sonny Bono Copyright Extension Act and the Digital Millennium Copyright Act were passed, ushering in a new era of international enforcement and zero tolerance for any deviation including piracy. For an extensive analysis of the DMCA see Litman (2000). For a useful survey of Hollywood's international campaigns see Miller *et al.* (2001).

17 The IIPA List is under four headings. The two relevant ones under its special 301 are the Priority watch list and watch list, which is used for most offenders including India and China.

18 See http://www.iipa.com/pdf/IIPA2007PressReleaseonUSTRSpecial301decisions FINAL04302007.pdf visited on June 1, 2007.

19 Fair use in the USA follows the three-step test laid down in Berne, of which creative reuse is one, but not the only one.

20 For a summary of all the bizarre cases pursued by the US RIAA against individuals see the page maintained by the Electronic Frontier Foundation at http://w2.eff.org/IP/P2P/riaa-v-thepeople.php.

21 The statistics are available on the website of the IIPA and the MPA. Loss statistics are based on cost projections of media costs, assuming, of course, that every person who bought pirated media would have also bought a legal copy. For arguments that piracy is actually beneficial to industry see Gu and Mahajan (2005).

22 P2p networks are a significant part of rising internet usage. In 2004 P2p networks were up to 60 percent of global traffic. See http://www.morganstanley.com/institutional/techresearch/pdfs/Webtwopto2006.pdf visited on May 1, 2007.

23 Liang (forthcoming). Liang argues that in the eyes of the liberal public domain, piracy suggests neither a model of creative authorship, nor does it fall within the normative claims of the public domain. For Liang, legalism and liberal constitutionalism limit the application mainstream public domain discourse in postcolonial contexts of unmarked populations.

24 Online downloads through P2P networks have been increasing among middle-class Internet subscribers in India.

25 The portable radio is an interesting site which suggests a prehistory to new media gadgets.

26 I refer to the cultural experience. To be sure, there are loosely organized pirate networks and coalitions; their staying power has been fragile due to harassment and raids by the police.

27 I prefer to use this concept to simply illuminate strategies of the pirate form rather than mobilize the entire corpus of Deleuze's work, which has now

congealed into a global theoretical current. The productivity of the pirate form recalls Deleuze and Guattari's claim that assemblages are primarily of desire rather than power – in contrast to Foucault. See Patton (2000) for an extended discussion.

28 "As the Video Virus Spreads," *Times of India*, Bombay, January 22, 1984.

29 Innovative imitation of film music was quite central to the audio boom, along with the commodification of local and regional music.

30 This was the age before the internet and widespread use of digital technology.

31 See Miller *et al.* (2001).

32 Although Canclini admits to a brute egalitarianism produced by video culture (along with North Americanization), his tone in this essay is comparable to that of cultural elites in many parts of the postcolonial world that reacted with dismay when the old "national" consensus came apart in the 1980s.

33 A major difference was that unlike India, Nigerian video emerged in the wake of an economic crisis that devastated the older film industry. Video then went on to set up a revival of a unique cultural landscape incorporating regional and local forms and also low-cost experimental video which made its way into international art house releases.

34   The recent suspensions of five producers of the Film Producers' Guild of
       India ... brought to the fore the skirmish going on in Bombay's film
       circles. Of the suspended producers B R Chopra, Ramanand Sagar, Subodh
       Mukerjee, Shakti Samanta and Shanti Sagar B R Chopra is known to con-
       sider the Guild's anti-video stance somewhat too rigorous and restrictive. The
       President of the Guild, G P Sippy, on the other hand, has a furious antipathy
       towards both the "irresponsible" growth of national video.
                                    (Kajal Basu, *Sunday Observer*, September 18, 1983)

35 The notification was issued under Sections 4 and 7 of the Indian Telegraph Act of 1885, and Sections 4 and 10 of the Indian Wireless Telegraphy Act of 1933. For more discussion on video and the law see Mayur Suresh's useful paper (2002). Suresh points out that the repealed rules continue in force in the border states of Assam, Jammu and Kashmir, Mizoram, Manipur, Nagaland, and Tripura along with the Andaman and Lakshadweep islands. This is consistent with the governments' stricter security regimes for the periphery.

36 Restaurant Lee v. State of Madhya Pradesh, AIR 1983, Laxmi video versus State of Haryana AIR 1993 SC 2328.

37 This was finally upheld by the Supreme Court in 1993 in the case of Laxmi Video Talkies and others v. State of Haryana. Ibid.

38 The conversation was in June 1996, in the Tamil Nadu express to Chennai. Parts of this section are extracted from Sundaram (1999).

39 This was narrated to me by Pitroda at the Doors of Perception 2 conference, the Netherlands, 1998. At the time of writing the dynamic Pitroda is the Chairman of the Knowledge Commission in India. For Pitroda's story see the sympathetic narrative in Das (2002).

40 In 1999 on a trip for an architectural conference to Taiwan, I met two Delhi-based small businessmen who did these trips regularly; they showed me their suppliers' directory, and a list of small budget hotels in South East Asia printed in the old city of Delhi. Bangkok, Singapore, Taiwan, Hong Kong, and Shenzen were soon in the travel circuit. The Taiwan connection began with T-series importing equipment for its factories in the 1980s.

41 See Sundaram (1999).

42 See the entire story in *A Brief Biography of a Cable Operator* by Lokesh Sharma (2004). In a classic story of class and power, Shrikant ultimately lost his territory to the major players.

43 Industry legend (narrated by an anti-piracy enforcement agent) has it that Gulshan Kumar presented the late Indira Gandhi with an audio cassette of her speeches to win favors. Kumar was murdered in 1997 allegedly by the Mumbai underworld.

44 This applied more to audio than to video. Pirate film releases were always more tightly controlled than audio.

45 The T-series release was stopped by an injunction in 1995. See High Court of Delhi, Interim Application No. 217 of 95 and Suit No. 2924 of 1994. The judge ruled that

> the defendants are not to use in the carton or inlay card or any other packaging material a design, colour scheme, layout and getup similar to that of the plaintiffs; not in the title to use the words "Hum Aapke Hain Kaun" simpliciter or any combination of words including "Hum Aapke Hain Kaun" which would be calculated to lead to the belief that the defendants' record was the plaintiff's record. The unoffending alternate title must also contain underneath it a declaration in sufficiently bold letters that the record is not from the original sound track but only a version record with voices of different artists. The word "not" should be underlined.

Notice the play between the word "original" and "version", symptomatic of the cultural debate in public life.

46 See the enforcement site http://www.filmpiracy.com/filmpiracy%20black/main.swf. This shows alleged differences between pirate and original media.

47 See Sarai Reader 5 Bare Acts, p. 285.

48 The shattering of "aura" as mass copies flooded the market was Benjamin's artwork essay's central modernizing thrust.

49 I visited Sadaf in Karachi's Rainbow Center in April 2004. The first release films camera prints come to Sadaf through broadband connections from Dubai, where they are remastered and sent to India via couriers and the Internet. Recent MPA-instigated raids on Karachi's Rainbow Center have not harmed the flow of films to India.

50 See her "Portrait of an Artist" in the PPHP archive, July, 2005, also published in *Media Nagar 02*. Muqabla is a popular form of conversational quawali that Tasleem claimed to have innovated with film tunes and explicit allusions. The videos are shot in a studio and feature a range of remixed compositions, including hits like "Coca Cola."

51 Ibid.

52 Khadeeja Arif confirms this in her report of Tasleem's travels and public performances.

53 In 1994, a case came up before the Monopolies and Restrictive Trade Practices Commission (MRTPC) on the legality of advertising in video. I.A. No. 33 of 1994 Decided On, December 23, 1994. Appellants, Mehmood Pracha vs. Respondent, Video Master. While the case was ostensibly about the mutilation of the original by the copy due to advertising, the timid judgment of the MRTPC allowed advertising to continue unabated.

54 The recent crowding of the mainstream TV screen with moving information and advertising in US and Indian TV networks in the past years was actually introduced in the pirate video in India way back in the 1990s.

55 Officers with near-magisterial powers appointed by the Court to ensure court orders are being followed and with authority to summon the police.

56 By 2001 local TV crime news shows, the staple of the late night 11 p.m. slot in India, were inserting stories of raids on pirate establishments with help from enforcement agents.

57 For police raid statistics see the compilations in the IIPA India reports.

58 See http://www.screenindia.com/fullstory.php?content_id=13126 Accessed on January 4, 2007.

59 In 1984, the punishment for copyright violation was drastically increased from a maximum of one year for a first offender to a maximum of three years' imprisonment for repeats. This is designed specially for piracy; a minimum one-year imprisonment is mandated. The demand from enforcement lobbies is to make these more stringent.

60 T-series is considered among the more effective enforcement agencies, limiting piracy to 40 percent of its products. Given T-series' own history, it perhaps possesses an insider intelligence of the trade that is not forthcoming to many other agencies. T-series has twenty-five people in its Delhi office – more than the current staff of the Economic Offenses wing in 2006. Interviews with T-series lawyers, PPHP archive.

61 Interesting parallels exist with "Collection Agents" employed by MNC Banks, ie persons to whom the recalling of loans is contracted out and who call, threaten, browbeat, pretend to be process servers of the Court, pretend to be mafia, and use every other trick to get debtors to repay loans. The Supreme Court has deplored the practice, but it continues apace nonetheless.

62 See " 'Anti-piracy' Men in Extortion Racket" by S. Ahmed Ali *Times of India*, Mumbai edition, December 24, 2006.

63 Satish Kapoor, Prime Protection, East of Kailash, Delhi. The following section draws from the tape archive at PPHP Delhi. Interviews by Ravi Sundaram, Bhagwati Prasad, Yamini Jaishankar, and Jawahar Raja.

64 State of Andhra Pradesh v. Nagoti Vekatatraman, 1996(6) Supreme Court Cases 409.

65 Competing detectives sometimes produced fake POAs from clients for the police, who became doubly careful, and demanded that the paperwork be complete before any raid. This was true particularly of the late 1990s.

66 Smaller factories might produce CDs and VCDs for all producers, legal and non-legal.

67 This is from Jawahar Raja's remarkable interview with "VS," a former investigator with the MPA. PPHP archive.

68 Ibid.

69 Where the local operator is so small that he or she can shift or shut up shop at the first whiff of trouble, serving him with the Court summons, presents its own problems. Several suits for injunction were stuck at the first stage of the serving of summons on the alleged copyright violators as they were untraceable. Some of the original complainant-detectives also vanished.

70 Often the settlements involve merely the payment of a nominal sum and an apology. The motivation seems to be more to secure an admission of guilt than to gain monetary recompense for loss of value.

71 Field investigators claim that larger factories producing master disks or mass reproduction are an important component in piracy.

72 Bhagwati Prasad first showed me this license. See also Yamini Jaishankar and Bhagwati's Prasad's interview with the T-series "license distributor," Rajeev Khurana, April 8, 2003, Delhi. PPHP Archive. Khurana suggested that much of piracy was not necessarily illegal but "alegal," an in-between zone. That this came from someone devoted to enforcement is in itself remarkable.

73 The research by Bhagwati Prasad (2003b) showed that there are at least thirty-seven versions of the explicit tune "Kaante Laaga," ranging from dance to devotional forms.

74 Deleuze put it beautifully: "This indefinite life does not itself have moments; close as they be to one another, but only between-times, between-moments" (2001, p.29).

75 Akhtar, the worker who we met with Lokesh Sharma in the last chapter, pointed out that his factory Cotina was a household firm when it began copying Philips radios successfully. Very soon Cotina began to be overwhelmed by copies of its own radios with the import of cheap Chinese parts. Says Akhtar, "Every original has its duplicate. Now even there is duplicate of the duplicate." New radios called Motina began to appear and threatened Cotina's existence.

76 "Capitalist production seeks continually to overcome these immanent barriers, but overcome them by means which again place these barriers in its way and on a more formidable scale. The real barrier to capitalist production is capital itself" (Marx, 1967, p.250).

4 Death of the accident

1 Included in the collection *Paul Gomra ka Scooter* (2002). I have used the English translation in *Short Shorts Long Shorts* (2003) for ease of access by readers.

2 Transport Department, Government of NCT of Delhi. Available at <http://transport.delhigovt.nic.in/transport/tr0g.htm> accessed June 10, 2005. The figure is surely more, as many vehicles are registered in UP and Haryana.

3 Western car travel has been variously seen as a detachment from space (Richard Sennet), privatized escape from the street (Zygmunt Bauman), a movement through non-place (Marc Auge). This can be seen increasingly in urban India, where globally designed cars now move towards air-conditioning and private audio systems, creating "sound envelops" away from the street. There is always the danger however of a perspectivalism in reverse in such accounts, where the "outside" exists solely for the objectification of the driver's vision and the stability of the "private" zone is taken for granted.

4 This was the focus of Guy Debords's attack in his "Theses on Traffic." See Knabb (1981, pp.56–58) for the entire document. For a larger discussion see Sadler (1999, pp.24–25).

5 The tram system came to an end in the 1960s. The tracks still exist in the old city, slowly giving way to road modernization. For some, the tram system evokes nostalgic memories of the old city before 1947. Ravi Dayal writes, "And yes, people went to *Shahar* (the old city) to see and ride in trams, perhaps the ricketiest, slowest and oldest trams in the world, but the only ones in north India. Not even Lahore could boast of trams" (2001).

6 Like the Railway Ministry at the national level, the Delhi Transport Department has functioned as a site for distributing favors to constituents.

7 Edward Gargan, *New York Times*, June 12, 1993: "New Delhi Journal; And Now, Killer Buses: It's Just Too, Too Much" (p.A4).

8 Ibid.

9 "Delhi Residents Fume Over 'Killer Buses'," *Associated Press*, June 23, 1993.

10 "Four Year Old Boy, Mother, Run Over By Bus," *Times of India*, October 2, 2000.

11 "Road Accident Sparks off Mini-Riot," *Times of India*, Delhi edn, September 26, 2000.

12 "Students go on Rampage after Accident," *The Hindu*, September 21, 2000.

13 Pooja Kumar, "Caught in Jam, Blueline Victim was 15 Mins too Late", *Indian Express*, May 21, 2004, available at: <http://cities.expressindia.com/fullstory.php?newsid=85157>, accessed January 26, 2004.

14 This form of student protest was inherited from the days of the state-owned DTC. In the 1980s when I was at Delhi University it was *de rigueur* for male students to stone buses after conflicts with DTC staff. In the late 1980s the anti-Mandal agitators targeted DTC buses leading to significant damage of the fleet, and probably playing a part in the shift to the Redline system.

15 *The Sunday Pioneer*, February 25, 2001, p.8.

16 From "Eyes of the Crowd" from *The Book Box* texts from Cybermohalla, Sarai-CSDS, Delhi, 2003, available at: http://www.sarai.net/practices/cybermohalla/public-dialogue/books/book-box/crowd_eng.pdf, accessed April 3, 2006.
17 Ibid.
18 Vinod Nair, "Delhi, A Killer Metro?," *The Times of India*, October 12, 1999, p.6.
19 See Cybermohalla, "Eyes on the Crowd", op.cit.
20 Letters, *Times of India*, June 16, 2000.
21 "Blueline Conductor Stones Passenger," Express News Service, May 27, 2005.
22 Cybermohalla, "Eyes on the Crowd." This deployment of machine technology combined with the harassment of women in public transport was an integral part of travel culture in Delhi. In the 1980s women's movements had campaigned against sexual assaults in the city, including its buses. The stories of assaults on women in road culture seem to have shifted more from inside the bus to the road itself: newspapers report women picked up and assaulted in moving cars by young men, in parking lots, and in all potential dark city spaces.
23 Cybermohalla, "Eyes on the Crowd."
24 *Mid Day* (Mumbai), December 4, 2002.
25 I owe this phrase to Schnapp (2003).
26 Joginder Singh Arora to Ajay Jha in *Gulf News*. September 8, 2003.
27 Pooja Dubey of *The Pioneer* reported on October 22, 2001,

> The poor passengers have often to give in to the whims and fancies of the bus drivers who often divert their vehicles to commercially more viable routes. While some buses resort to divert their routes others change their routes completely. "Recently a Blueline bus (Route no 310) in which I was traveling changed its route and via Delhi Gate. This has become a regular practice and no one has taken any action on this.

28 Urvashi Gulia, "The Buck Stops with the Passengers," *The Pioneer*, March 22, 2002.
29 Ibid.
30 Buses would sometimes stop at petrol stations to fill up with passengers in tow. This was common practice in all private transport vehicles in Delhi, and auto-rickshaws were the biggest culprits. This practice declined after buses were forced to shift to CNG by the Supreme Court, and a nightly time-cycle began at CNG stations.
31 Mayank Tewari, "Stand in Queue, Please!," *The Pioneer*, August 17, 2001.
32 Ibid.
33 This is a technology that has since been utilized with great effect by the Delhi police during encounter killings.
34 See Dinesh Mohan (2004). The main reformers congealed around the Transport Research and Injury Prevention Programme (TRIPP) at IIT Delhi. The TRIPP group and Mohan in particular have been critical of the city planners' obsession with flyover construction designed to enhance speed. He has successfully pushed for a high-speed bus service (BRT) with special lanes in Delhi.
35 Two years later, the charges were finally filed against the driver. Addition Sessions judge Prem Kumar noted that the driver could not be charged with culpable homicide, but with a lesser offense of death caused by negligence. He said that the police report after the accident revealed that the driver might have lost control after the bus "went over a pile of sand on the bridge. Since the evidence showed no intention on the part of the driver to kill the children, the accident was solely due to the driver's rash driving and his losing control over the vehicle" (*The Times of India*, March 5, 2000).
36 Supreme Court of India, MC Mehta v. Government of India and others delivered December 1, 1998. Emphasis added.

37 The move to natural gas transformed the road's temporal cycle: as gas refills took longer, buses filled tanks at night: Initially the change caused a major crisis as supplies were short, long lines of angry bus- and car-drivers waited endlessly outside gas stations at night, many sleeping over in vehicles. Both gas kits and electronic speed governors increased costs for a large number of vehicles. The violence of this transition has yet to be documented adequately.

38 The police guidelines for children, distributed in schools, alluded to a chaotic world: "At the bus stand, always follow the queue. Board the bus only after it has come to a halt, without rushing in or pushing others. While in the bus, shouting or making a noise is definitely bad manners. Such behavior can also distract the driver." Available at: <http://www.delhitrafficpolice.nic.in/guidelines-for-children.htm>, accessed July 10, 2005.

39 "This technology not only monitors the movements of buses but also keep records of speeding, improper halts, skipping of bus stops and so on. Besides, daily and monthly reports of schedules and trips per shift can be maintained and assessed for viability of a route" (*Indian Express*, December 2, 2004). The Delhi government citizens charter on transport also lists this new system as part of its future plans. Available at <http://dtc.nic.in/ccharter.htm>, accessed June 15, 2006.

40 Government of India, Department of Road Transports and Highways (Road Safety Cell) Circular No. RT- 25028/2/2003-RSC, February 19, 2004. This is a rare insight into the internal perceptual apparatus of government.

41 April 6, 2001. See also *The Hindu*, April 7, 2001, for another explosion report. The fear of CNG explosions has not however gone away. In an early morning explosion in south Delhi, police and eyewitness accounts contradicted each other. The witness claimed the explosion was due to a CNG cylinder exploding, while the police called it a "bomb blast." *Indian Express*, Delhi, March 15, 2006.

42 Cited in Creed (1998).

43 Delhi's police stations have filled up with smashed and seized vehicles after the automobile boom of the 1990s.

44 The Furturist Manifesto, available at: <http://www.cscs.umich.edu/~crshalizi/T4PM/futurist-manifesto.html>, accessed January 5, 2005.

45 Marinetti's work on the speed-machine put him in a diverse spectrum of European avant-garde writers who were fascinated by technological power at various points in their work. This ranged from the Russian constructivists Soviet artist as engineer, Gramsci's work on Americanism and Fordism, Benjamin's artwork essay, and urbanists from Loos to the Bauhaus. See Wollen (1993) for a wider discussion of some of the writers here.

46 See Ballard's Introduction to *Crash* (1973).

47 Delhi Police website, available at: <http://delhipolice.nic.in/home/backup/Jan2006.htm>, accessed June 17, 2006. The overall number of fatalities on the road does not seem to have declined. This report was released to the press on January 6, 2006.

48 "Fatal Mishap Hits Traffic on Ring Rd," *Indian Express*, Delhi, January 25, 2006, available at <http://cities.expressindia.com/fullstory.php?newsid=167183>, accessed February 22, 2006.

49 Andy Warhol used repetitive crash photos to suggest similar conditions.

50 Early cinema produced both crash movies and execution films. See Doane (2002).

51 Benjamin suggested that this desire for violent gratification was supplied by fascism. In the conclusion of the artwork essay he wrote, "Mankind, which was in Homer's time an object of contemplation for the Olympian gods, is now one for itself. Its self alienation has reached such a degree that it can experience its own destruction as an aesthetic pleasure of the highest order" (1969, p.242).

52 I finally located the story, available at: <http://cities.expressindia.com/fullstory.php?newsid=85157>, *Indian Express*, May 21 2004.

53 I use the term first deployed by Mark Seltzer (1998), though my purpose is wider.

5 Conclusion: an information city?

1 The classic theory of fetishism in Marx presumed that capitalist commodity culture generated a process that transformed human relationships and concepts into impersonal and atomized objects, while objects appear endowed with personified and fantastic spiritual powers. The commodity fetish enacted social relations, which were fantastically inscribed in the powers of the object itself. The task of radical theory was to unmask this double inversion – of people as things and things as magical.

2 Thanks to Ravikant Sharma (who introduced me to both stories) and fellow members of the Sarai workshop on markets and commodities for the discussion on the stories.

3 In September, 2007 *The Indian Express* reported:

> A year ago, when town planners, bureaucrats and politicians were grappling with the twin monsters of sealing and demolition, Union Minister for Science and Technology Kapil Sibal had instructed his staff to look for a techno-logical solution to the problem. A year later, the team is ready to unfold the benefits of this artificial intelligence, a unique feature of which is the ability to detect unauthorized construction in any part of the city on a computer screen.

September 13, 2007, available at http://www.expressindia.com/latest-news/Illegal-construction-You-are-being-watched-from-above/216193/, accessed September 25, 2007.

4 The Right to Information Act was passed in 2005. It mandates a "time-bound" response to requests for government information. For a copy of the Act see http://righttoinformation.gov.in/, accessed May 1, 2007.

5 In a similar language, the "overcoded" form of the classic Masterplan is now extinct. The current 2002 Masterplan acts more like an urban filter and gate, rather than as a vision for the city.

6 The tactics are those of doubling: fake IDs and ration cards, multiple Sim cards for mobile phones. It is a game of evading the urban gatekeepers, more difficult for the urban poor and minorities.

7 Albert Mayer wrote *The Urgent Future* after he returned to the USA, calling the endless urban sprawl "stupid and inhumane." He suggested that it was "the oozing together of already amorphous cities into a sort of lava flow hundreds of miles in dimension" (1973, p.3). Planning was Mayer's way to save the future.

8 As discussed in Chapter 2, Jagmohan showed a significant necrophilic interest in Shahjehanabad, and affirmed it, if only to carry out a mass displacement of its poor to the periphery of the city.

9 "Today it is not the city but rather the camp that is the fundamental biopolitical paradigm of the West" (Agamben, 1998, p.181). Given the brutality of Delhi's displacement of its informal working-class settlements in recent years, the shadow of bare life also hangs over the modernizing non-West.

10 A large part of northern regional music and video is now produced in Delhi.

11 See Benjamin, *Arcades* (1999a, p.459).

Bibliography

Archives

The Delhi State Archives (DSA)
The Ford Foundation Archives, New York (FFA)
The Albert Mayer Papers, University of Chicago Library, Chicago (AM papers)
MCD Archives, Land and Estate Department
The Sarai Archive, Delhi

Newspapers

The Hindu (Delhi)
The Hindustan Times (Delhi)
New York Times (New York)
The Pioneer (Delhi)
The Statesman (Delhi)
The Times of India (Delhi)

Governmental and non-governmental published documents

Bharat Sevak Samaj, 1958. *Slums of Old Delhi, A Survey*, by, Atma Ram and Sons, Delhi
Delhi Development Authority (DDA), 1962. *Masterplan for Delhi*, Work Studies Vols 1, and 2, Delhi
Delhi Development Authority, 1972. *Report on Nehru Place*, text by Jagmohan
Delhi Development Authority, 1990. *Masterplan for Delhi: Perspective 2001*, Delhi
Delhi Improvement Trust, *1951 Annual Administration Report 1950–1*. New Delhi
Ford Foundation, 1959. The Ford Foundation and Foundation-supported projects in India, New Delhi (Mimeo)
Ford Foundation, Gaither Report: Report of the Study for the Ford Foundation on Policy and Program, online at http://www.fordfound.org/archives/item/0113
Government of NCT of Delhi, 2006. *Delhi Human Development Report 2006 Partnerships for Progress*, Oxford University Press, Delhi
Government of India, Ministry of Home Affairs, 1978. *Report of the Slum Clearance, Demolitions and Firing in Turkman Gate during the Emergency*
Government of India, 1978. *Shah Commission of Inquiry*, Interim Report, Vol 2

International Intellectual Property Alliance (IIPA), 2003. *Special 301 Report India.* www.iipa.com

Janvadi Adhikar Manch, 2001. "How Many Errors Does Time Have Patience For?" Delhi (Mimeo)

Ministry of Health, 1956. "Report of Committee Investigating Epidemic of Jaundice (Infectious Hepatitis) in New Delhi, India, December 1955 to January 1956," Ministry of Health, Delhi

Ministry of Health, 1956. Interim General Plan of Greater Delhi, Ministry of Health, Delhi

Ministry of Information and Broadcasting, 1951. *Film Enquiry Committee Report of 1951*, Ministry of Information and Broadcasting, Delhi

Ministry of Information and Broadcasting, 1966. *Report of the Committee on Broadcasting and Information Media*, New Delhi

Municipal Corporation of Delhi, 1962. *Three Years of the Municipal Corporation of Delhi: 1958–61*, Delhi

Municipal Corporation of Delhi, 1962. *Evaluation Study of the Formation and Working of Vikas Mandals*, Department of Urban Community Development, Municipal Corporation of Delhi

National Council for Applied Economic Research, *1973 Techno-economic Survey of Delhi*, NCAER, Delhi

Report of the Advisory Committee on Slum Clearance, 1958. New Delhi

Report of the Delhi Improvement Trust Enquiry Committee, Government of India, 1951, Delhi

Report of the Delhi Municipal Organization Enquiry Committee, 1948. Government of India Press, New Delhi

Report on the Relief of Congestion in Delhi, 1936. Vols I and II, Government of India Press, Simla

Town Planning Organization, 1958. *Slum Clearance and Urban Renewal in Delhi*, Ministry of Health

Town and Country Planning Organization, 1970. *Land Values in Delhi*, TCPO, Delhi

Town and Country Planning Organization. 1973. *Review of Master Plan for Delhi*, New Delhi (Mimeo)

Books and articles

Agamben, Giorgio (1998) *Homo Sacer*, Stanford, CA: Stanford University Press.

Amin, Ash and Nigel Thrift (2002) *Cities: Reimagining the Urban*, London: Polity Press.

Anderson, Benedict (1991) *Imagined communities: reflections on the origin and spread of nationalism*, London, Verso.

Appadurai, Arjun (ed.) (1986) *The Social Life of Things: Commodities in Cultural Perspective*, New York: Cambridge University Press.

—— (1996) *Modernity at Large: the Cultural Dimensions of Globalization*, Minneapolis: University of Minnesota Press.

—— and Carol A. Breckinridge (2005) "Public Modernity in India," in *Consuming Modernity: Public Culture in a South Asian World*, ed. Carol Breckenridge, Minneapolis: University of Minnesota Press.

Arrighi, Giovanni (1994) *The Long Twentieth Century*, New York and London: Verso.

Augé, Marc (1995) *Non-places: Introduction to an Anthropology of Supermodernity*, trans. John Howe, London: Verso.

Bachelard, Gaston (1994) *The Poetics of Space*, trans. Maria Jolas, with a new Foreword by John R. Stilgoe, Boston, MA: Beacon Press.

Ballard, J.G. (1973) *Crash*, New York: Farrar, Strauss & Giroux.

Banga, I. (ed.) (1991) *The City in Indian History*, New Delhi: Manohar Publications.

Barthes, Roland (1984) *Camera Lucida: Reflections on Photography*, London: Flamingo.

Baudrillard, Jean (1983) "The Ecstasy of Communication," in Hal Foster (ed.) *The Anti-aesthetic: Essays on Postmodern Culture*, Port Townsend, Washington D.C.: Bay Press.

Bauman, Zygmunt (1998) *Globalization: The Human Consequences*, New York: Columbia University Press.

—— (2000) *Liquid Modernity*, London: Polity Press.

Baviskar, Amita (2003) "Between Violence and Desire: Space, Power, and Identity in the Making of Metropolitan Delhi," *International Social Science Journal* 55 (1), pp.89–98.

Bayat, Asef (1997) "Un-Civil Society: The Politics of the 'Informal People'," *Third World Quarterly* 18 (1).

—— (2000) "From 'Dangerous Classes' to 'Quiet Rebels' Politics of the Urban Subaltern in the Global South," *International Sociology* 15 (3), pp.533–557.

Bayly, C. A. (1983) *Rulers, Townsmen and Bazaars: North Indian Society in the Age of British Expansion, 1770–1870*, Cambridge: Cambridge University Press.

Beck, Ulrich (1992) *Risk Society: Towards a New Modernity*, London: Sage.

Ben Atar, Doron (2004) *Intellectual Piracy and the Origins of American Power*, New Haven, CT: Yale University Press.

Benjamin, Solomon (1991) *Jobs, Land and Urban Development: The Economic Success of Small Manufacturers in East Delhi*, Boston, MA: Lincoln Institute of Land Management.

—— (2005a) "Touts, Pirates and Ghosts," in *Bare Acts*, Sarai Reader 5, Delhi.

—— (2005b) *Lifestyle statement & Marxist manifestos*, CASUMM Working Paper. Unpublished.

—— (2005c) *"Productive Slums": The Centrality of Urban Land in Shaping Employment and City Politics*, Boston, MA: Lincoln Institute of Land Management.

Benjamin, Walter (1969) *Illuminations*, New York: Schocken Paperbacks.

—— (1992) Selected Writings Volume I: *Metaphysics of Youth, Writings 1912–1926*, ed. Michael Jennings and Marcus Bullock, Cambridge, MA: Belknap Press, Harvard University Press.

—— (1999a) *The Arcades Project*, Cambridge, MA: Harvard University Press.

—— (1999b) Selected Writings Volume II: *Crisis and Criticism, Writings 1926–1934*, ed. Michael Jennings, Howard Eiland, and Gary Smith, Cambridge, MA: Belknap Press, Harvard University Press.

—— (2002) Selected Writings Volume III: *Paris, Capital of the Nineteenth Century, Writings 1935–1938*, ed. Michael Jennings and Howard Eiland, Cambridge, MA: Belknap Press, Harvard University Press.

Benkler, Yochai (2007) *The Wealth of Networks: How Social Production Transforms Markets and Freedom*, New Haven, CT: Yale University Press.

Berlant, Lauren (2000) *Intimacy*, Chicago, IL: University of Chicago Press.

Berman, Marshall (1988) *All That Is Solid Melts into Air: The Experience of Modernity*, New York: Penguin Books.

Bhatia, Gautam (1996) "The Problem," *Seminar* 445, Special Issue, September.

Blanchot, Maurice (1987) "Everyday Speech," *Yale French Studies* 73, pp.12–20.

Blom Hansen, Thomas (2001) *Wages of Violence: Naming and Identity in Postcolonial Bombay*, Princeton, NJ: Princeton University Press.

Bopegamage, A. (1957) *Delhi: A Study in Urban Sociology*, Bombay: University of Bombay.

Bose, Ashish (1978) *India's Urbanization: 1901–2001 Institute of Economic Growth*, New Delhi: Tata McGraw-Hill.

Boyer, Christine (1983) *Dreaming the Rational City: The Myth of American City Planning*, Cambridge, MA: MIT Press.

Boyle, James (1997) *Shamans, Software, and Spleens: Law and the Construction of the Information Society*, Cambridge, MA: Harvard University Press.

—— (2003) "The Second Enclosure Movement and the Construction of the Public Domain," *Law and Contemporary Problems* 66, p.33.

Braudel, Fernand (1992) *The Wheels of Commerce (Civilization and Capitalism: 15th–18th Century – Volume 2*, Berkeley: University of California Press.

Buck-Morss, Susan (1990) *The Dialectics of Seeing: Walter Benjamin and the Arcades Project*, Cambridge, MA: MIT Press.

Canclini, Néstor García (2001) *Consumers and Citizens: Globalization and Multi-cultural Conflicts*, Minneapolis, MN: University of Minnesota Press.

Canetti, Elias (1962) *Crowds and Power*, New York: Viking Press.

Caro, Robert A. (1974) *The Power Broker: Robert Moses and the Fall of New York*, New York: Vintage.

Castells, Manuel (2000) *The Rise of the Network Society: Economy, Society and Culture*, London: Blackwell.

Chakrabarty, D. (1991) "Open Space/Public Place: Garbage, Modernity and India," *South Asia* (1), pp.15–31.

Chakravorty, S. (1999) "From Colonial City to Global City? The Far-from-complete Spatial Transformation of Calcutta," in P. Marcuse and R. van Kempen (eds) *Globalizing Cities*, Oxford, Malden, MA: Blackwell.

Charney, Leo and Vanessa Schwartz (eds) (1995) *Cinema and the Invention of Modern Life*, Berkeley: University of California Press.

Chartier, Roger (1994) *The Order of Books: Readers, Authors, and Libraries in Europe Between the 14th and 18th Centuries*, Stanford, CA: Stanford University Press.

Chatterjee, Partha (1993) *The Nation and Its Fragments*, Princeton, NJ: Princeton University Press.

—— (2004) *The Politics of the Governed: Reflections on Popular Politics in Most of the World*, New York: Columbia University Press.

Chattopadhyay, Swati (2000) "Expedient Forgetting: Architecture in Late-twentieth-century Indian Nationalist Imagination," *Design Book Review* 43.

Chitrasen (1961) "A City Without Character," *Panchshila*, November

Chopra, Anil. "Is This An Original?" *Playback and Fast Forward* (Bombay), May 1988, p.56.

Clark, T.J. (2000) "Reservations of The Marvellous," *London Review of Books*, June 22, pp.3–9.

Clinard, Marshall (1963) "The Sociologist and Social Change in Underdeveloped Countries," *Social Problems* 10 (3), pp.207–219.

—— (1966) *Slum and Community Development: Experiments in Self Help*, New York: The Free Press.

Colomina, Beatriz (1994) *Privacy and Publicity: Modern Architecture as Mass Media*, Cambridge, MA: MIT Press.

Correa, Charles (1959) "Architectural Expression" in Seminar on Architecture, Lalit Kala Academy.

Correa, Charles, Pravina Metha and Shirsh B. Patel (1965) "Planning for Bombay," *MARG* 18 (3), pp.30–56.

Crary, Jonathan (1986) "J. G. Ballard and the Promiscuity of Forms," *Zone* 1–2, pp.159–165.

—— (1992) *Techniques of the Observer, On Vision and Modernity in the 19th Century*, Cambridge, MA: MIT Press.

Creed, Barbara (1998) "The Crash Debate: Anal Wounds, Metallic Kisses," *Screen* 39 (2).

Crouch, David (1998) "The Street in the Making of Popular Geographical Knowledge," in Nicholas R. Fyfe (ed.) *Images of the Street: Planning, Identity, and Control in Public Space*, New York: Routledge.

Cybermohalla Labs (2007) *Bahurupia Shehr*, Delhi: Rajkamal Prakashan.

Dalrymple, William (2007) *The Last Mughal: The Fall of a Dynasty: Delhi, 1857*, New York: Alfred A. Knopf.

Darnton, Robert (1982) *The literary underground of the Old Regime* Cambridge, MA: Harvard University Press.

Das, Gurcharan (2002) *India Unbound: The Social and Economic Revolution from Independence to the Global Information Age*, New York: Anchor.

Davis, Mike (2006) *Planet of Slums*, London, New York: Verso.

Dayal, J. and Bose, A. (1977) *For Reasons of State: Delhi Under the Emergency*, Delhi: Ess-Ess Publications.

Dayal, Ravi (2001) "A Kayastha's View," *Seminar* 515.

Dayan Daniel and Elihu Katz (1994) *Media Events, the Live Broadcasting of History*, Cambridge, MA: Harvard University Press.

De Certeau, Michel ([1984] 2002) *Practice of Everyday Life*, trans. Timothy J. Tomasik, Berkeley: University of California Press.

—— (1998a) Timothy J. Tomasik translated. *Practice of Everyday Life* Vol.2, trans. Timothy J. Tomasik, Minneapolis: University of Minnesota Press.

—— (1998b) *Culture in the Plural*, Minneapolis and London: University of Minnesota Press.

Debord, Guy (1994) *The Society of the Spectacle*, Brooklyn, NY: Zone Books.

Deleuze, Gilles (1990) *Postscript on the Societies of Control*, October 59 (Winter), pp.3–7.

—— (1992) *The Logic of Sense*, New York: Continuum Books.

—— (2001) *Pure Immanence: Essays on a Life*, New York: Zone Books.

—— (2006) *Control and Becoming*: in conversation with Antonio Negri, at http://www.generation-online.org/p/fpdeleuze3.htm, accessed December 10, 2006.

Deleuze, Gilles and Felix Guattari (1988) *A Thousand Plateaus*, London: Athlone Press.

—— (1995) "Capitalism: A Very Special Delirium," http://www.generation-online.org/p/fpdeleuze7.htm.

Delhi Development Authority (DDA) (1961a) *Work studies relating to the preparation of the Master plan for Delhi*, Volume One, DDA, Delhi.

Delhi Development Authority (DDA) (1961b) *Work studies relating to the preparation of the Master plan for Delhi*, Volume Two, DDA, Delhi.

Deshpande, Satish (1993) "Imagined Economies: Styles of Nation Building in Twentieth Century India," *Journal of Arts and Ideas* 24(5), pp.5–35.

Dewan-Verma, Gita (1993) *Slumming India*, Delhi: Penguin Books.

Dimmendberg, Edward (2004) *Film Noir and the Spaces of Modernity*, Cambridge, MA: Harvard University Press.

Doane, Mary Anne (1990) "Information, Crisis, Catastrophe" in Patricia Mellencamp (ed.) *The Logics of Television*, Indianapolis: Indiana University Press.

—— (2002) *The Emergence of Cinematic Time: Modernity, Contingency, the Archive*, Cambridge, MA: Harvard University Press.

Donald, James (1999) *Imagining the Modern City*, Minneapolis: University of Minnesota Press.

Down to Earth, (2000) "Masterplan for Anarchy," Vol 9, No 15 Sunday, December 31. Available HTTP http://www.downtoearth.org.in, accessed July 3, 2007.

Dupont Veronique (2000) "Spatial and Demographic Flows of Delhi Since 1947," in Denis Vidal *et al.*, *Delhi: Urban Space and Human Destinies*, Delhi: Manohar Publications.

Dupont, Veronique, E. Tarlo and D. Vidal (2000) *Delhi: Urban Space and Human Destinies*, New Delhi: Manohar Publishers and the French Research Institutes in India.

Ehrenberg, Ilya (1999) *Life of the Automobile*, London: Serpents Tail Reprint Edition.

Eisenstein, Elizabeth (1980) *The Printing Press as an Agent of Change: Communications and Cultural Transformations in Early Modern Europe*, Cambridge: Cambridge University Press.

Elias, Norbert (1993) *The Civilizing Process*; translated by Edmund Jephcott. Oxford, UK and Cambridge, Mass.: Blackwell.

Ellin, Nan (1997) *Architecture of Fear*, New York: Princeton Architectural Press.

Elsaesser, Thomas (2006) "Early Film History and Multimedia: An Archaeology of Possible Futures?", in Wendy Chun and Thomas Keenan (eds) *New Media, Old Media*, New York: Routledge.

Escobar, Arturo (1995) *Encountering Development: The Making and Unmaking of the Third World*, Princeton, NJ: Princeton University Press.

Evenson, Norma (1996) "An Architectural Hybrid," in Sujata Patel and Alice Thorner (eds) *Bombay: Mosaic of Modern Culture*, Delhi: Oxford University Press.

Farooqui, Mahmood, (2006) " 'Jahan se Dekhiye Yak Shor-e Shor-angez Nikle Hain (A Riot of Turbulence, Wherever You Look)': The Dehlvi Ghadar," *Turbulence, Sarai Reader 06*, Delhi: CSDS, pp.254–270.

Fishman, Robert (1992) "The Regional Plan and the Transformation of the Industrial Metropolis," in David Ward and Olivier Zunz (eds) *The Landscape of Modernity*, London: Russell Sage Foundation.

Foster, Hal (2002) *Design and Crime and Other Diatribes*, New York: Verso.

—— (2006) *Prosthetic Gods*, Cambridge, MA: MIT Press.

Foucault, Michel (1977) *Discipline and Punish: The Birth of the Prison*, New York: Vintage Books.

—— (1984) *The Foucault Reader*, ed. P. Rabinow, Harmondsworth: Penguin Books.

—— (1986) "Of Other Spaces", *Diacritics* 16, Spring, pp.22–27.

—— (1988) "The Dangerous Individual," in Lawrence Kritzman (ed.) *Michel Foucault, Politics Philosophy Culture*, New York: Routledge.

—— (1991) "Introduction" to Georges Canguilhem, *The Normal and the Pathological*, Cambridge, MA: MIT Press.

Frankel, Francine R. (1978) *India's Political Economy, 1947–77: The Gradual Revolution*, Princeton, NJ: Princeton University Press.

Friedberg, Anne (1993) *Window Shopping: Cinema and the Postmodern*, Berkeley: University of California Press.

Frisby, David (1986) *Fragments of Modernity*, Cambridge, MA: MIT Press.

Frith, Simon and Lee Marshall (2004) *Music and Copyright*, Edinburgh: Edinburgh University Press.

Frow, John (1997) *Time and Commodity Culture*, New York: Oxford University Press.

—— (2002) " 'Never Draw to an Inside Straight': On Everyday Knowledge," *New Literary History* 33(4), pp.623–637.

Fuller, C. J. and Veronique Benei (2000) *The Everyday State and Society in Modern India*, New Delhi: Social Science Press.

Gaines, Jane (2006) "Early Cinema's Heyday of Copying," *Cultural Studies* 20(2–3), pp.227–244.

Geddes, Patrick (1946) *Patrick Geddes in India*, London: Percy Lund Humphries.

Ghosh, Anindita (2006) *Power in Print: Popular Publishing and the Politics of Language and Culture in a Colonial Society*, Delhi: Oxford University Press.

Ghosh, Bijit (1968) "Delhi 1981 AD: Promises for a Heartless City," *Shakti*, February.

Gilloch, Graeme (1996) *Myth and Metropolis: Walter Benjamin and the City*, London: Polity Press.

Ginsburg, Faye D. (ed.) with Lila Abu-Lughod and Brian Larkin (2002) *Media Worlds: Anthropology on New Terrain*, Berkeley: University of California Press.

Goodfriend, D. (1989) "The Tyranny of the Right Angle: Colonial and Post-colonial Urban Development in Delhi," in P. Singh and R. Dhamjia (eds) *Delhi: The Deepening Urban Crisis*, New Delhi, Bangalore: Sterling Publishers.

Gooptu, Nandini (1996) "The Problem of the Urban Poor Policy and Discourse of Local Administration," *Economic and Political Weekly*, December 14, pp.3245–3253.

Gordon, Leonard A. (1997) "Wealth Equals Wisdom? The Rockefeller and Ford Foundations in India," *Annals of the American Academy of Political and Social Science*, Vol. 554.

Govil Nitin (2004) "War in the Age of Pirate Reproduction," *Sarai Reader 04: Crisis Media*, Delhi: CSDS.

Graham, Stephen and Simon Marvin (2001) *Splintering Urbanism, Networked Infrastructures, Technological Mobilities and the Urban Condition*, London: Routledge.

Grumbach, Antoine (1978) "The Theatre of Memory," *Architectural Design Profile* 48, pp.8–9.

Gu, Bin and Mahajan, Vijay (2005) "How Much Anti-piracy Effort is Too Much? – A Study of the Global Software Industry" (February). McCombs Research Paper. Available at SSRN: http://ssrn.com/abstract=825165, acessed July 3, 2006.

Gupta, Narayani (1998) *Delhi Between Two Empires: Society, Government and Urban Growth, 1809–1931*, Delhi: Oxford University Press.

—— (2006) "A 'Notified' Future for Delhi's Past, South Asia," *Journal of South Asian Studies* 29(1), pp.101–115.

Hacking, Ian (1990) *The Taming Of Chance*, Cambridge: Cambridge University Press.

Hansen, Mark (2004) *New Philosophy for New Media*, Cambridge, MA: MIT Press.

Hansen, Miriam Bratu (2004) "Room-for-play: Benjamin's Gamble with Cinema," *October* 109 (Summer), pp.3–45.

Harootunian, Harry (2000) *History's Disquiet: Modernity, Cultural Practice, and the Question of Everyday Life*, New York: Columbia University Press.

Hart, Keith (2000) *The Memory Bank: On Money, Machines, and the Market*, London: Profile.

Harvey, D. (1989) *The Condition of Postmodernity: An Enquiry into the Origins of Cultural Change*, Oxford: Blackwell.

Haug, Wolfgang Fritz (1987) *Commodity Aesthetics, Ideology, and Culture*, New York: International General.

Haynes, Jonathan and Onookome Okome (1998) "Evolving Popular Media: Nigerian Video Films" *Research in African Literatures*, Vol. 29, No. 3. (Autumn), pp.106–128.

Hebdige, Dick (1993) "Training Some Thoughts on the Future," in J. Bird, B. Curtis, T. Putnam, G. Robertson and L. Tickner (eds) *Mapping the Futures*, New York: Routledge.

Heidegger, Martin (1971) "The Thing," in *Poetry, Language, Thought*, trans. and Introduction by Albert Hofsadter, New York: Harper & Row.

Horkheimer, Max and Theodor W. Adorno (1988) *Dialectic of Enlightenment*, New York: Continuum.

Hosagrahar, Jyoti (2005) *Indigenous Modernities*, London: Routledge.

Hoselitz, Bert (1962) "The Role of Urbanization in Economic Development: Some International Comparisons," in Roy Turner *et al.* (eds) *India's Urban Future*, Berkeley: University of California Press.

Hughes, Stephen (2000) "Policing silent. Film exhibition in colonial south India," in Ravi S. Vasudevan (ed.), *Making Meaning in Indian Cinema*, New Delhi: Oxford University Press, pp.39–64.

Hull, Mathew (2009) "American Technologies of Democracy in Post-colonial Delhi," in *Comparative Studies of Society and History*, forthcoming.

Huyssen, Andreas (1986) *After the Great Divide*, Bloomington: Indiana University Press.

Irving, Robert (1983) *Indian Summer: Lutyens, Baker and Imperial Delhi*, New Haven, CT: Yale University Press.

Jacobs, Jane (1961) *The Death and Life of Great American Cities*, New York: Random House.

Jagmohan (1975) *Rebuilding Shahjahanabad, The Walled City of Delhi*, Delhi: Vikas Publishing.

—— (1978) *Islands of Truth*, New Delhi: Vikas Publishing.

Jain, A.K. (1990) *The Making of a Metropolis: Planning and Growth of Delhi*, New Delhi: National Book Organization.

Jain, Kajri (2003) "New Visual Technologies in the Bazaar, Reterritorialisation of the Sacred in Popular Print Culture," in *Shaping Technologies, Sarai Reader 03*, Delhi: CSDS, pp.44–57.

Jain, Sonu (2001) "Video 'Pirates' in Lead Role, Cops Play Villains," *Indian Express*, December 19.

Jameson, Fredric (1991) *Postmodernism, or, the Cultural Logic of Late Capitalism*, Durham, NC: Duke University Press.

—— (2003) "Future City," *New Left Review* 21 May.

Jaszi, Peter (1994) "On the Author Effect: Contemporary Copyright and Collective

Creativity," in Martha Woodmansee and Peter Jaszi (eds) *The Construction of Authorship: Textual Appropriation in Law and Literature*, Durham, NC: Duke University Press.

Johns, Adrian (1998) *The Nature of the Book: Print and Knowledge in the Making*, Chicago, IL: University of Chicago Press.

Julier, Guy (2000) *The Culture of Design*, Thousand Oaks, CA: Sage.

Kalia, Ravi (1999) *Chandigarh: The Making of an Indian City*, Delhi: Oxford University Press.

Kaur, Ravinder (2007) *Since 1947: Partition Narratives Among Punjabi Migrants of Delhi*, Delhi: Oxford University Press.

Kaviraj, Sudipto (1997) "Filth and the Public Space: Concepts and Practices about Space in Calcutta," *Public Culture* 10, pp.83–113.

—— (2000) "The Modern State in India," in Zoya Hasan (ed.) *Politics and the State in India*, Thousand Oaks, CA: Sage.

Kearns, Gerry and Chris Philo (eds) (1993) *Selling Places: The City as Cultural Capital, Past and Present*, Oxford: Pergamon Press.

Khanolkar, Prasad (2005) "Duplicacy; The Robinhood of Global City", Unpublished Paper, Sarai Archive.

Khati, Sanjay (1989) *Pinti Ka Sabun, Hans*, April, Delhi.

Khilnani, Sunil (1998) *The Idea of India*, New Delhi: Penguin Books.

King, A. (1976) *Colonial Urban Development*, London: Routledge & Kegan Paul.

King, Ross (1996) *Emancipating Space: Geography, Architecture, and Urban Design*, New York: Guilford Press.

Kittler, Friedrich (1999) *Gramophone, Film, Typewriter*, Stanford, CA: Stanford University Press.

Knabb, Ken (1981) *Situationist International Anthology*, Berkeley, CA: Bureau of Public Secrets.

Knox, Paul (1992) *The Restless Urban Landscape*, Englewood Cliffs, NJ: Prentice Hall.

Koolhaas, Rem (2002a) "Junkspace," *October 100 (Spring)*, pp.175–190.

Koolhaas, Rem (2002b) "Fragments of a Lecture on Lagos," in Okwui Enwezor, Carlos Basualdo, Ute Meta Bauer, Susanne Ghez, Sarat Maharaj, Mark Nash and Octavio Zaya (eds) *Documenta11_Platform4. Under Siege: Four African Cities Freetown, Johannesburg, Kinshasa, Lagos*, Germany: Ostfildern-Ruit.

Koolhaas, Rem and Bruce Mau (1997) *S,M,L,XL*, New York: Monacelli Press.

Kracauer, Siegfried (1995) *The Mass Ornament: Weimar Essays*, trans. and ed. Thomas Y. Levin, Princeton, NJ: Princeton University Press.

Kumar, Jainendra (2000) "The Philosophy of the Bazaar", originally "Bazaar Darshan" (date uncertain) trans. Ravikant in *Hindi: Language, Discourse, Writing* 1(2), July–September, pp.286–291.

Kumar, Kanchan (2003) "Mixed Signals: A History of Radio Broadcasting Policy in India," in The community radio list, http://mail.sarai.net/pipermail/cr-india/2003-June/005911.html, accessed June 3, 2004.

Kumar, Rakesh (2002a) "Palika Seems Tired at 23," PPHP Broadsheet no. 2, Sarai, Delhi. Available at http//www.sarai.net/research/media-city/field-notes/media-markets/palika-story, accessed February 1, 2005.

—— (2002b) "Shiv Sagar and the Delhi Porter's Union," http://www.sarai.net/research/media-city/field-notes/media-markets/shiv-sagar/, accessed July 3, 2005.

Kundu, A. (ed.) (2000) *Inequality, Mobility and Urbanization*, New Delhi: ICSSR and Manak Publications.

Lalit Kala Academy (1959) Seminar on Architecture, Lalit Kala Academy, New Delhi.

Lang, John, Madhavi Desai, and Miki Desai (1997) *Architecture and Independence: The Search for Identity: India, 1880–1980*, New Delhi: Oxford University Press.

Larkin, Brian (2004) "Degraded Images, Distorted Sounds: Nigerian Video and the Infrastructure of Piracy," *Public Culture* 16(2), pp.289–314.

Lash, Scott (2002). *Critique of Information*, London: Sage.

Latour, Bruno (1987) *Science in Action: How to Follow Scientists and Engineers through Society*, Cambridge, MA: Harvard University Press.

—— (1993) *We Have Never Been Modern*, Brighton: Harvester Wheatsheaf.

Le Corbusier (1972) "Architecture or Revolution," in *Towards a New Architecture*, New York: Praeger.

—— (1978) *The City of Tomorrow*, New York; Dover Publications.

—— ([1929]1996) "A Contemporary City," in R.T. Le Gates and F. Stout (eds) *The City Reader*, London: Routledge.

Lefebvre, Henri (1971) *Every Day Life in the Modern World*, New York: Harper & Row.

—— (1991) *The Production of Space*, trans. Donald Nicholson-Smith, London: Blackwell.

Legg, Stephen (2007). *Spaces of Colonialism: Delhi's Urban Governmentalities*, Oxford: Blackwell.

Lelyveld, David (2005) "Upon the Subdominant: Administering Music on All-India Radio," in Carol Breckenridge (ed.) *Consuming Modernity: Public Culture in a South Asian World*, Minneapolis: University of Minnesota Press.

Lessig, Lawrence (2004) *Free Culture: How Big Media Uses Technology and the Law to Lock Down Culture and Control Creativity*, New York: Penguin Books.

Liang, Lawrence (2005) "Porous Legalities and Avenues of Participation," in *Bare Acts, Sarai Reader 05*, Delhi: CSDS, pp.6–15.

—— (2009) "Beyond Representation: The Figure of the Pirate," in Peter Jaszi, Martha Woodmansee, and Mario Biagioli (Eds) *(Con)texts of Invention*, Chicago, IL: University of Chicago Press.

Litman, Jessica (2000) *The Demonization of Piracy*, online reference at http://www.personal.umich.edu/~jdlitman/, accessed May 7, 2005.

Locke, John (2003) *Two Treatises of Government and A Letter Concerning Toleration*, New Haven, CT: Yale University Press.

Manovich, Lev (2002) *The Language of New Media, Cambridge*, MA: MIT Press.

Manuel, Peter (1991) *Cassette Culture: Popular Music and Technology in North India*, New Delhi: Oxford University Press.

MARG (1946) "Planning and Dreaming," No. 1 Inaugural Issue, Bombay.

Markovits, Claude, Jacques Pouchepadass, and Sanjay Subrahmanyam (2003) *Society and Circulation: Mobile People and Itinerant Cultures in South Asia, 1750–1950*, Delhi: Permanent Black.

Marx, Karl (1967) *Capital, Volume III*, New York: International Publishers.

—— (1976) [1867] *Capital: A Critique of Political Economy*, trans. Ben Fowkes, Harmondsworth: Penguin Classics.

Masselos, Jim (ed.) (2003) *Bombay and Mumbai: The City in Transition*, 9–13, New York: Oxford University Press.

Mayer, Albert (1936) "Green Belt Towns for the Machine Age," *New York Times*, February 2.

—— (1956) "New Way of Life in Britain's New Towns," *New York Times*, January 29.

—— (1962) "Some Operational Problems in Urban and Regional Planning and

Development," in Roy Turner (ed.) *India's Urban Future*, Bombay: Oxford University Press.

—— (1973) *The Urgent Future*, New York: McGraw-Hill.

Mazumdar, Ranjani (2007) *Bombay Cinema, an Archive of the City*, Minneapolis: University of Minnesota Press.

Mazzarella, William (2003) *Shovelling Smoke: Advertising and Globalization in Contemporary India*, Durham, NC: Duke University Press.

Mbembe, Achille and Janet Roitman (1995) "Figures of the Subject in Times of Crisis," *Public Culture* 7, pp.323–352.

McCarthy Anna (2001a) "From Screen to Site: Television's Material Culture, and Its Place," *October*, Vol. 98.

—— (2001b) *Ambient Television: Visual Culture and Public Space*, Durham, NC: Duke University Press.

McLuhan, Marshall ([1964] 1994) *Understanding Media*, Cambridge, MA: MIT Press.

Mehrotra, Rahul (2002) "Bazaar City: A Metaphor for South Asian Urbanism," in *Kapital and Karma: Recent Positions in Indian Art*, Vienna: Kunsthalle Wien.

Mehta, Suketu (2004) *Maximum City: Bombay Lost and Found*, New York: Alfred A. Knopf.

Menon, A.G.K. (2000) "The Contemporary Architecture of Delhi, The Role of State as Middleman," in Denis Vidal *et al.*, *Delhi: Urban Space and Human Destinies*, Delhi: Manohar Publications.

Menon, Nivedita and Aditya Nigam (2007) *Power and Contestation: India since 1989*, London: Zed Press.

Merleau-Ponty, Maurice (1969) *The Visible and the Invisible*, Evanston: Northwestern University Press.

Metcalf, Thomas (2002) *An Imperial Vision: Indian Architecture and Britain's Raj*, New York: Oxford University Press.

Miller, Daniel (1987) *Material Culture and Mass Consumption*, Oxford: Blackwell.

Miller, Toby (1998) *Technologies of Truth: Cultural Citizenship and the Popular Media*, Minneapolis: University of Minnesota Press.

Miller, Toby, with Nitin Govil, John McMurria, and Richard Maxwell (2001) *Global Hollywood*, London: BFI.

Mitchell, Timothy (2002) *Rule of Experts: Egypt, Techno-politics, Modernity*, Berkeley: University of California Press.

—— (2004) *The Properties of Markets*, Working Paper No. 2, Cultural Political Economy Research Group, University of Lancaster.

Mohan, Dinesh (2004) *The Road Ahead: Traffic Injuries and Fatalities in India*, TRIPP, Delhi: Indian Institute of Technology.

Moore, Sally (1973) "Folk Law and Social Change: The Semi-autonomous Social Field as an Appropriate Subject of Study," *Law & Society Review* 7(4), pp.719–746.

Morris, Meaghan (1990) "Banality in Cultural Studies," in P. Mellencamp (ed.) *Logics of Television*, Bloomington: Indiana University Press.

Nair, Janaki (2005) *The Promise of the Metropolis: Bangalore's Twentieth Century*, New Delhi: Oxford University Press.

Nandy, A. (2001) *An Ambiguous Journey to the City: The Village and Other Odd Ruins of Self in the Indian Imagination*, New Delhi: Oxford University Press.

Nangia, S. and Torhat, S. (2000) *Slum in a Metropolis: The Living Environment*, New Delhi: Shipra Publications.

Nehru, Jawaharlal (1959) Opening Address, Seminar on Architecture, Lalit Kala Academi, pp.5–9.

—— (1972) *The Discovery of India*, Mumbai: Vikas Publishing.

Nietzsche, Friedrich (1967) *The Will to Power*, trans. Walter Kaufman and R.J. Hollingdale, New York: Random House.

Nigam, Aditya (2001) Industrial Closures in Delhi, available at <http://www.revolutionarydemocracy.org/rdv7n2/industclos.htm>, accessed June 6, 2004.

Nora, Pierre (1989) "Between Memory and History: Les Lieux de memoire," trans. Marc Roudebush, *Representations* 26 (Spring).

O'Conner, Alice (2001) *Poverty Knowledge: Social Science, Social Policy and the Poor in Twentieth-century US History*, Princeton, NJ: Princeton University Press.

Olalquiaga, Celeste (1992) *Megalopolis: Contemporary Cultural Sensibilities*, Minneapolis: University of Minnesota Press.

Oldenburg, Veena Talwar (1985) *The Making of Colonial Lucknow, 1856–1877*, Delhi: Oxford University Press.

Patel, Sujata (1995) "Bombay's Urban Predicament," in Sujata Patel and Alice Thorner (eds) *Bombay: Metaphor for Modern India*, Delhi: Oxford University Press.

Patel, Sujata and Alice Thorner (eds) (1996) *Bombay: Mosaic of Modern Culture*, Delhi: Oxford University Press.

Patton, Paul (2000) *Deleuze and the Political*, New York: Routledge.

Pearson, Keith Ansell (1997) *Viroid Life, Perspectives on Nietzsche and the Transhuman Condition*, London: Routledge.

Perry, Clarence (1939) *Housing for the Machine Age*, New York: Russell Sage Foundation.

Picon, Antoine (2000) "Anxious Landscapes: From the Ruin to Rust," *Grey Room* 01 (Fall), pp.64–83.

Plant, Sadie (1992) *The Most Radical Gesture: The Situationist International in a Postmodern Age*, London: Routledge.

Prakash, Gyan (1999) *Another Reason: Science and the Imagination of Modern India*, Princeton, NJ: Princeton University Press.

—— (2002) "The Urban Turn", in the *Sarai Reader* 2, The Cities of Everyday Life, Delhi and Amsterdam.

Prakash, Uday (2002) *Paul Gomra ka Scooter*, Delhi: Vani Prakashan.

—— (2003) *Short Shorts Long Shorts*, Delhi: Katha.

Prasad, Bhagwati (2003a) "Piracy: Judte Rishte, Phaylta Bazaar," *PPHP Laghupatrika*, Sarai Delhi.

—— (2003b) "Sangeet Udyog ka chota khiladi," *PPHP Laghupatrika*, Sarai Delhi.

Prasad, M. Madhava (1998) *Ideology of the Hindi Film: A Historical Construction*, New Delhi: Oxford University Press.

Raban, Jonathan (1998) *Soft City*, London: Harvill Press.

Rabinow, Paul (1989) *French Modern: Norms and Forms of the Social Environment*, Cambridge, MA: MIT Press.

Radnoti, Sandor (1999) *The Fake: Forgery and its Places in Art*, London: Rowman and Littlefield.

Rajadhyakshya, Ashish (2003) "The 'Bollywoodization' of the Indian Cinema: Cultural Nationalism in a Global Arena," *Inter-Asia Cultural Studies* 4(1).

Rajagopal, Arvind (2001a) "The Violence of Commodity Aesthetics: Hawkers, Demolition Raids, and a New Regime of Consumption," *Social Text* 19(3), pp.91–113.

—— (2001b) *Politics after Television: Religious Nationalism and the Reshaping of the Indian Public*, Cambridge, New York: Cambridge University Press.

Rao, M. S. A. (ed.) (1974) *Urban Sociology in India*, Hyderabad, India: Orient Longman.

Raqs Media Collective (2005) "X Notes on Practice: Stubborn Structures and Insistent Seepage in a Networked World," in Geoff Cox and Joasia Krysa (eds) *Data Browser 02: Engineering Culture*, New York: Autonomedia.

Ravindran, K.T. (1996) "Why Planning Failed," *Seminar* 445.

Raynor, Gregory K. (2000) "Engineering Social Reform: The Rise of the Ford Foundation and Cold War Liberalism, 1908–1959," Ph.D. Dissertation, New York University.

Razzaz, Omar (1994) "Contestation and Mutual Adjustment: The Process of Controlling Land in Yajouz," *Jorden. Law & Society Review* 28(1), pp.1–74.

Rifkin, Jeremy (2000) *The Age of Access*, New York: Penguin Books.

Rodowick, D.N. (2007) *The Virtual Life of Film*, Cambridge, MA: Harvard University Press.

Rose, Mark (1993) *Authors and Owners: The Invention of Copyright*, Cambridge, MA: Harvard University Press.

Ross, Kristin (1996a) "Streetwise: The French Invention of Everyday Life," *Parallax* 2, pp.67–75.

Ross, Kristin (1996b) *Fast Cars, Clean Bodies: Decolonization and the Reordering of French Culture*, Cambridge, MA: MIT Press.

Rossi, A. (1982) *Architecture in the City*, Cambridge, MA: MIT Press.

Roy, Ananya and Nezar Al Sayyad (2004) *Urban Informality: Transnational Perspectives from the Middle East, Latin America, and South Asia*, Lanham, MD, Oxford: Lexington Books.

Roy, Dunu (2004) "From Home to Estate," *Seminar* 533.

Roy, Srirupa (2002) "Moving Pictures: The Postcolonial State and Visual Representations of India," *Contributions to Indian Sociology* 36, p.233.

Sadler, Simon (1999) *The Situationist City*, Cambridge, MA: MIT Press.

Sassen, Saskia (2001) *The Global City*, Princeton, NJ: Princeton University Press, (new edn of 1991 book).

—— (2007) "Toward a Multiplication of Specialized Assemblages of Territory, Authority and Rights," *parallax* 13(1), pp.87–94.

Schivelbusch, Wolfgang (1986) *The Railway Journey*, Berkeley: University of California Press.

Schnapp, Jeffery T. (1999) "Crash (Speed as Engine of Individuation)," *Modernism/Modernity* 6(1).

—— (2003) "Three Pieces of Asphalt," *Grey Room* 11 (Spring), pp.5–21.

Seigworth, Gregory J. (2000) "Banality for Cultural Studies," *Cultural Studies* 14(2), p.234.

Seltzer, Mark (1998) *Serial Killers: Death and Life in America's Wound Culture*, New York: Routledge.

Sen, Jai (1975) "The Unintended City," *Seminar* 200, pp.33–40.

Sennett, Richard (1990) *The Conscience of the Eye: The Design and Social Life of Cities*, New York: W. W. Norton.

—— (1996) *Flesh and Stone: The Body and the City in Western Civilization*, New York: W. W. Norton.

Shah, Amrita (1997) *Hype, Hypocrisy, and Television in Urban India*, Delhi: Vikas Publishing.

Sharan, Awadhendra (2002) "Claims on Cleanliness, Environment and Justice in Contemporary Delhi," Delhi/Amsterdam *Sarai Reader 02: Cities of Everyday Life*.

—— (2006) "In the City, Out of Place, Environment and Modernity, Delhi 1860s to 1960s," *Economic and Political Weekly*, November 25, pp.4905–4911.

Sharma, Kalpana (2000) *Rediscovering Dharavi*, New Delhi: Penguin Books.

Sharma, Lokesh (2004) *A Brief Biography of a Cable Operator*, http://www.sarai.net/research/media-city/field-notes/cable-tv-networks/biography, accessed June 8 2006.

Shetty, Prasad (2005) "Stories of Entrepreneurship", Unpublished manuscript, CRIT, Mumbai.

Shwartz, Hillel (1996) *The Culture of the Copy*, Cambridge, MA: MIT Press.

Simmel, G. (1971) "The Metropolis and Mental Life," in D. Levine (ed.) *On Individuality and Social Form*, Chicago, IL: University of Chicago Press.

Simon, Frith and Marshall, Lee (eds) (2004) *Music and Copyright* (2nd edn), Edinburgh: Edinburgh University Press.

Simone, Abdou Maliq (2006) "Pirate Towns: Reworking Social and Symbolic Infrastructures in Johannesburg and Douala," *Urban Studies* 43(2), pp.357–370.

Singer, Ben (1995) in *Cinema and the Invention of Modern Life*, Leo Charney and Vanessa R. Schwartz (ed). Berkeley, University of California Press, pp.72–102.

Singh, K. and Steinberg, F. (1996) *Urban India in Crises*, New Delhi: New Age International Limited, Human Settlement Management Institute, New Delhi.

Singh, P. and Dhamjia, R. (eds) (1989) *Delhi: The Deepening Urban Crisis*, New Delhi, Bangalore: Sterling Publishers.

Soderstrom, Ola (1996) "Paper Cities: Visual Thinking in Urban Planning," *Ecumene* 3 (3).

Soja, Edward (1989) *Postmodern Geographies: The Reassertion of Space in Critical Social Theory*, London: Verso.

Srinivas, S.V. (2000) "Is There a Public in the Cinema Hall?" *Framework* 42 (summer), available at http://www.frameworkonline.com/42svs.htm, accessed May 3, 2003.

Stark, Ulrike (2007) *An Empire of Books: The Naval Kishore Press and the Diffusion of the Printed Word in Colonial India, 1858–1895*, New Delhi: Permanent Black.

Stone, Alucquere Rosanne (1991) "Will the Real Body Stand Up: Boundary Stories about Virtual Cultures," in Michael Benedikt (ed.) *Cyberspace: The First Steps*, Cambridge, MA: MIT Press.

Subramaniam, Radhika (1998) "The Crowd in Bombay." Ph.D. dissertation, New York University.

Sundaram, Ravi (1999) "Recycling Pirate Modernity," *Third Text* 47 (Summer), pp.59–65.

—— (2000) "Beyond the Nationalist Panopticon: The Experience of CyberPublics in India," in John Caldwell, *Electronic Media and Technoculture*, London: Rutgers University Press.

—— (2004) "Uncanny Networks: Pirate and Urban in the New Globalisation in India," *Economic and Political Weekly*, January 6.

Suresh, Mayur (2002) "Policing the Networks and Practices of Video," available at http://mail.sarai.net/pipermail/commons-law/2004-September/000857.html, accessed April 2, 2006.

Sutton, Francis X. (1997) "Ford Foundation: The Early Years," *Daedalus* (Winter).

Swamy, Harini (1991) "In the Big music Bazaar," *Times of India*, July 21.

Tafuri, Manfredo (1976) *Architecture and Utopia: Design and Capitalist Development*, Cambridge, MA: MIT Press.

Tarlo, Emma (2003) *Unsettling Memories: Narratives of the Emergency in Delhi*, Berkeley: University of California Press.

Taussig, Michael (1992) *The Nervous System*, New York: Routledge.

TERI (2002) *Restructuring Options for Urban Public Transport in India*, New Delhi: Tata Energy Research Institute.

Thomas, V.J. (2000) "Road Accidents," in S. Parsuraman and P.V. Unnikrishnan (eds) *India Disasters Report: Towards a Policy Initiative*, Delhi: Oxford University Press.

Thompson, Emily (2002) *The Soundscape of Modernity: Architectural Acoustics and the Culture of Listening in America, 1900–1933*, Cambridge, MA: MIT Press.

Topalov, Christian (1990) "From the Social Question to 'Urban Problems'," *ISSJ* 125, Tales of Cities.

—— (2003) " 'Traditional Working-class Neighborhoods': An Inquiry into the Emergence of a Sociological Model in the 1950s and 1960s," Osiris, 2nd Series, Vol. 18, *Science and the City*, pp.212–233.

Turkle, Sherry (1995) *Life on the Screen: Identity in the Age of the Internet*, New York: Simon & Schuster.

Urry, John (2004) "The 'System' of Automobility," *Theory Culture and Society* 21, pp.25–39.

Vaidhyanathan, Siva (2001) *Copyrights and Copywrongs: The Rise of Intellectual Property and How It Threatens Creativity*, New York: New York University Press.

Vasudevan, Ravi (ed.) (2000) *Making Meaning in Indian Cinema*, New Delhi: Oxford University Press.

—— (2004) "Disreputable to Illegal Publics: Cinematic Allegories in Times of Crisis," in *Crisis Media, Sarai Reader* 03, Delhi: CSDS, pp.71–79.

Venturi, Robert Denise, Scott Brown, and Steven Izenour (1972) *Learning from Las Vegas*, Cambridge, MA: MIT Press.

Vida, Denis *et al.* (eds) (2000) *Delhi: Urban Space and Human Destinies*, Delhi: Manohar Publications.

Vidler, Anthony (1994) *The Architectural Uncanny: Essays in the Modern Unhomely*, Cambridge, MA: MIT Press.

—— (2000) *Warped Space: Art, Architecture, and Anxiety in Modern Culture*, Cambridge, MA: MIT Press.

Virilio, Paul (1986) *Speed and Politics*, New York: Semiotexte.

Virlio, Paul (2002) *Foreword to The Museum of Accidents*, Online reference at http://www.onoci.net/virilio/pages_uk/virilio/avertissement.php?th=1&rub=1_1 accessed on July 20, 2006.

—— (1989) *War and Cinema*, London: Verso.

—— (1997) "The Overexposed City," in Neil Leach (ed.) *Rethinking Architecture: A Reader in Cultural Theory*, London: Routledge.

—— (2005) *Desert Screen: War at the Speed of Light*, London: Continuum International Publishing Group.

Wallerstein, Immanuel (1983) *Historical Capitalism*, London: Verso.

—— (1991) "Braudel on Capitalism, or Everything Upside Down," *Journal of Modern History* 63, pp.354–361.

Wang, Shujen (2003) *Framing Piracy: Globalization and Film Distribution in Greater China*, Boulder, CO: Rowman & Littlefield.

Ward, Janet (2001) *Weimar Surfaces: Urban Visual Culture in 1920s Germany*, Berkeley: University of California Press.

Wark, Ken (1988) "Technological Time: Cruising Virilio's Over-exposed City," *Arena* 83.

Warner, Michael (1993) "The Mass Public and the Mass Subject," in Brice Robbins (ed.) *The Phantom Public Sphere*, Minnesota: University of Minnesota Press.

Wigley, Mark (2001) "Network Fever," *Grey Room* (Summer), pp.82–122.

Williams, Raymond (1973) *The Country and the City*, New York: Oxford University Press.

Wollen, Peter (1993) *Raiding the Icebox: Reflections on Twentieth-century Culture*, London: Verso.

Woodmansee, Martha and Peter Jaszi (eds) (1994) *The Construction of Authorship: Textual Appropriation in Law and Literature*, Durham, NC: Duke University Press.

Wright, Frank Lloyd (1958) *The Living City*, New York: Horizon Press.

Zukin, Sharon (1991) *Landscapes of Power: From Detroit to Disney World*, Berkeley: University of California Press.

Index